J. M. Reid

Sketches and Anecdotes of the Old Settlers and New Comers

The Mormon Bandits and Danite Band

J. M. Reid

Sketches and Anecdotes of the Old Settlers and New Comers
The Mormon Bandits and Danite Band

ISBN/EAN: 9783337296353

Printed in Europe, USA, Canada, Australia, Japan

Cover: Foto ©Thomas Meinert / pixelio.de

More available books at **www.hansebooks.com**

Sketches and Anecdotes

OF

The Old Settlers,

AND

New Comers,

The Mormon Bandits

AND

Danite Band,

BY

COL. J. M. REID, Attorney at Law.

KEOKUK, IOWA.
R. B. OGDEN, PUBLISHER,
1876.

THIS BOOK IS RESPECTFULLY DEDICATED TO

COL. J. M. SHELLEY,

OF KEOKUK, IOWA, THE PIONEER WHOLESALE DRY GOODS MERCHANT OF THE DES MOINES VALLEY, WHO IS BETTER KNOWN TO THE PEOPLE TO-DAY AS A PRIVATE CITIZEN THAN ANY PUBLIC MAN IN THE STATE. WITH THE REGARDS OF THE WRITER FOR HIM PERSONALLY, WHICH IS SHARED BY THE PEOPLE WHO APPRECIATE HIS INTEGRITY AS A MERCHANT, HIS CHARACTER AS A MAN, HIS HIGH ORDER OF TALENT AND SUPERIOR BUSINESS CAPACITY, AND WHO FEELS THAT HE IS ALSO ONE OF THEMSELVES, AN "OLD SETTLER."

KEOKUK, Dec. 1876.   THE AUTHOR.

KEOKUK WHEN AN OLD MAN.

From a Daguerreotype presented by KEOKUK himself to JOHN BURNS, Esq.
of Keokuk, Iowa.

PREFACE.

We propose in these pages briefly to give sketches and anecdotes of the Old Settlers of Iowa, and its borders, most of which have come under our own personal observation. Those incidents, now part of the history and traditions of the past, which happened before our time, we have from the Old Settlers themselves, with most of whom as Lawyers, Judges, Politicians, Merchants, Mechanics and Farmers, residing in Southern Iowa, we have been personally acquainted. We want it distinctly understood we do not claim this to be a history or to be correct in all its details. From the hasty manner in which it has been written we have depended principally upon our own recollection, not referring in but few instances to documents, giving dates, which are not very important for this work.

We promised our subscribers no illustrations but have given them one of Joe Smith the Mormon Prophet, in full uniform as Lieutenant-General, one of Old Keokuk with his son at his feet, in his full dress war costume as he appears when a young man in the National Picture Gallery at Washington, also one of Black Hawk, the War Chief of the Sacs and Foxes, as sketched by a U. S. officer at the close of the Black Hawk War, while he was a prisoner of war in 1833.

If you are pleased with our sketches we shall be satisfied; some future Macaulay may elaborate on what we have written and write up the Old Settlers in better style than we have done. We begin it, let those who have the time, the ambition and an interest in keeping up the dear memories of our past unwritten history, complete what we have commenced.

We leave our sketches with you, read them and take them for what they are worth.   THE AUTHOR.

KEOKUK AS A YOUNG CHIEF

In the great Council at Washington when Mr. POINSETT was Secretary of War.

THE OLD SETTLERS.

CHAPTER I.

"The big black bull ran down the meadow,
And he shook his tail and jarred the river,
And he pawed the dirt in the heifers' faces
　＊　　＊　　＊　　＊　　＊　　＊
　　Long time ago.--Hoose anna! Hoose anna ha!"

The Star of Empire, its birth place in Buncombe County, North Carolina.—Immigration to Posey County, Indiana.—How the Hoosier State got its name.—Old Settlers of the Upper Mississippi Valley, etc.

The infant in his swaddling clothes has no dreams of greatness. He blubbers and cries, eats, drinks and grows to be a big lubberly boy, and toddles about holding on to chairs, and smashes his playthings; falls down and in his fall knocks the claret from his nose, and cries again at the sight of blood, and awakes the sympathy of his kind-hearted mother. This agony is soon over, and still he grows, gets more noisy, while his mother indulges him in his mischievous pranks. In time he is a school boy and plays hookey and makes himself the best boy at school and gets to the head of his class, which he steps up to in triumph. And the boy above him cries out "you Ben. Rankin, you never would have got up head if I hadn't had a sore toe!"

A country grows to greatness as a child grows to manhood. It has its days of ginger-bread and molasses; its verdant know-nothing, barefooted period. It was so with the North Carolinians, the State which boasts of the county of Buncombe, which the old geographies used to say was the largest in territory of any county in the Union. Its population was sparse; hunted and trapped, and raised a little corn, tobacco and cotton, and the inevitable black-eyed peas, and tapped the tall pine trees by cutting a slab out of one side so the sap ran down and became turpentine. They burnt tar kilns and understood the habits of animals, and when in the woods their eyes had habitually an upward cast as if looking up in the tops of the trees for bees. They never change their habits or customs, and the dresses of the women and the men too were homespun, and with them the center of the world was North Carolina. Scotch presbyterians, their old hewed log churches, two stories high, with a porch in front, had stood for a century, and the roofs were covered with mosses. Near by is an unfenced grave yard, where if you look at the inscriptions on its venerable head-boards of cedar or pitch-pine, all are "Macs" who are buried there. Their barren clay hills are fenced into little patches of fields, and as you pass by on the road you see the old fashioned shovel plow standing in the furrow, and when at work in the field the horse is harnessed with a husk collar, and iron linked trace chains used by father and son from the primitive days of the revolution, and will be used still till Gabriel blows his trumpet for the morning of the resurection. The tombstone of one minister of one of these antiquated graveyards was a marble slab, and we had the curiosity to read its inscription, and found he had died at the advanced age of one hundred and three years, and had been seventy years a minister of that church, preaching of faith and foreordination. You come to cross-roads where the black-lettered finger-boards point out the way and tell the number of miles to the county seat. The learned read them and for those who cannot read is a cedar post with notches cut in it to tell them the way, for all can count. But there is a better time coming for the land of tar and turpentine.

The young men who take tobacco to market, with their return bring news of another country, and they resolved to go west; they follow the Star of Empire. And let us tell you a little secret, that the great Star of Empire you read of, though never yet traced to any country, had its paternity in Buncombe county. Its progress was westward and its first abiding place was Posey county, Indiana, which has made both Buncombe and Posey immortal. Many of the people who followed the Star, wandered out here into the valley of the upper Mississippi, from Carolina and the Hoosier State, and they are thus connected with our sketches of the old settlers. A word, then, about the way they came, and we shall hurry forward as we do not wish to keep you too long in expectancy for your beards to grow before the gates of Jericho.

Many walked all the way barefooted, but those who came with the Star of Empire had a tandem team of two horses hitched one in front of the other to a cart, the women and half-grown girls, barefooted, wearing sun-bonnets and copperas-colored dresses, bringing up the rear, riding on horses and ponies. The cart loaded with thirteen children, ranging from fourteen years of age down to the baby in its mother's arms, where it squalls while she spanks it with one hand and adjusts the corn cob pipe in her mouth with the other. The tow-headed children were of all sizes, and when they stood up in a row like the children at school, tapered from the head of the class to the foot like a pair of stair steps. At the sharp crack of a rifle, in the road behind, all are in fidgets, lifting the wagon "kiver" at the side, and peeping out wondering if "daddy" has shot a "bar." The cart stops, the horses prick up their ears at the report of the rifle, and twenty lean, hungry hounds come bounding up the road till they reach the heels of their master who has killed a buck in the brush by the road side. While they stop the mother gets out the kettle, puts up two sticks in the ground, forked at the tops, a pole is put across and lodged in the forks, and on this pole over a fire is hung the kettle in which is soon boiling the venison for their dinner. The future sovereign, and his boys, big enough to help, having skinned and dressed it all ready; the children gather around and look with hungry eyes while the pot boils, waiting for that dinner of venison and corn-pone which the mother bakes in the spider over the coals. So, day after day they make their weary way until they arrive in Posey on the *Way-bash*, (Wabash.)

They have a welcome reception—all new comers had in those days. The politicians flock in and make the acquaintance of the tar-heeler, soon to be a voter, and measure him with their eyes, taking in at a glance his long arms, great paws of hands, and feet—such feet—too big for number 13 brogans, and with no particular shape, but spread out, well, just like the roots of the hickory grubs of his native state, on top of the ground, and against which, he had no doubt many a time stumped his toes. The neighbors inspect the family and the last pattern of sun-bonnets, and take a mental inventory of the tow linen-shirts of the boys, and the narrow home-spun skirts of the women at their advent into Posey, and compare the ages of the children with that of their own.

The tar heelers exchange tobacco with their new made neighbors of Posey, giving their native twist for New Orleans plug. The country district schools gets new scholars, bare-footed and bare-headed. Quilting parties and dances on the puncheon floors have new visitors, and the brawny arms of our tall, gaunt North Carolinians, with their butternut clothes, fawn-skin spotted vests, and coon-skin caps come in good play at the log rollings and house raisings, on the *heav-o-he!* and big lift. They are delighted with the country, the "craps" and the rich soil, and send back glowing accounts of their rising fortunes to their old neighbors who come west in wagons, on foot and on horseback, with their big bored rifles, carrying eighty bullets to the pound of lead, and big leather saddle bags, in time to make up the next party for a coon hunt.

The ghosts of all the Macs must have haunted the church yards at their going, while the skeletons of the dead turned over uneasily in their pine coffins, it was so out of the usual order of things. "Everything is lovely and the goose hangs high," till autumn tinges the foliage of the trees with its variegated colors of saffron and gold, and frosts the papaws and persimmons on which the possums feast, and hooking their tails around a limb at night, with their heads down, sleep and dream of the name of O'Possum given their family by the naturalist; but here in the muddy bottoms of the Wabash the original "O" is left off as the O'Flannigans, the O'Daughertys and the O'Rourkes left it behind when they immigrated from the green emerald isle. But the fever and ague, unknown in Carolina, comes as the leaves are scattered on the ground to die; the teeth of our tar-heeler chatters and he feels he has no friends, as every victim of the ague feels, but others are soon shaking around him, and he consoles himself that he has companions in misery.

It is said the legislature of Indiana, not to be ungrateful, passed an act exempting from execution a barrel of whisky for the head of a family where he had no cow. Such was their experience in Posey; they shook with the ague, went to horse races and shooting matches for a quarter of beef, attended funerals and foot races. They were not slow to learn, but traveled on broad horns with the products of Posey, corn, whisky and hoop poles to New Orleans. One strayed to Louisville, Ky., where his ungainly appearance, his long stringing strides, his linsey-woolsey wampus with a strap about the waist, fastened by a big brass button in front, attracted the attention of a crowd of loafing men and boys on the levee; they followed him and hooted at him. He turned upon them, and with glaring eyes, while he jingled the silver in his pocket, shook his fist at them, and bade defiance, for he was a Putnam in courage and did not fear his weight in wild cats. He took a big drink, and swore a big oath, and still they followed him till he could stand it no longer, and as he jumped up and down, smacked his heels together and cried out, "I'm a hus-sar! I'm a hussar!" That was a clincher, they laughed and left him and told the story of the *hussar*, which being corrupted to Hoosier gave name to the Hoosier State.

The Virginians came to Kentucky with their traditions and settled at the "heads of the hollers." All these people and the hoosiers heard of the pukes and the Black Hawk purchase, and loading their big wagons with their household goods and household gods, with their fiddles and a barrel of soft soap took their way here to the valley of the Mississippi, making themselves merry as well as ready for wash-day. They slept in the wagons, and when the wolves howled about their camp fires on the great prairies of Illinois, they felt as independent as the historic bob-tailed bull in fly time.

The big girls had muscle and with their sleeves rolled up did not hesitate to charge on a wash-tub, kill a chicken and churn, and fry dough-nuts as a treat for their sweet hearts in blue jeans. The days work over they join in the Virginia reel or French four or played Sister Phoebe, who is said to have sat under the juniper tree. This was better than talking about their neighbors; no one did that but the old ladies at tea parties, who after roundly abusing some ancient maiden, and reciting the catalogue of her faults, wound up with, *well, well! after all she's a good girl! a good girl!* There were no breach of promise cases, no divorces, no suits for slander, no enterprising women hunting for trouble, no Flora McFlimsys with nothing to wear. They settled their disputes without law and by arbitration or by a knock down, till the legislature of Wisconsin, then having jurisdiction over the "Black Hawk Purchase," passed an act abolishing trial by battle. Nearly all the county office holders came from Kentucky, those from Knox County, Ohio, monopolized, with a few exceptions, those of the territory and then of the state, and were succeeded by the enterprising Washington County Pennsylvanians.

It used to be the custom here, in "early times," to select for every character of any special note in the place, some *soubriquet* or nick-name—such as the whim of its donors might deem appropriate; upon the same principle, it is presumed, that Napoleon was dubbed by his idolizing soldiery, the "Little Corporal;" Jackson, "Old Hickory;" and Taylor, old "Rough and Ready." Thus we had here, some eight or ten years ago—the originals of which every Old Settler will readily call to mind from the *soubriquet*—The tall Cedar of Lebanon; Devil Creek; Citizen; Dot and go 1; Joe Doane; Doublehead; Compromise; Government; Pompey; Sweet William; Split Dog; Big Muddy; Dont'y; Flitterfoot; Cousin William; Old Juns; Rouser; Little Pee Dee; Fat Boy; Peril; Oh! la me; Peezzle Weezzle; Wharf Rat; *Little* Reed; Red Fox; Heels; Terror; Dornicks; B——s Bill; Berkshire; Osprey; Jurisprudence; Little Duff; Pacing Johnson; Dabney; Picayune Andrews; R. B; and Bucket No. 1; Bucket No. 2; Bucket No. 3; etc., etc., etc.

Among the well known "Institutions" of Keokuk in early times, and still remembered also in connection with her public men, was "Rat Row," a string of log cabins stretched out upon the ground between the fine store houses now fronting upon the levee, and the river; the "Shot Tower," a noted frame building, somewhat upon the lantern order of architecture, that formerly embellished the ground now occupied by the Hardin House; the ancient "Wharf Boat," fitted up for the accommodation of passengers on their arrival and departure; the "Rapids" hotel—sometimes under the noted management of "Sweet William"—the Astor House of the aspiring young City, and where "Peril" the "Tall Cedar," and others, did sometimes congregate to concoct and perform their exploits; the old "Mansion House"—the rival of the "Rapids"—catered for in those days by the inimitable "Pompey;" the "Old Elm Tree," a short distance above the old Packet Depot, to which most of the Steamboats landing here were in the habit of "making fast;" the "Painted Rocks," down near the first Pork House, a favorite place of resort—until their beauty and romance were destroyed by the barbarous innovations of modern stone quarries—of ardent young "lovyers" upon any pleasant Sunday afternoon; the "Fleet of Tow Boats," used for carrying freight over the rapids in low water, and for hauling which, when the supply of rope on hand fell short—as happened not unfrequently—the native grape vine, found in abundance along the river bank, or the bark of the paw-paw and the hickory, was put in requisition as a substitute.

The tall Cedar of Lebanon was General Jesse B. Browne.
Devil Creek, William A. Clark, first Mayor of Keokuk.
Citizen, A. Browne, Commission Merchant.
Dot and go one (1,) Capt. Silas Haight.

A. Holland, Capt. Trotter.
Joe Doan, Squire Samuel Van Fossen.
Doublehead, Colonel John Hills.
Compromise Roberts, Robert Roberts.
Government, Captain Adam Hine.
Pompey, L. B. Fleak.
Sweet William, William Coleman.
Split Log, Colonel Mitchell, of Missouri.
Big Muddy, Lou. Collins, of Muddy Lane.
Donty, Dr. Birdsell.
Flitterfoot, Valencourt Vanorsdall.
Cousin William, William F. Telford.
Old Jums, James H. Wise.
Rouser, Captain William Holliday.
Little Pee Dee, P. D. Foster.
Peril, Dr. O'Hara.
Terror, Dr. Hogan.
O! la, me, John A. Graham.
Red Fox, General H. T. Reid.
Peezle Weezle, William C. Graham.
Little Reed, J. P. Reed
Heels, Lyman E. Johnson.
Dornicks, Calohill E. Stone.
Taller, Dr. Thos. M. Sullivan.
Burns' Bill, William C. Rentgen.
Pacing Johnson, J. Nealy Johnson.
Berkshire, William Timberman.
Black Hawk, Israel Anderson
Osprey, George C. Anderson.
Jurisprudence, Joseph A. Clark.
Dearduff, Little Duff,
R. B., Ross B. Hughes.
Dabney, Zephaniah Meeker.
Billy Confang, William Morrison.
Horse Head, Dr. D. Hoover.
Picayune Andrews, James Andrews.
Bucket No. 1, Isaac R. Campbell.
Bucket No. 2, Henry J. Campbell.
Bucket No. 3, Captain Jim Campbell.
Beef McCready, John McCready, of the country.
Chips, J. B. Thurman.
Wharf Rat, Capt. Daniel Hine,
Sheeps, George A. Hawley.
Anti Christ, John McKean.
Jiggery Jones, Joab Jones.
Garry, Lewis R. Reeves.

THE OLD SETTLERS.

Garret, C. F. Davis.
Lawyer Greasy, L. E. H. Houghton.
Wapsi, Hugh W. Sample.
Old Continental, Peter Eicher.
Black Bill, Bill Thompson.
Off Ox of Democracy, J. C. Hall.
Old Blueface, Palmer of Iowa City.
Cock-eye, Henry W. Starr.
Bow-legs, W. H. Starr.
Old Timber, J. W. Woods.
Eleana Perdew, Kil Kenny.
Uncle Toby, Francis Semple.
Peach Blossom, Phillip Viele.
Old Tilthammer, Peter Miller.
The Old He Possum, Josiah Clifton.
Old John A. Murrell the Law Pirate, M. M. Morrill.
Ghost of Buster, Daniel F. Miller.
Old Buck, Captain William Edwards.
Chief of the Blackfeet, Dr. J. D. Elbert.
King of the Hairy Nation, Dr. John J. Sellman.
Cottonwood, John Hill.

Besides the foregoing there were numerous others such as "Skillet Head," "Trigger Leg," etc., etc., in Iowa, Illinois and Missouri.

Dr. Samuel C. Muir who built the first cabin in what was afterwards Keokuk, was the partner of Isaac R. Campbell who bought old "Rat Row," the quarters of the North American Fur Company, after Farnham died, the agent who established the trading post of that company. Mr. Campbell now lives in St. Francisville, Mo., and was born, as he states, in Oneida Co., New York, in 1798. His ancestors were Scotch with a mixture of Welch blood, but he shows unmistakably his Scotch descent, and for a man of his advanced age has a very remarkable memory of persons and events which happened in the pioneer days of Keokuk when he knew all the Old Settlers. He came West and built a saw mill between Canton and LaGrange, Mo., in 1827, was here where Keokuk now stands the same year and again in 1828. He moved to a place called the "Rising Sun" then, afterward called Commerce, and now Nauvoo, Ill., in 1827. Dr. Muir was his partner from April, 1831, till he died of cholera in 1832. Mr. Campbell was the first administrator on an estate in Lee County, that of Antaya, a Half-Breed Sac and Fox Indian, and the husband of Euphrosine Antaya; he died of Cholera just before the death of Dr. Muir, that epidemic prevailing here in 1832 to an alarming extent considering the sparse population.

Dr. Muir was educated as a physician and surgeon at the University of Edinburg, Scotland, and was a surgeon in the United States Army stationed at the military post of Fort Edwards on the high point on the Illinois shore, just in front of the present residence of Mr. Henry Albers at Warsaw, Ill., the location of the fort being about five miles below Keokuk, and its situation being such as to command an extensive and sweeping view of the river in front and for miles both up and down. Dr. Muir, it is said, was a very able surgeon and a learned man. He was taken sick, and during a severe illness was nursed and tenderly cared for by a full blooded Sac and Fox Indian Squaw, who once saved his life while a prisoner of war, and upon his recovery became so much attached to her that he married her. To this the government made objections, and on the fact being reported to the War Department at Washington, he was dismissed from the service or permitted to resign for the good of the service, which is equivalent to dimissal. He was held in such high estimation as a surgeon, that General Scott and other officers of the army offered to have him restored to his full rank, with all arrears of pay, amounting then to twenty-five hundred dollars, a large sum in that day, when the government paid all its officers in gold. They insisted on his returning to the army, in which he was a favorite, his professional services being highly esteemed; but Dr. Muir considered he had been badly treated and indignantly refused to be reinstated under any circumstances, but thanked General Scott and the other officers for the kindly interest they had taken in his behalf, from their personal friendship to himself, which he highly appreciated. Just before his death he had been on a visit with Mr. Campbell and others to see some patients near the residence of Moses Stillman, and when they were on their return home, just in front of the residence of Daniel Hine, he stopped suddenly, put his hand upon his stomach and said to his friends, I believe I am taking the cholera! They immediately proceeded home, and on the way he gave them full instructions what to give him, prescribing for himself.

They got the medicines as he directed, but he refused to take anything at all, and lingered till next morning when he died. During the night Dr. Isaac Galland was called to see him, but said it was then too late, no human power could give him any relief as he was then in the agonies of death. He was the first white man to die in Keokuk. —— Palean, a Frenchman, who also died of cholera, for whom one of our streets is named, and Edward Brishnell were also at different times the partners of Mr. Campbell, and John Gaines, who was one of the first County Commissioners, was his clerk, and a man of good business qualities, making an efficient clerk. He was afterwards also Justice of the Peace.

During the Black Hawk War in 1832, Jenifer T. Sprigg, who surveyed the Half Breed Tract, was made Captain of a Military Company of Volunteers numbering thirty-four men; Isaac R. Campbell, First Lieutenant and Quarter Master; Horton McFerson, Second Lieutenant, Conlee, Ensign and Dr. Muir, Surgeon. This was the first military company ever raised in Keokuk. Jenifer T. Sprigg was a Major in the war of 1812, a brave man as his selection to command and the testimony of Lieutenant Campbell indicates. He participated in the battle of Bladensburg, called the Bladensburg races, which was no evidence of his want of courage as he was not in command, but was due no doubt to the inefficiency of his commanding officer.

Quarter-master Campbell built a block house at Keokuk and received a large quantity of pork and supplies for the army from St. Louis during the Black Hawk War, and also supplied the posts at Nauvoo and St. Francisville

THE OLD SETTLERS. 15

Mo., Keokuk being the most accessible point reached by steamers and the chief base of all supplies. For their patriotic services this company and its officers were never paid. The Military post at Montrose, commanded by Col. Kearney and Mason as Fort Des Moines from 1834 to 1837, for three years got its supplies from Keokuk. Captain Sumner, a General in the war of 1861, who was every inch a soldier, was stationed at Montrose, also Captain Jessie B. Browne, who subsequently figured as a politician after his resignation from the service, of whom many good stories are told, his sobriquet being, "The Tall Cedar of Lebanon," and Ben S. Roberts, then a young lieutenant, afterwards captain in the Mexican War in which he distinguished himself by capturing General Torrejohn, whose sword is in the Adjutant-General's office at Des Moines, and for this the State Legislature voted him a sword and its thanks. He was a Brigadier-General of note in the late war; was Chief of General Pope's staff at the second battle of Bull Run; was the principal witness against General Fitz John Porter when he was court-martialed and dismissed from the service, and afterwards a commandant of this State with headquarters at Davenport. "Benny," as he was familiarly called, was a character, and one of the best story-tellers we ever heard, and could relate many very amusing incidents about the military post and the Old Settlers. When first assigned to duty, after he graduated at West Point, he reported to the Commanding officer at Montrose in full dress, inexperienced and verdant, with full beard and hair a little too long to comply with the strict requirements of the army regulations. Kearney, a bluff old soldier, immediately ordered him to get his hair cut and get cleanly shaved. He was sent with a detail of men to build a log cabin for quarters, and put it up, and then found it had no doors or windows, and notwithstanding that they could be cut out after the cabin was built, he ordered his men to tear it down and cut out the doors and windows much to the amusement of the pioneer soldiers; and he used to tell this story on himself. From some cause, it is said, from having charge of Government funds in paper which became depreciated and left him a defaulter, he was dismissed from the service but tendered his services to the government at the breaking out of the Mexican War and was made Captain of a company of Mounted Rifles. He was subsequently restored to his full rank with arrears of pay from the date of his dismissal, and promoted in the line of his rank the same as if he had remained in the service all this time. While out of the service he practiced law at Fort Madison and was a Justice of the Peace, and made a deed for a town lot in that city to his mother-in-law, Mrs. Sperry, himself, and certified as Justice of the Peace to the acknowledgement before himself, which is on our county records. At the close of the Mexican War, having a law suit in the Court at Fort Madison, involving the validity of the decree title, in which suit in chancery he claimed an interest in the Half Breed tract, not admitted in the decree, he came into court in full dress uniform as a Captain, with his blue coat and pants and brass buttons, with belt sword and epauletts to make an argument and create an impression, which he did, as the New York Company compromised with him and paid him over three thousand dollars to quit. While in the service on the plains he got thrown from his horse and severely injured, in consequence of which he lost his voice for some time and could only speak in a whisper. He got leave of absence and went to Washington to look after a soft place, and while there kept interviewing Old Marcy, then Secretary of War, till one day the Secretary said to a friend "he had got tired of hearing that whispering, it followed him every place he went," for "Benny" was perservering. So he sent him to command a post on the frontiers in New Mexico, just what he wanted, for if he could not be in Washington, "Benny," who loved a little authority, no matter how brief, went to his post. Here he set to work and in a short time captured a lot of Mexican thieves and outlaws who had been making raids into our territory, and created a big sensation by hanging them all. It was a summary proceeding, and there is no doubt he served them right, for if they did not deserve to be hung for the offences with which they were charged, did deserve it upon general principles, and as amusements were at that remote quarter very scarce, it made a good time and a public day for the soldiers. All of these old-time officers, stationed at Montrose then, often visited Keokuk on business or pleasure.

General James C. Parrott, now Post-master, was first Sergeant in a Company of U. S. Dragoons, stationed there in 1834, and has resided in the county except when temporarily absent, and as Colonel of the 7th Iowa Infantry in the war of 1864-5, ever since, and ranks with William Skinner, formerly County Commissioner, as one of our oldest settlers. Valencourt Vanorsdall, who came here with his brother, and brother-in-law Moses Stillwell, being the oldest settler now living, his first residence dating as far back as 1828. They settled on the original claim of Dr. Muir, which he had leased to Otis Reynolds, an old steamboat captain, and John Culver, both of St. Louis. They employed Moses Stillwell as their agent, and he came here with his family that year, and in 1831 Margaret Stillwell, afterwards Mrs. Dr. E. R. Ford, was born, said to be the first white child born in Keokuk.

John Gaines, to whom we have heretofore referred as the clerk of Isaac R. Campbell, Alexander Hood, and William McBride, both noted as roughs, and Major Thomas W. Taylor came the same year, and Nathan Smith, of St. Francisville, Mo., now seventy years of age, came here in 1833, and gives a graphic account of the Old Settlers of that day. Born in Washington County, Pennsylvania, he came west to Galena, then a village, in 1826, was there some two years in the lead mines, and was some ten years with the Sac and Fox Indians at Galena, Rock River, St. Joseph, Mo., Keokuk and up the Des Moines River and other places, as a trader, interpreter and a scout, and spy for General Gaines, and afterwards for General Atkinson in the Black Hawk War. He carried the mail on horseback from Rock Island to Quincy, Ill., when there was but two houses on the route in 1829-30, that of John White, at Nauvoo, the father-in-law of Isaac R. Campbell, and that of Major Marston who had been an officer of the army at Fort Edward, and then lived below the present town of Warsaw, Ill. He well knew Black Hawk and Keokuk, and General Gaines, of whom he had a high opinion of as a soldier, for his manly decision of character, and also General Atkinson, from whom he carried the commission to Colonel Henry Dodge to raise volunteers to fight the Indians. He speaks of

THE OLD SETTLERS.

Atkinson as a weak and undecided man, without the soldierly qualities of Gen. Gaines, and adds that Dodge did all the fighting which is no doubt true. We will have occasion again to refer more fully to Black Hawk and Keokuk and our officers and others who participated in the Black Hawk War. The officers at Montrose were great friends of Campbell, particularly Sumner and Browne, and the latter always stopped with him often for days at a time. These two officers on different occasions would come with details of soldiers for corn to feed the horses of the U. S. Dragoons at that post, and when Sumner and Browne came they always were liberal with the soldiers, giving them all the whiskey they could drink or stow away in their canteens, and also took a liberal supply themselves, as Campbell was generous with his whiskey, which he had to keep in those days or not keep a store, but never drank a drop himself. As a consequence the corn for the horses was strewed along the road from Keokuk to Montrose. We spoke of Alexander Hood as a desperado and a rough; he was married to a daughter of Dr. Muir, a half-breed woman, who was not to blame in any way for his short comings. On one occasion he had been to St. Louis and left his wife at the house of Mr. Campbell, and had just returned on the steamer "Warrior," then lying at the wharf. He came in the store and loafed about for several hours, quarreled with his wife, and talked of dividing their personal property and separating from her, and finally left and came back about midnight intoxicated, got a lighted candle and wanted Campbell to get up, but before he had time to do so, approached the bed on which he was lying with his infant daughter, and stabbed at him with a long Spanish dagger which fortunately missed him, but stuck in the pillow near the little girls head. Campbell arose at once and seized his rifle, which was not loaded, attacked Hood, striking him a furious blow, for he was then a young and powerful man, and he fell, and in falling fell outside of the door where he laid motionless and bleeding as if dead. The mate of the boat came up and saw him and said, if he was not dead it was a great pity he had not been killed. Mr. Campbell was afraid he had killed him. Captain Browne was then stationed near by and he sent a messenger to him immediately to send him a surgeon. Browne inquired what the surgeon was wanted for. The messenger told him. Tell Mr. Campbell, said Browne, I will not send him any surgeon for that d——d rascal, and tell him from me, if he has not killed him to kill him any way. Alexander Hood did not die, but was ever in a muss or a fight, and had a row with one John Hamilton, of Warsaw, shooting him in the mouth but did not kill him, his gun being loaded with nails. The people were indignant, and for some time he kept clear of Warsaw. One night, however, he ventured to go down there disguising himself as an Indian to take observations. It was some time before he was recognized but was finally discovered and the word went about the town that Alexander Hood was there. A crowd had now collected and found him in a saloon drinking and carousing, and instantly arrested him. The excitement was great; and threats were made of lynching him, and the crowd decided to hang him. A rope was produced. He begged and plead for his life; affairs were getting desperate; he talked in Indian, in English and French, to no purpose; they resolved to string him up. Just then, in the nick of time, Dr. Wilkinson, a prominent and influential citizen, appeared upon the scene. The crowd swayed open, and made way for him as he walked up to Hood and addressed him in French. Hood begged him to save him; he would suffer any punishment to save his life. The Doctor addressed the crowd deprecating lynch law and pointing out its bad effects on the reputation of the town abroad. Others came to the rescue, and then he proposed a compromise; he was to be whipped and turned loose. Hood readily assented to this; he was glad to do anything to save his life. The contract was thus settled and agreed upon, and the lynchers further confirmed it by a loud hurrah. One man, by his pluck and daring had battled successfully against a host and carried the day before him, and saved a life. Alexander Hood acknowledged he owed his life to Dr. Wilkinson. But the end was not yet; he was taken to the brush, followed by his persecutors, stripped to the buff, and retribution meeted out to him, which he richly deserved. He got thirty lashes upon the bare rump, well laid on, every stroke bringing the claret which flowed like a rivulet. He yelled like a wild Indian, and as the black snake whip came down with a whack, resounding through the air, it and his cries were heard for near a mile, and at every stroke he bounced up high in the air. The agony was soon over; and in less time than it takes to tell it, with his back excoriated and bleeding, sober and penitent as a whipped dog with his tail between his legs, he went sneaking away on his road homeward, cheered by the lynchers who gave him a parting salute and his orders as an exile never to return. The surgeon, who dressed his wounds on his return home at daybreak, told us his back was clotted with blood and looked very much as if a map of buffalo paths, leading to a big spring, had been laid out upon it.

CHAPTER II.

Sketches of Keokuk, the Indian Chief. His Public Services and power as an Orator. His Wives and his Attempted Assassination. Imitating Henry Clay. His Mother, La Lotte, a Half-Breed.—The Hairy Nation and its King.—Soap Creek.—Anecdotes of Dr. Rogers, an Old Surgeon, who puts a Wooden Leg on a Hog.—Mickey Curtayne, the Irrepressible Irish Constable.—Jackson holding a Steamboat.—Bill Price, the desperado.

KEOKUK, as the Chief of the Sac and Foxes, belonged to the peace party, and was opposed to the mad councils of The Black Hawk, who thirsted for revenge by war upon the whites. He was a friend of the whites, and the best authorities say, cool and collected, with the far seeing gifts of the statesman and diplomatist; he negotiated difficult treaties with much judgment and skill, evincing rare talent and perception of the savage characters with whom he had to deal. "He was a large and finely formed man, his manners were dignified and graceful, and his elocution in public speaking and conversation energetic, expressive and animated. His flow of language and rapidity of utterance remarkable, yet his enunciation so clear and distinct that not a syllable was lost. His voice was powerful and agreeable, and his countenance prepossessing. It is not often so fine a looking man as this forest chief has been seen, or one whose deportment has been so uniformly correct." The old pictures we see of him here, first painted and then photographed from a bad painting, are the pictures of an old Indian, and may have borne some resemblance to him when taken, as an old man emasculated by age, but have little resemblance to him in the prime of life. The portrait taken of him at Washington, with his young son at his feet, when in his full vigor and the zenith of his power, shows him to be a man. This was at a time too, when he was in council and in the presence of Mr Poinsett, then Secretary of War, and the hostile Sioux, who were his enemies, when criminations and recriminations were bandied bitterly between parties. The Sioux accused him of bad faith, and said that they could not depend on treating with him any more than the boy, his son, at his feet, that the ears of his people had to be pricked with sticks. The speeches were bitter on both sides, and the secretary by a conciliatory speech, but to no purpose, tried to make peace between them. Keokuk, in his great speech, which was interpreted at the end of each sentence, in reply, told the Sioux chiefs that when they had invaded the country of the Sioux they had shown themselves men, that they had taken many scalps and could give the times and places when they took them, and that the heads of the Sioux wanted to be bored with hot irons. The Sioux and other Indians, except Keokuk and his party, were rigged out with blue coats and brass buttons at this conference held in a church at Washton, D. C., their clothing being presented to them and are thus painted. Keokuk was dressed in the war-like garb of an Indian chief, and his chiefs according to their rank with their wampum, war paint and Indian insignias such as eagle feathers, &c., of their greatness, while in one hand he holds a long round stick, decorated apparently with ribbons; this was his battle flag which he holds in state as a king upon his throne, as his royal baton or scepter, as his badge of authority, as Canute is pictured rebuking the waves with the memorable "thus far shalt thou go and no farther, &c." He had the power to organize and command, to discipline his men and hold them in subjection, and this was remarked of him at Washington. While the other Indians were disorderly and went about riotously, his won the confidence and regard of all by their dignity and general good behavior; this was, no doubt, due to the chief, and it is from such evidence as this all experienced military officers would form the opinion that he was an able chief, able to successfully command and make a military force effective, requiring executive ability in the chief to conceive and enforce obedience, the *esprit de corps* or animating spirit of all collective bodies. To show his strategy in a case of emergency, an instance is related when he and his party, numerically weak and not on the war path were on the march. By accident or through his advanced scouts, he discovered the Sioux were all ready to march and attack his village by surprise, though the tribes were at peace. The treacherous Sioux were rigged out, armed and painted for war; with savage yells and ceremonies to work themselves up into warlike frenzy before beginning the march; recounting their deeds of valor, they were joined in the wardance. Keokuk saw the situation at a glance, and haulting his braves at a safe distance, he gave them their orders to remain till his return. Splendidly mounted on a nigh mettled horse he set out, and before they were aware of it, while they were in a high state of excitement, he was in their midst, his sudden and unexpected appearance striking them with as much astonishment as if the lightnings of heaven descending in their fury had stricken and shivered to atoms the upright center pole of their war lodge. Keokuk, in a voice of thunder, called for the chief, who advanced, and as he came toward him, cried out, there is a traitor in the camp! I have heard you are ready to make war on my village! I am not ready to believe it! The chiefs had laid their hands on his legs; their object was doubtless to make him prisoner. The principal Sioux chief had not spoken. Keokuk saw the storm rising, and with the glance of his eagle eye took in the situation and was equal to the emergency. Suddenly digging his spurs into the flanks of his horse, he galloped away, riding down or releasing himself from the grasp of his enemies who held him, and giving the war whoop as he flew; several shots were fired at him, but without effect; he reached his little party, the Sioux pursuing, but being afraid of falling into an ambuscade, they approached in view but withdrew without an attack, and Keokuk and his braves, now safe, returned to their village.

Again he demonstrated his military ability and sagacity as a ruler and leader when the odds were largely against him. The prophet, an intriguing Indian, pretended to have dreams and visions, and used his influence so to work on their superstitious credulity as to incite the British, a faction of the Sauks or Sacs, afterwards the Black Hawk Band, to war with the whites in 1831, which finally culminated in the Black Hawk War of 1832, resulted in the battle of Bad Axe, the total defeat and death of Black Hawks warriors, he and only a few others escaping; but it is not our intention to speak of it here, as it will more properly come under the head of our notice of Black Hawk himself, the great war chief.

Keokuk, as we have said, was ever faithful and the friend of the whites But a faction, led by the prophet, endeavored to imbroil him and his tribe in the war, to which he was bitterly opposed. He promptly notified our government of the fact and desired to have his loyaly tested and the government satisfied. For this purpose he requested that a white man, who spoke the Sauk language, be sent to live in their midst and take observations, he being in the meantime under the protection of Keokuk who confided everything to him. He knew too well what would be the fatal results of such a war. But his young braves thirsted for blood to be distinguished or die in battle. Keokuk protested against this but held them in check by his great influence. But there came a day, a time when he stood solitary and alone. Emissaries came from the prophet, the tools of designing men, and made speeches of the most inflammatory character to these Indians, supplied them with whiskey, and incited them by a rehearsal of their wrongs and a desire for vengence to such a pitch of frenzy and madness, that with one voice they declared for war, and demanded that he, as their chief, should lead them. The critical period had come, and he directed the representative of the government to hide himself before the brewing storm he saw coming on should culminate in a whirlwind, carrying all before it. For him to remain was certain death, and the life of Keokuk, now that the excitement, controled by this foreign element, ran to its highest, was trembling in the balance like the sword of Democles suspended by a hair. Keokuk was unmoved and silent till called upon to respond to their call to lead them; they were then west of the Mississippi River, in what is now Iowa. Slowly he arose, and every eye was turned upon their chief. Had he mistaken the shouts of the mob for the trumpet of fame, to meet its execrations the next? Folding his blanket slowly across his breast, he stood in an attitude of grandure and defiance. All eyes were still directed to their chief they had unanimously chosen as their leader in a war on the whites east of the Mississippi River. They awaited his answer; it was decisive; he would go, he would lead them, but upon *one* condition only, that was, that they would first kill all their squaws and children, destroy all their property, and armed for the fight recross the Mississippi River, never to return, but to fight and to die there by the graves of their fathers! The excitement died away, the sober second thought returned to his people, and the partisans of war were not willing to make the sacrifice, and Keokuk, the Peace Chief, thus won over to himself his people, who decided with him against war, and were thus saved from certain extermination.

Nathan Smith, who has heretofore been mentioned as for a long time interpreter and a spy among the Indians, was at Keokuk's camp or village, on the Iowa River, during the troubles resulting in the Black Hawk War. There was great excitement in the village, and night after night Keokuk assembled the people of his tribe in the Council House and made speeches to them—his speeches were opposed to war—he told them its consequences, and as Smith understood every word he uttered, and was in the habit of hearing the best public speakers, he says that he never heard an orator equal to Keokuk. His influence with his people was great; they knew him to be brave, but it was with difficulty he restrained them from their natural love of war. He made several journeys to Washington and was much trusted for his integrity and fidelity to our government.

Keokuk was a quarter blood, not a full blooded Indian, a Sac or Saux. This is not generally known, but it is nevertheless a well authenticated fact which is settled beyond any controversy. His mother was La Lott, a half-breed Indian woman, as appears from a letter dated at Rocky Island, as it was then called, but now Rock Island, on the 9th of June, 1830, addressed to Gen. William Clark, then superintendent of Indian Affairs at St. Louis, Mo., which was written out by Thomas Forsythe, Indian Agent for Keokuk, Taimah and other chiefs, and explained and signed by six of them in number, all uniting in the letter, which is a curiosity, and to show that what we assert is true, as a historical fact we now publish it for the benefit of the public, as it has always been taken for granted that this noted chief was of pure Indian blood. To the Caucasian element in his composition he no doubt owed much of that sagacity which distinguished him, that prophetic foresight which enabled him to see the future, utter extinction of his nation, which by his wisdom in council he sought to defer, for he was what Maribeau was to France, the Rienzi, the last of the tribunes of his race, was to Rome. The letter speaks of the half-breeds of the Sac and Fox nation of Indians, viz.:

To GENERAL WILLIAM CLARK,
    Superintendent of Indian Affairs at St. Louis, Mo.:

FATHER—Last year while at Prairie du Chien, we wrote a letter to our Great Father, the President of the United States, requesting him to have the lands surveyed which we give to our relations, the half-breeds of our nation, as the treaty made at the city of Washington, on the 4th of August, 1824, but as yet have received no answer.

Father—Above are the names (a list of names precedes the letter) and ages of the half-breeds of our nations who were in existence when we made the treaty and to whom we give the tract of land, and to none others whatever

Father—We wish you to interest yourself for our relations, the half-breeds of our nations who are mentioned in the above list, to have their land surveyed and equally divided, it being perfectly understood at the before mentioned treaty that the late Maurice Blondeau was to have his choice of any place in said tract so granted.

Father—We wish you to remove all the white people now on that tract of land, which we intend for the use of the half-breeds of our nations, and not allow any white people of any description to settle and live on that land, except a father, a husband or a wife of any of the half-breeds, or any agent or agents appointed by the President.

Father—We wish you to prevent any white person or half-breed from keeping spirituous liquors for sale on any part of the above mentioned tract of land, on any account whatever, but to any white people or half-breeds, who wish to sell goods to Indians or others, we can have no objections to them being allowed to remain any where on this tract of land, *provided you choose to give them a license.*

    Signed,   Pershapaho, his X mark.
            Pukkenami, his X mark.
            Wabawlaw, his X mark.
            Tiamah,   his X mark.
            Keokuck, his X mark.
            Moccopawn, his X mark.

It will be seen that there were post-traderships at that day, and they in the letter to the Indian agents at that day, had an eye to business; as old Bullion said of Douglas's Nebraska bill, it had a stump speech in its belly, so the latter had *licences to trade* in the belly of this Indian letter to General Clark, also a surveying contract, but here follows the remarkable part of the letter about Keokuk's mother:

"The above chiefs also request that La Lott, (Keokuk's mother), a half-breed, shall have a share in the above mentioned lands, that is to say that Thomas Abbott's and La Lott's land may join together at a place called the Orchard, at the head of the Des Moines Rapids.

Explained and signed before me this 9th of June, 1830, at Rocky Island.
    Signed,   THOMAS FORSYTHE,
                 Indian Agent.

THE OLD SETTLERS.

From the name La Lott, Keokuk's mother, was either a French woman or his father a Frenchman, as the name La Lott is evidently a French name, hence his vivacity and the impetuous fiery magnetism of his oratory resulted from his French, not so much as from his Indian origin, whence he derived his cunning and quick perception of the savage reared like a wild animal in the wilderness.

The savages are dark copper-colored, and while Black Hawk was unmistakably a full-blooded Indian, with all the war-like instincts of his race and the marked physognomy, narrow forehead, high cheek bones, erect carriage and lithe spare figure. Keokuk's complexion was of a lighter color, his face and forehead high, broad and intellectual, thus showing a wide difference in the character and make up of the two men. The one was the proud savage warrior, who turned neither to the right nor to the left, whose gaze was like the eagles upon the sun without flinching, whose tread was as proud as that of the Roman gladiator entering the arena of death.

In the language of the great and fallen cardinal, his ideal though that of the savage, and differing from our own ideal of right, was to "be just and fear not."

Keokuk's reflective faculties led him to look in advance and to take measures with statesman-like foresight, to accomplish his ends.

Both desired the good of their people, but there was this difference; one thought it was glory enough to die on the war path and to die as a brave; the other saw in war with the whites nothing but misfortunes and calamities.

The old chief Keokuk lived for a long time in a little bark hut in the present city of Keokuk. At Washington, D. C., he made the acquaintance of Mr. Clay, whom he greatly admired. Clay always carried a gold-headed cane tucking it under his arm. Taking a fancy to Keokuk he presented him with a silver-headed cane like his own with a sword in it, and Keokuk imitating Mr. Clay, always carried that cane as Mr. Clay carried his own, under his left arm.

About four hundred Indians were camped near Athens, Mo., on the Des Moines River, Sac's and Foxes, after the Black Hawk War, and as is well known, till his return from captivity, Black Hawk was hostile to Keokuk, as were also many of the Foxes. Keokuk had superseded him, and was one of the peace party. Till Black Hawk's return they believed he had betrayed them, which was not true, as the Black Hawk learned to his satisfaction. Sharing in this hostility of his chief, a Fox Indian, madened with whiskey, resolved to assassinate Keokuk at the camp during a festival.

With this object in view he stealthily walked behind him and seized the head of the cane, presented by Mr. Clay, drew out the sword, and before Keokuk could prevent it, stabbed him with the intention of running the blade through his heart.

The sword was of very fine steel and as limber as a Damascus blade carried by the Crusaders and Moors.

Instead of piercing his heart it struck a rib and glanced off passing around, inflicting a painful but not a fatal wound. On Black Hawk's return great de.

monstrations were made over him and a big dinner was given him at Sammy Bartlett's, at St. Francisville, at which Black Hawk and Keokuk, and their families were present and here they made friends. Mrs. Louisa Briggs and Mrs. Harriet Conway were cooks, the latter the mother of Mrs. Charlie Grumman, of the Alexandria Commercial.

The Indians made great rejoicings. Keokuk's old wife was there and assisted the cooks to take a large door off of its wooden hinges for a table. Keokuk was decked out in a calico shirt, silver rings and brass medals, carrying the inevitable silver-headed cane, with his young squaw wife, for whom he had discarded his old one, his last one being about thirty years of age. The chiefs and their two sons were seated in the places of honor at each end of the table, and at the conclusion of the feast thanked Mr. Bartlett and Jerry Wayland always their friends, saying "great big white men live heap years."

The war-hoop of the "big Injin" had hardly died away when the "Waybash" and Posey sent its recruits here to help populate the country.

They landed at Keokuk, went up the "divide" in their prairie schooners to Ottumwa, the capital of Soap Creek, forded the Des Moines and crossed over into the land of promise the "Hairy Nation," since celebrated for its wealth, its men of genius and talent, and its fund of humorous stories to which there is no end. The future capital of the Hairy Nation was destined to be Bloomfield, Davis County.

The King of the Hairy Nation at that day was Dr. John I. Sellman, and there used to be an old picture of moving the capital in which his likeness as senator stood out in bold relief and could easily be recognized; also that of R. R. Harbor, of "Proud Mahaska," and Gill Fulsom, of Iowa City, a prominent and eccentric lawyer.

The Hairy Nation has ever since its early settlement sustained the reputation it then made, for hospitality, courage, enterprise and fun. The people of the Hairy Nation were a great people; most of the early settlers were from Hoosier. Dr. Sellman, who was the leading democratic politician, and an eminent physician, was, as we have said, called the King of the Hairy Nation. Most of its people then wore beards, which was not usual, and long hair, and many of them coon-skin caps and fawn skin vests. He was a man of great natural ability, but was eccentric and original as he was talented, he feared no man, and was very popular, as he understood the people, and was born to be a leader. He could look at a man and read him, and make a diagnosis of his disease and prescribe for him without going to books to study up his case, and many of the old settlers to-day will not employ any one else. His original sayings were legion, one in particular, when speaking of some "new comer" who was a little too fresh in his longings for office, and put himself forward, he would say, "We tramped the dog fennel and smart weed long before he came here!"

Dr. McKay Findley, now President of the Bloomfield Bank, was an able physician, a genial, whole-souled gentleman, with much business capacity, and cared nothing for dress, and used to visit his patients barefooted, with his pants rolled up to his knees so he could better wade through the mud.

THE OLD SETTLERS. 25

Harvey Dunlavy, a lawyer and a Scotchman, had aspirations for Congress; he never got there, but went to the legislature; he believed Bloomfield was the center of creation and ought to have a member of Congress. His son is credited with capturing General Marmaduke.

When the war of the rebelion came on, the Hairy Nation was among the first to rush to the front and furnished many gallant officers and soldiers, among the rest Col. James Baker, killed at Corinth, Col. Henry H. Trimble, wounded at Pea Ridge, an able lawyer and judge; Gen. J. B. Weaver, a gifted public speaker and prominent lawyer; Gen. Cyrus Bussey, an orator of rare talent; Col. Sam Moore, a soldier of courage and capacity, and Col. George Duffield, without a peer as a humorist, brimful of fun, and here let us tell a story on him. When Col. Bussey organized the 3d Iowa Cavalry, George was Captain and soon made Major. An old hotel keeper, named Martin, wanted to be made an officer Duffield understood his weakness and gave him to understand indirectly that he was to be made a Major. Martin put on a boiled shirt, got cleanly shaved, came down to Keokuk, put on his best clothes, stopped at the hotel where all the officers put up, and in due time received a commission as major, purporting to come from Governor Kirkwood. (It was bogus of course.) He was highly elated, showed his commission confidentially to many of his friends. For several days he walked about feeling that his time had come at last. But no one called him major. He opened his eyes and smelt a rat and took himself off home. George says he never commissioned him, but that will do to tell to the marines.

Dr. John D. Elbert, who lived near Pittsburg above Keosauqua after you cross the river on the wagon road to Bloomfield, at an early day was considered a skillful surgeon and no doubt was then the best in the country.

He was a Virginian by birth, affable and polite to every one, and very hospitable after the old Virginia style, and always invited you to stop at his house and take dinner and stay all night, and was the prince of hosts. He was a gentleman of the old school, was large and portly, weighing near three hundred, and had a very dark skin and very black hair and eyes, and from being very much the complexion of the Indians, used to laugh and style himself chief of the Blackfeet. The doctor aspired to be a politician and was once elected senator.

He went to the capital and returned home during the holidays and made a visit to see his constituents at Keosauqua, the county seat.

Being in the habit of making a great many gestures with his hands, and seeing a crowd on the side walk, who rather hesitated in approaching him, he saluted them repeatedly, as they came, and as he threw out his hands gesturing to them rapidly, cried out, fellow citizens! approach your senator! approach me as usual! I am nothing more than a common man!

Judge John A. Drake went to the Hairy nation from Fort Madison, at an early day, and laid out the town, became wealthy, and, though a whig, was personally very popular in the democratic Hairy nation, and could be elected as Probate Judge or Senator when he chose.

When living at Fort Madison he was a Justice of the Peace, and Dr. Joel C. Walker, ex-clerk of the U. S. District Court, under Judge Mason, tells a good story on him. Drake knew every one, and knew the reliability of witnesses, and who it would do to believe, and when a case came before him soon made up his mind without hearing all the evidence. On one occasion there was a suit up before him on an account for fourteen dollars and twelve and a half cents. The defendant in the case set up as a defense to save costs that he had tendered plaintiff the money. To make a tender good as a legal tender at that day, the money tendered must be in coin, gold or silver. The witnesses for the defense were sworn, and one old fellow named Keim, (whom Drake would not believe at any rate,) was sworn to prove the tender. Old Keim lisped when he spoke. And when called up was put on the stand and sworn, and asked by the attorney for the defense if he saw the money paid. Y-e-e-s sir! said Keim, I did! How much was it? I didn't count it, replied Keim, but judging from the size of the pile, there was about fourteen dollars and a bit!— Some silver money and some paper money! As the witness testified, Drake kept nodding his head to him, saying yes sir! yes sir! while at the same time he was writing up his judgment for the plaintiff.

His son "Marion" was a Lieut. Col. and Brigadier General in the late war, and is now a prominent citizen and president of the M. I. & N. R. R. at Centerville, and has the jovial characteristics and humor of his father. He distinguished himself for his personal courage as an officer in the army. He was the law partner of Amos Harris, a prominent politician, who went to Kansas, after representing Apanoose county in the Senate, and being the democratic candidate for congress.

Centerville has an ex-congressman, Major Waldron, formerly of Lee county, and ex-attorney general Baker, of Mo., previously of Chariton, Iowa. On one occasion, our first visit to Centerville, we recollect of meeting Judge Tannehill, then a young attorney, and a certain old Dr. Potts, who believed in witches, and nailed a horse shoe over his door to keep them away. General T. I. McKenny, who was full of fight, had, when here in business, a dispute with Major Waldron about an unsettled account. They both grew excited, and the lie passed between them. Mc, who was a small man, but full of grit, and would fight with his fist, a pistol, or any other way, if it was against his weight in giants, dared the Major to go back of the store, in the alley, and fight it out. They went, and after two or three blows the Major, who was physically larger and more powerful, caught him and threw him, and dealt him such a terrible blow in the ribs that took away his breath, while he choked him, but Mc would not surrender, and if it had not been for the bystanders separating them, the Major would have made short work of the valiant General.

Chariton was once a rural district of the "Hairy Nation," where the democracy and whigs held their congressional conventions.

At a convention where Gus Hall was nominated for congress, a hotel keeper at that place charged extortionate rates to the delegates—double fare. Some complained, and St. John, who kept the house, grew insolent. Dr. Wm. H. Davis, of Fort Madison, who had been Surgeon General, of the fillibustering army of William Walker, "the grey-eyed man of destiny," who was a very powerful man, (and once adjourned his court, as Justice of the Peace, fifteen minutes, to whip Bill Thurston, a pettifogging lawyer,) struck him a powerful blow in the face, and in drawing back cut his knuckles so badly in the glass of a show case, that his hand bled profusely, when sheriff Wm. H. Leech, of Lee county, forgetting he was over a hundred miles from home, commanded the peace as sheriff of Lee county. In the interim, while they were parleying, Gus Goodrich, who had not paid his bill at all, cooly stepped up and demanded that St. John repay him the double fare he had paid, and made him pay it over.— Great excitement prevailed, and the people of Chariton were so indignant that it was difficult to restrain them from lynching St. John on the spot.

This was before the days of railroads, and all the prominent politicians of the district were at this convention. Hall and his friends, George Gillespie, Judge Johnstone, Judge Trimble, and their friends, Dr. Elbert, Judge Townsend and Perry, Judge Hendershot, Dr. James D. Eads, and others less noted, who had then, and have since, figured conspicuously.

The business of the convention over, Hall made a speech, in which he told the story of the "pig and the pup," while others amused themselves by playing poker, and Gus. Goodrich paid his addresses to Sally, a big, bouncing, red faced chambermaid,

Peter Rougy, a German living in Marion township, had Dr. Lowry, an old practicing physician of West Point, Lee county, as his family physician. He lived in the country five miles west of the town of West Point. Peter had never been sick himself, but the Doctor had been in the habit of coming out to his house in the country when called to visit his family. Peter got sick himself with fever and ague. Before daylight one morning in September, 1847, the clatter of horses hoofs were heard in the streets of West Point; it was Peter Rougy. He came to town in a full gallop. He had a high fever on at the time. Stopping in front of Dr. Lowry's house he called out, halloo! The Doctor in a few minutes appeared and inquired what was wanting. (Peter) I'm sick with the fever and ague, and want you to go out to my house to see me!

When Death and Haight ran the Old Mill on the levee, Mr. James Hurst, known now and highly regarded as an old settler, and Thommy Holt, went to the mill on business where they saw some castor beans, out of which castor oil is manufactured. They had never seen any before, and thought they were very pretty, therefore they must be good. They bought some and took them home, and had them cooked for dinner, and ate heartily of them. The oil in the beans soon created a revolution in their stomachs and intestines; they became deathly sick and lively in their movements. The beans physiced them severely, but they wondered what could bring on this seveie and continued purging. They got frightened at last, thought they might have been poisoned. The doctor came and the secret was out. They knew beans when the bag was open before this, but never after feasted on castor beans, and to this day laugh about it and tell the story of the castor beans.

DR. S. ROGERS.

Noted for his genius and eccentricity of character, was an old settler of Keokuk, and one of its first physicians. He had great natural talent; was a fine writer; could tell a good story; was brimful of wit, and could write good poetry by the yard on the impulse of the moment. He was an Irishman, or at least of Irish descent, and came here at an early day to practice medicine, and put the following advertisement in the *Register*, June 5, 1847:

"Dr. S. ROGERS.

As I have never experienced much difficulty in treating the various maladies incident to the human family, in consequence of not understanding their nature, I would wish to be troubled as little as possible with all other diseases except ague and fever.

The chief calamities of life generally fall upon the poor, therefore I solicit none of their patronage; but am the humble servant of the wealthy part of the community, because there is some prospect of obtaining a reward for my services. Dr. S. ROGERS."

He was a great drinker at one time, and guzzled large quantities of cheap corn juice, and told funny stories to the crowds gathered together in the numerous restaurants, eating houses, and other houses frequented by the river rats along rat row.

A full grown hog was frequently seen with a herd, and sometimes alone in the brush, or skirmishing for garbage or grains of corn dropped on the levee. This hog had a hard time of it, and was minus a leg; one of his hind legs was off above the middle joint. Old Dr. Rogers took pity on the hog; it was too bad, he said, to have that hog run about in this way; he wanted a new leg.— Some of the party thought the Doctor was only joking, but they caught the hog and brought him to him. The Doctor took his measure for a wooden leg, got a piece of board, took his knife and carved out a complete wooden leg, and fitted it on the hog, which was then turned loose and walked about as if he had four good legs, only he walked a little lame. This made a good deal of fun at the time, and was much commented upon, but it helped to spread his fame as a Surgeon, and his practice at one time was extensive. He finally quit using corn juice, and as a substitute, to keep up the excitement of his system, he commenced using opium and morphine, which he took in almost incredible quantities, and in a state of stupor would go to sleep in a chair or any other place he happened to be. In 1867 Dr. Bartlett assisted him and he raised money enough to take him to Washington Territory, where General McKenny gave him an appointment as physician for the Indians. From using so much morphia, or from the want of it, he became insane, and finally died in the territorial lunatic asylum.

"MICKEY" CURTAYNE.

There was a little Irishman who came to Keokuk in 1855; he had come direct from Ireland to New York, and stayed there two years before he came here, and was at first employed as a porter in a store. "Mickey," for by that name he was known, was a good worker then, but his five years in this country having expired in 1858, he was naturalized, and as "Mickey" aspired to be a politician, he was very active in drumming up voters at elections, and was himself nominated and elected Constable. He was much impressed with his importance, and rushed about serving papers, and got a little office on which he put up a sign "Michael Curtayne, Constable, and Collector for Iowa, Illinois, and Missouri." Mickey one day had a subpoena to serve on a man as a witness in a suit, and called out to him as he walked along the street, "hold on till I level a sub-peen on yees!"

He served an execution levying on some cattle, and made this return:— "Leveled on five cows, one of which was a 'muly bull.'"

Mickey was nominated as the chamber maid of the Salt River Packet by the Governor Belknap, of the mock legislature, but not confirmed. Mickey was indignant that his name should be used in this way. He got married to a demi-rip; she whipped Mickey and drove him off, and he got a divorce. He served in the grey beards in the war of 1861; got to be Corporal, and was, when last heard of, still thirsting for office as policeman, in Louisville, Kentucky.

HOLDING A STEAMBOAT.

In 1840 a little steamer hove in sight, coming up the river, and landed near the foot of Main street, the line was thrown out and one of the deck hands came ashore by the stage plank, and, seizing the line, was about tying it around a post put there for that purpose. A big country boy named Jackson was standing on the wharf watching the boat, and saw it land. It looked like a very small boat to him. He was verdant and did not understand the power of steam. So when the deck hand came ashore, he had hold of the line, and the deck hand was about to take it up to tie up the boat, but Jackson, who wanted to be clever and accommodating, spoke out and said, "let it alone, and never mind, I can hold her!"

BILL PRICE.

Bill Price was married to a half-breed squaw, and was among the first and oldest settlers, and lived here at the same time with Isaac R. Campbell, John Gaines, and till long after Campbell left, and Gaines died, and was well known as a turbulent character, always getting into fights and whipping some one, for he was a bully, and sometimes he got whipped himself. Once a man named Jackson, whom he had been imposing upon for some time, whipped him badly, but a party of Price's enemies who wanted him whipped, first got him drunk, and then put Jackson up to whip him, which he found was then an easy job, and after that Price let him alone. He was vindictive and revengeful, and would watch his chances to get even, and sometimes took a gun and watched, shooting men from the brush. Price's Creek was named for him, and on one occasion he ordered his brother Lindsay to watch from the brush at this creek and shoot a man. The man passed that way but Lindsay, who saw him, did not shoot him, and when old Bill found it out he gave him a terrible thrashing. A stranger named Green, from Ohio, who settled near West Point, stopped here on his way to Fort Madison, got off the Steamboat to go up on the side hill to get a fresh drink of spring water. He stooped down to drink, but happening to look up in the brush above him, what was his astonishment to see a man there with a rifle, taking deliberate aim at him. He did not shoot, but drawing up his rifle said, "excuse me, stranger, I took you for another man."—

The stranger from this little adventure at the beginning got a bad impression of the country, but soon got over it, and settled on a farm near West Point, where he died.

Many stories of his fights and troubles with different people are told of him.

He finally got sick and found he was going to die, at his place above town, on the river, at the mouth of Price's Creek. Sending for two of his neighbors, who, by the way, never associated with him, Robert Roberts, a farmer who stood high in the community, and Archy Gilliland, a good old seceder, he told them that he felt that he was about to die, and he had sent for them to talk to them, and that now he wanted to tell them he had been a very bad man, and in his life time he had done a great many bad things, but he had also done a great many good things; that he had been thinking seriously of his past life; of the bad things and the good things he had done, he had studied it all over and found that the good he had done overbalanced the bad, and he had settled with God, and was ready to die, and was going to heaven, or, as Roberts put it, he had balanced his books and settled with God.

LEAVES FROM THE DOCKETS OF THE OLD JUSTICES OF THE PEACE.

On the 18th of March, 1847, Charley Moore, a big blacksmith, was before the Court for assault and battery on Ed. N. Ingham, who was a very insolent and noisy little hack-driver. He whipped him and was fined.

On the 6th of May, 1847, Alex. M. Stilwell was arrested for bastardy, on the complaint of one Emily Barton, he came before the court, asked leave to have a talk with the prosecuting witness, which was granted, the information was withdrawn, the suit dismissed, and defendant paid the costs.

One Chandler charged one Jones with assault and battery before E. Cole, J. P. Jones was fined and ordered committed till the fine and costs were paid. The record concludes "Jones has left the State."

The docket of Cole, General Browne, and many other Justices, were frequently all in the handwriting of Sam. T. Marshall, attorney at law, when they had their offices with him.

CHAPTER III.

LIEUTENANT-GENERAL JOSEPH SMITH,
The Mormon Prophet.

Joseph Smith, the Mormon Prophet.—The Notorious Bill Hickman.—Murder of Miller and Leiza by the Hodges, their trial and Execution.— "Mill" Walker who kept the Robbers Roost, and his Wealth at his Death in Old Silver and Gold Coins.—Edward Bonney and the Murder of Colonel Davenport, Capture and Execution of the Murderers— Expulsion of the Mormons and Addresses to the People of Lee County, etc.—Whipping Horse Thieves.—The Bully Osprey, the Powder Packet to Nauvoo.—Captain George C. Anderson.

The most successful religious impostor ever born in America, first saw daylight in the Green Mountain State, and had his birth place at Windsor, Sharon County, Vermont, on the 23d of December, 1805, and was not quite thirty-four years of age when he was killed at Carthage, Hancock County, Ill., on the 27th of June, 1844. He removed with his father's family to Palmyra, Wayne County, N. Y., in April, 1815, and in March, 1820, claimed that his mind was much affected at a revival held by a Rev. Mr. Lane, of the Methodist church. He pretended to have received his first vision while praying in the woods, when God the Father and Jesus Christ appeared to him coming down from the heavens and told him his sins were forgiven and that he was chosen of God to reinstate His kingdom and reinstitute the gospel and that none of the denominations were right.

In September, 1823, he fell from grace and swore and swindled and lied as usual, and was frequently intoxicated. Then an angel appeared to him while still in bed, and told him of the existence of the history of the ancient inhabitants of America, engraved on plates of gold, and directed him where to find them. On the 22d of September he went as directed and claimed to have found them in a hillside between Manchester and Palmyra, in Western New York, in a stone box. He attempted to take them, when a great contest between the devil and angels took place about him; the devil finally got whipped and retreated, and the same day he received the plates from the hands of an angel. In 1828–9 they were translated by Oliver Cowdry acting as clerk, who, with Smith, it is claimed, were baptized by John the Baptist, who appeared to them and ordained them as priests, and commanded them to baptize and afterwards reordain each other. In 1830 the Mormon Church was established, and June of that year its first conference held at Fayette, New York. In August, Parley P. Pratt and Sidney Rigdon were converted to Mormonism. In January, 1831, the church was commanded to move to Kirtland, Ohio, where Rigdon had made many converts.

In May, following, the elders were sent out by twos to preach. Smith started a wild cat currency bank, "The Kirtland Safety Society Bank," also a store and a mill; his bank failed, and on the 22d of March he was mobbed, tarred and feathered. The failure of the bank was to be expected as no capital was invested in it, but in this venture the Prophet was like all other operators in wild cat currency.

"Zion" had been established in Independence, Mo., and thither he and Rigdon went, running away from their creditors at night. Soon nearly all the Mormons followed in 1834. "The Church of Jesus Christ of the Latter Day Saints," flourishing in Missouri, with varying fortunes, the temple at Kirtland went on to completion in 1836; the foundations of a new temple was laid at Independence, Mo., in 1839, and on the 9th of May, of that year, Smith, by invitation of Dr. Isaac Gayland who presented him with a large tract of land at Commerce, Ill., resolved to settle and remove his people there on account of growing troubles with the people in Missouri.

He received a convenient revelation called the "Saints" about him, and sold them the lots of the city which he named Nauvoo, at high prices.

THE OLD SETTLERS.

In 1841 the city was incorporated, the Nauvoo Legion organized, and Joseph Smith made Lieutenant-General, and the foundation stones of a new temple laid by him with great military parade. Smith had an army at one time when inspected by General Singleton, of six thousand men in line under arms and all well armed and equipped.

The Lieutenant-General had a numerous staff of high rank, and it was amusing to see the gaudy uniforms, gilt buttons, gold lace and shoulder straps, they wore, representing every rank from Major General down to Lieutenant Colonel, an army of Staff-officers. It was never surpassed, and may have been paralelled in the ridiculous figure cut by ex-governor Bob Stewart, at St Louis, when appointed to recruit a regiment as Colonel by that dress parade hero, who parted his hair in the middle (Fremont). In many cases his staff ranked the Colonel, if shoulder straps indicated rank, some wearing the stars of a Brigadier, others that of a Major-General.

On grand review ladies on horseback accompained the Lieutenant-General and staff.

Under the act of incorporation the Mayor had power to try writs of habeas corpus, and when a Mormon was arrested for any crime he was promptly discharged. Dr. J. C. Bennett was a General in the legion and made Mayor of Nauvoo. But he made the mistake of appropriating to himself one of the loves of the Prophet, and Joseph who could not brook interference in his monopoly of spiritual wifedom or polygamy, cut him off from the Church. Bennett filled the paper with abuse of Smith, who replied; the laws started a paper in Nauvoo, "The Expositor," on account of an insult in the way of dishonorable proposals to the wife of one of them, attacked him in their paper, and on the 6th of May, 1844, Smith had the press destroyed. This resulted in his arrest on the charge of treason, destroying the liberty of the press which could not have been sustained had he come to trial, but his career was cut short by his death in jail at Carthage, on the 27th of June, 1844, by a disguised party of men upon whom he fired first with his revolver. The attorneys for Joe Smith were General Hugh T. Reid, at that time of the firm of Reid & Johnstone, of Fort Madison, and Jim Woods, of Burlington. He was to pay Reid & Johnstone a thousand dollars fees, none of which they ever received. During his arrest and after his imprisonment in jail, Smith told General Reid that if he thought there was any danger he could have his friends release him by breaking the jail. Reid on the assurances of Governor Ford of Illinois, who promised protection, told him he did not apprehend any danger, and that night he and Hiram, his brother, were killed. Next day, when the attorneys came to Nauvoo, where the remains of the dead prophet and his brother were brought, there was great consternation, the Mormons expecting an immediate attack from the Gentiles. They were all badly frightened and preparing ways and means of escape.

The prophet at his residence in the Mansion House had a secret passage leading from the house through the doors of a closet to a stairway and thence underground to his stables across the street so he could escape on horseback in case of a sudden emergency. His widow married Major Bideman and is still living at Nauvoo, a tall, dark, masculine looking woman, and his oldest son, Joseph, is the leader of the Reformed Mormon Church at Plano, Ill., which branch of the church is opposed to polygamy.

THE DANITE BAND

Was first organized under the name of the "Daughters of Gideon," in far west Missouri, before the removal of the Mormons to the city of Nauvoo, Ill., and their name was subsequently changed to the "Danite Band," of which D. W. Patton, whom Joe Smith styled "Captain Fearnot," was first commander. In a fight with the citizens or militia under Captain Bogart, he was killed near Richmond, Clay County, Mo. The Mormons indulged in many Bible quotations, and any ignorant fanatical Mormon could quote Scripture by the chapter. Hence it is not strange that the name of the Danite Band, at one time under the leadership of the Mormon Bill Hickman, the terror of Lee County, should derive its name from a scriptural quotation, Genesis XLIX, 17: "Dan shall be a serpent by the way, an adder in the path, that biteth the horses heels so that his rider shall fall backward."

When the Mormons at Nauvoo were in the zenith of their power and in high feather with the politicians of Illinois, they numbered no less than two thousand members. They held secret meetings of their conclave and called themselves the "Destroying Angels." They were bound together by secret oaths of the most terrible character, and the punishment of traitors to the order was death. John A. Murrel's band of pirates, who flourished at one time near Jackson, Tennessee, and up and down the Mississippi River above New Orleans, was never so terrible as the Danite Band, for the latter was a powerful organization and was above the law. It made its threats of death and they were not mere idle threats, but were carried into execution. They went about after night in gangs on horseback, like another "Ku Klux Klan," clothed for the occasion, in the disguise of white gowns, and wearing red girdles. Their faces were covered with masks to conceal their identity. Bill Hickman, afterwards their captain, once lived near Nashville, on the Rapids. He owned a fast and blooded stallion and was frequently absent. He was not communicative, but decided and silent, came and went like a shadow.

Tall, raw-boned, sandy haired and of a florid complexion, he was strong and sinewy, and in height about six feet, though appearing taller. His cold grey piercing eye proclaimed him a villian of the deepest dye, who hesitated at nothing from larceny to murder.

Like a pestilence which walks abroad at noon-day, he, with his fast horse, was omnipresent on the roads and at all public gatherings, a keen observer of all passing events, a secreet spy upon the actions and conversations of the Mormons as well as his hereditary enemies, and the enemies of the Mormon Church, (whom he considered or affected to consider the chosen people of the Lord,) the Gentiles upon whom he made relentless war to the knife, and from the knife to the hilt. He and his followers accordingly seized and appropriated their property wherever they found it by stealth or by force.

With them the earth was the Lord's and the fullness thereof, and what was the Lord's belonged of right to the Latter Day Saints.

The followers of Joseph Smith, the prophet, believed in Polygamy, as do the followers of Brigham Young; the followers of young Joseph Smith believe not in plurality of wives, and reject the bad and criminal teachings of the first Mormons and their secret orders, and those left in this country now, it is proper to say are good citizens and honest people, against whom there is no word of reproach. They are not answerable for what has been done by Bill Hickman and his Danite Band of Destroying Angels, who were murderers and outlaws of the worst character.

They would steal before your eyes in the day time, and if a Mormon coveted your cow or horse he went and took it; if he wanted your meat he entered your smoke-house in force and carried it away. If you resisted he made war on you and notified you to leave the country.

If you remained, your property was destroyed or carried off and your life was imperiled; they did not hesitate to take life, it was cheap. A country man surrounded by Mormon neighbors, had a large lot of wood hauled and corded up; the Danites coveted it and came with wagons to haul it off. He shot one of them and fled; they took the wood nevertheless, and he never dared to return, as they threatened his life. This was just what they wanted; they then appropriated his house, goods and possessions, and kept them till they were driven from the country.

Bill Hickman, amongst the least of his numerous crimes, was a thief, and before he became noted as a murderer, stole many horses, and was caught with one of them in his possession and arrested; he also stole meat from old John Wright, was indicted and sent to jail in Lee County, Iowa. The indictment for larceny against the notorious Bill Hickman is still among the files of the Court in the Clerk's Office of the District Court at Fort Madison, for which he has never been and never will be punished.

In 1843 the Mormons and Mormon sympathisers or Jack Mormons, by which name they were more familiarly known, at that day were numerous in Lee County, and from that day till finally driven from the country by the uprising and indignation expressed by the people till they were finally expelled altogether, many remaining who could not well get away till as late as the year 1847.

The death of Joe Smith, the Mormon Prophet, only paralyzed their operations temporarily but did not stop them. Robberies and murders were as frequent as ever. Murders for money were of the most startling ever known, and the bold character of the perpetrators have never had their paralel in the annals of crime in this or any other country. As late as 1845 things had come to such a pass that the people of the country kept their stable doors locked and the doors of their houses bolted and barred to keep out the threatened intruders against whose raids, if they had anything of value, particularly in the way of money or jewelry, they could not at any time consider themselves safe.

Lonely and isolated places were particularly subject to the visitations of these midnight marauders, who had their spies in day time "looking up sights," traveling through the country dressed in the homespun garb of farmers, or disguised as mechanics or laborers, carrying tools of their trade, so as better to delude the unsuspecting people, who like all people on the frontier are free to give information about themselves and their neighbors. Edward Bonney, more familiarly known as the man who created a great sensation as the author of a little book called the "Banditti of the Prairies, or the Murderers Doom," over thirty years ago, then lived at Montrose where he kept a livery stable. He was frequently at Nauvoo and traveled much on the river on steamboats, and had an extensive acquaintance with all classes of people, knew in detail all the secret operations of "Danites" and their confederates. Time has left little doubt but what he was an unmitigated scoundrel and the scheming projector of all the operations of the band, which resulted in getting money. Though not himself a Mormon, he knew them all, consulted with and advised the perpetrators of crime, and no doubt shared the proceeds of their villiany. When they failed he pursued and arrested them to get the reward, and when they were hung or sent to the penitentiary their mouths were closed against him forever. Though not personally present at the perpetration of a crime, putting little facts and circumstances together, and still greater revelations which have since come to light; there is little doubt that he was an accessory generally before and always after the fact. The most startling event which put the whole country in a tremor of excitement was the murder of Miller and Leiza, two Germans at their log cabin on Sugar Creek, about three miles west of West Point and nearer Franklin, the center of Lee County, Iowa, by the two brothers William and Stephen Hodges, Mormon preachers and one Tom Brown, the latter being arrested, on the night of Saturday, May 10, 1845, over thirty-one years ago, but well remembered with its horrible details by all the Old Settlers of that day. Leiza came to Iowa first and made the improvement, the log cabin on the place, where they settled, where the murder took place. He was at that time unmarried but returned to Ohio and married the daughter of old John Miller. They all moved to Iowa acccompained by a brother-in-law and his wife, and came on a steamer by way of the river. Bonney, who it will be seen, appeared as a witness on the indictment, and took an active part in having the murderers arrested and convicted, was heard to remark at West Point that he came up with them on the same boat from St. Louis, and that from their big German boxes and general surroundings that they were a better class of Germans than generally came to the country, and *that they must have plenty of money!* He was no doubt on the look-out. The Hodges had worked in West Point helping to build the Court House, and were well acquainted in that vicinity. Stephen Hodges a short time before stayed all night at the house of Samuel B. Ayres, then county treasurer and collector, who was absent at the time. Several thousand dollars in money was at the time in a trunk in the house, and Mrs. Ayres naturally felt afraid it would be stolen. She knew Stephen Hodges well, and believing him honest spoke to him about it, and felt safe that he was to stay there that night. Strange to relate the money was not disturbed. He was then on his way prospecting, and the next night the house of Jerry Smith on Sugar Creek, was entered and he was made to deliver his money by two masked men. They failed in getting much; he had sold a farm but had left the money at Adolphus Salmons, in West Point. The robbers on this occasion were

Stephen and William Hodges, a confederate lying in wait on the outside in case of alarm.

That night they returned from Smiths' and remained till morning and during the next day in concealment at the house of "Mill" Walker, so named from his owning a little water mill on Sugar Creek near his house. One of them ventured out to the house of Miller and Leiza, near by, carrying a whip and pretending to look for cattle, got a drink of water and tried to get a ten dollar bill changed. Mill Walker was a suspicious character and petty-fogged before Country Justices of the Peace. Suspicious characters, strangers were often seen coming from or going to his house. Nothing was ever established connecting him in any way with robbers or murderers, but he no doubt kept the robbers roost where they stopped and laid their plans in concealment, while he was their confidential counselor and advisor and the receiver of the money realized from their robberies, this being fully settled from the fact that at his death in Quincy, Ill., three years ago, he left behind, concealed under his cellar floor nearly one hundred thousand dollars in specie which he could not have accumulated by any honest means in the different kinds of business in which he was known to have engaged since leaving Lee County.

This money was put up in rusty tin sardine and oyster boxes and cans, and consisted of the old coins in circulation in 1845 and previously, such as Mexican silver dollars, half dollars, Spanish doubloons, etc., which, his widow who knew their place of concealment had brought out, opened and counted by her lawyers and deposited in bank.

A redeeming trait in the character of Walker, after he went to Quincy, was that he was very generous to the poor, and made no parade about it. He would often haul in a load of wood, and without saying a word throw it over into the door yard of some very poor person. This probably was done by way of atonement for his crimes.

The excitement consequent upon the robbery of Jerry Smith had hardly died away when the murder of Miller and Leiza was committed.

Court was then in session.

THE MURDER OF MILLER AND LEIZA BY THE HODGES.

The District Court of the Territory was then held at West Point. Charles Mason was Judge, and Dr. Joel C. Walker Clerk. L. D. Stockton was the regular District Attorney, but Gen. Hugh T. Reid was appointed district prosecutor pro tem, drew the indictments, and conducted the prosecution throughout, from its beginning till the close of the trial, which resulted in their conviction, sentence, and final execution.

William Hodges, Stephen Hodges, and Thomas Brown, were indicted by the Grand Jury at West Point, May 15th, 1845, for the murder of John Miller, by stabbing him on Saturday night, the 10th of May, 1845. Solomon Jackson was the foreman of that Grand Jury, and this indictment was exhibited and filed May 15th, 1845, in the court.

The names of the witnesses upon it were James L. Estes, then Sheriff, Robert McNair, Abraham K. Drollinger, Jacob Able, Peter L. Montjar, and Edward Bonney.

On the 21st of May, 1845, William Hodges and Stephen Hodges were brought into court, arraigned and plead not guilty, and the District Prosecutor immediately joined issue.

Leiza was not then dead, but died afterwards. On the same day they both filed a joint affidavit, praying for a change of venue on the ground that they could not obtain justice, as the people of the county were so prejudiced against them that they could not get a fair trial. This affidavit was sworn to before S. B. Ayres, J. P., and was signed by Stephen Hodges, but William Hodges made his mark.

The Court, in making the order for change of venue says, "that the cause be heard and determined in the District Court for the county of Des Moines, where the cause complained of does not exist, the same as originally instituted there, and that the Clerk certify the papers to the Clerk of the District Court of Des Moines county."

John Miller was a Menonite German Minister. The Society of Menonites wear clothing very much the same as the Dunkards, except instead of buttons they wear hooks and eyes on their coats. They all wear heavy beards.— Miller was stabbed through the heart by a huge bowie knife manufactured from a big file, such as was used in those days for sharpening mill saws. We saw the arsenal of huge bowie-knives taken by Sheriff James L. Estes, from the prisoners, afterwards at the old tavern, or hotel we would call it now, of Billy McIntyre, on Second Street, at Fort Madison, where he and Joseph C. Estes, his brother, then boarded.

The two Hodges were arrested on the 13th of May, 1845, at Nauvoo, taken to Fort Madison on the 14th, and put in charge of Captain Edwin Guthrie, then Warden of the Iowa Penitentiary, who was afterwards Captain of company K, Fifteenth U. S. Infantry, Mexican War, who was wounded in acting as guard for a supply train on the way from Vera Cruz to the City of Mexico, in the thigh, by an escopet ball at Pass La Hoya, and was taken to the Castle of Perote, where his thigh was amputated, and a second amputation became necessary, in consequence of which he died from physical exhaustion, caused by hemorrhage, or in other words, bled to death.

James M. Layton and Edward A. Layton were the two guards of the prisoners at the penitentiary.

On the 19th of May they were taken by Sheriff Estes from Fort Madison to West Point, and kept there till the 23d, and were taken up to Burlington by way of Fort Madison, thence on a steamer. Their guards during this time were Hawkins Taylor, E. B. Taylor, D. M. Sherman, Elijah T. Estes, Joseph Stotts, and Luke Allphin, for six days, at $2 per day.

They applied for a separate trial first, and then for a continuance, which were both refused.

On the 21st of June they were put upon their trial, sixty petit jurors being summoned. J. C. Hall, F. D. Mills, and Geo. Edmunds, Jr., appearing for the prisoners.

After a lengthy trial the jury brought in the following verdict, which is not dated, and the record does not say when it was returned:

THE OLD SETTLERS. 39

BURLINGTON, IOWA, T. 1845.

We, the jury, find the defendants, William Hodges and Stephen Hodges, guilty of murder. Joel Hargrove, foreman; James Snow, David Leonard, John Smith, William Bennett, Thomas Stought, Ely Walker, Robert Mickey, Isaac Chandler, Vincent Shelley, John D. Conover, Moses Nutt.

Forthwith, the record says, the Court demanded if they had anything to say, &c., and then pronounced sentence upon them: "That you be taken to the jail whence you came, and remain there till the 15th day of July next; that on that day you be taken by the proper officer of the county to some convenient place within the same, and between the hours of 10 o'clock a. m. and 4 o'clock p. m., be hanged by the neck until you are dead."

Dr. Freeman Knowles, who was then a practicing physician at West Point, a gentleman of high standing and character, with a remarkable memory of details, was a witness in this trial, and says it continued about a week. He is still living, and now a citizen of Keokuk.

The affidavit for continuance on account of the absence of material witnesses residing in Nauvoo, and St. Louis, Mo., was sworn to before John S. Dunlap, Clerk of the District Court of Des Moines county, on the 10th day of June, 1845. By these witnesses they alleged that they expected to prove that on the night of the 10th of June, 1845, the time the murder was committed, they were at home in Nauvoo, and that the cap found on the premises did not belong to either of them.

On the 15th day of July, 1845, both of the Hodges were hanged in a ravine now in the city limits of the city of Burlington. Till the last moment it was then said they expected to be pardoned or rescued. Sheriff McKenny made the following return of his doings, under the order of the court:

SHERIFF'S RETURN.

Territory of Iowa, }
    Des Moines county, }

In obedience to the within sentence, I did, on this 15th day of July, 1845, at 2 o'clock and 45 minutes p. m. of said day, in the presence of Dr. Enos Lowe, Dr. L. W. Hickok, Dr. J. S. Dunlap, Evan Evans, Col. Temple, and many other worthy and respectable citizens of said county of Des Moines and Territory of Iowa, at a place selected by me in said county, then and there hung by the neck, the said William Hodges and Stephen Hodges, until they were dead.   JOHN H. MCKENNY,
    Sheriff of Des Moines county, I. Ty.

Fees for this worst of all legal murders, $500.

It will be thirty-two years next 15th of July, since the Hodges were hung.

On the night of the murder Jacob Abel, a witness on the indictment, and a near neighbor of Miller and Leiza, first came on horseback to the house of Col. Wm. Patterson, a prominent citizen, living half a mile south of West Point on his farm, and gave the alarm.

The Colonel got out of bed, dressed himself, and sent his son Jo to the stable for his horse. Jo says he was so badly frightened, being then only a boy, he mounted the horse and rode out of the stable, and did not know whether he was on foot or on horseback. The Colonel got his rifle and they proceeded to West Point to find Sheriff James L. Estes.

It was past midnight, but not yet day light, when they found him, and the alarm was given. The Catholic church bell was rung, and every one supposing there was a fire rushed pell mell into the streets, or to the public square of West Point, and the buzzing of voices and the rushing of many feet could be heard in every quarter of the village. They all soon knew the cause of the alarm, that a murder had been committed, with its brief but startling details.— Col. Patterson, Sheriff Estes, and a party of men at once proceeded to the scene of bloodshed, and got there at day light. A most horrible sight was presented to them, and the deathly sick odor of blood—human blood—arose from the damp ground to their nostrils, and at first they shuddered and turned away. On examining the premises, old man Miller was found just in front of the door lying dead, stabbed through the heart by a big bowie knife, and his bloodless face upturned, looked from his open, glassy eyes with an excited stare upon them—like that of a soldier dying in the midst of a charge. A little deep, worn path, leading from the house to the smoke house, was filled with his heart's blood, which had flowed into it from the place where he had fallen. He was a brave man; had been a soldier who had seen service in Germany, and died game fighting for his life in the midst of excitement. Leiza was severely wounded but not yet dead; the door through which was a fresh bullet hole was yet spattered with blood; the last shot fired by the murderers passed through that door, and striking him under the shoulder blade, penetrated a vital part and internal hemorrhage caused his death, but his skull was also fractured by the cut of a knife. He, too, had resisted, and fought manfully; he was a stout and powerful young man in the prime of life. Had the other cowardly son-in-law Jacob Risser, come to the rescue, the murderers and assassins would have been defeated and repulsed. But he covered up his head in bed while the fight went on as he laid still on the floor in one corner of the cabin, and trembling with fright let his father-in-law and brother-in-law be murdered. Dr. Sala was sent for but pronounced the wounds of Leiza necessarily fatal. The family of the murdered men were in great distress, and their piteous cries and groans, their wailings, notes of grief and despair filled the air.

The crowd kept coming as the news spread; parties were formed rapidly, and patrolled the country in search of the criminals. The sheriff and party mostly Kentuckians, who had lived long on the border, found their tracks, that of three men, and where one of them had evidently been helped away, and had washed the blood from himself in a little ravine. A rimless cap was left behind, bound around with fur, "that fatal cap," as General Reid called it in his speech for the prosecution, by which they were identified and convicted, and suffered the penalty of death, which they so richly deserved.

The leading men in the pursuit were sheriff Estes, Col. Patterson, and afterwards Hawkins Taylor.

Traces of the murderers were found at Everharts, leading down towards Devil Creek bottom, thence by way of old Grant Reddens, who with his son

THE OLD SETTLERS. 41

Jack afterwards became notorious, another favorite stopping place of the gang, when all traces were lost. The sheriff and Col. Patterson, who was now armed with a big horse pistol, proceeded to Montrose, and at daylight awoke one Williams, landlord of a country tavern, who seeing the horse pistol, looked alarmed, till he recognized the parties. Their business was made known and soon the news of the murder spread through the village then filled with Mormons. Bonney heard of it, or probably knew it in advance, and came to Col. Patterson and asked if he could see that cap which sheriff Estes had in his saddle bags. Patterson and Estes held a consultation and concluded to show it to him. He had no sooner seen it than he said, "I know that cap as well as I know my jack knife; it belongs to Bill Hodges." People crowded about and tried to find out what was going on, but this conversation was private and heard by none but Patterson and Estes, who now had a clue to the murderers, whom Bonney asserted must be in Nauvoo. Thither the party accompanied by others who proceeded in a skiff rowed by W. S. Ivins, now of Keokuk.— The two brothers, Stephen and William Hodges, were living with their brother Amos, all suspicious characters, in the suburbs of the city. On the night of the 13th of May, with the assistance of one Markham, city Marshal of Nauvoo, the house was surrounded, and at day-light they were arrested and taken before a Mormon Justice of the Peace named Johnson. Almon W. Babbitt, a partner of George Edmunds, Jr., appeared for the prisoners, and the prosecution applied for a continuance till next day, on the pretext of getting witnesses from Iowa. In the meantime, on the 15th of May, 1845, an indictment was procured against them at West Point, and next day when the preliminary examination came on they were confronted with the indictment and held to await a requisition from the Governor of Iowa. But by the advice of their counsel, Babbitt, afterwards murdered by the Mormons, (while U. S. District Attorney of Utah, disguised as Indians,) they consented to go to Fort Madison, where they were safely lodged in the penitentiary.

While the prisoners were in jail at Burlington, Irwin Hodges, who was attempting to raise money to defend his brothers, publicly denounced and threatened Brigham Young, and tried to induce him to send men to break open the jail and release them. That night on his way home, early in the evening, he was met by two men, who assassinated him by stabbing him with his own knife, as they afterwards confessed when arrested on a criminal charge in Adams county, Illinois. One of them was arrested next day on suspicion, but as there was no evidence against him he was discharged. This trial was the most noted criminal trial which ever took place in the State, and created much comment at the time. General Reid prosecuted the prisoners with great vigor, and on the cross examination of the witnesses to prove an alibi for the defense completely entrapped them, as no two witnesses could agree as to the particular place the prisoners were at Nauvoo on the night of the murder. His closing speech of three hours was a masterly effort of great eloquence and power, and was listened to by the vast crowd in the court room and out side with breathless attention

The day the murderers were hung their father was permitted to come to see them from the Alton penitentiary, where he was under sentence for larceny, and after the execution one of their sisters eloped with Dr. Lyon, a married man, living then at Fort Madison, and went to Texas.

At the execution both the Hodges put on great bravado, and denied most explicitly that they were guilty.

Stephen spoke first; he was a tall finely formed, dark complexioned man, with black hair, with a loud ringing voice, in which there was not the slightest tremor when he spoke. Calm and collected as on an ordinary occasion he addressed the crowd who listened with great attention while he spoke.— Among other things he said "how can that jury who brought in a verdict of guilty sleep calmly on their pillows at night?" William spoke well but was excited and trembled slightly, and his voice was not so loud or his manner so decided.

They expected to be rescued, and till the last moment looked as if for some one to come. But no rescue came. The "New Purchase" ferry boat came in just before the execution, loaded down with passengers from Nauvoo, and its whistle was heard just before the execution, at the levee. The passengers had barely time to get to the scene of the execution before it took place. The sisters of the murderers were present. The condemned men were clothed in long white robes, their arms pinioned with cords at the elbows; they walked upon the scaffold after prayer by the Minister, Rev.———— of Mt. Pleasant, who gave out and sung the hymn:

"While the lamp holds out to burn,
The vilest sinners may return."

when the black cap was drawn down over their eyes, Sheriff McKenny cut the rope suspending the drops on which they stood, and their bodies shot downwards, swayed back and forth for a few minutes, Stephen drawing up his legs with a convulsive effort once only, and they were launched into eternity. Wild cries of despair from their sisters rent the air as they fell, and a death like stillness outside of this reigned in the crowd of thousands who covered the hill sides and filled the ravine below the scaffold, which was surrounded by militia under arms.

In their affidavit for continuance in the hand writing of Judge Hall, one of their attorneys, made on the 10th of June, 1845, they stated they could not proceed to trial on account of the absence of material witnesses, the first named being Artemus Johnson, George Broffit, Hiram Broffit, Willis Smith, Thomas Morgan, Geo. Kimball, and Lydia Hodges, who resided at Nauvoo, Ill., and that they expected to prove by these witnesses that on Saturday night of the 10th of May, 1845, they were at home in Nauvoo, all night; also that the cap found upon the premises was not the cap of either of said defendants. That they had promised Irwin Hodges, brother of defendants, to appear voluntarily and testify, but "on account of the alleged excitement existing in the community, they feared their presence would subject them to insult and abuse, and possibly violence," and that however they disliked the alternative they were compelled to believe the depositions of said witnesses would have to be taken or they would lose their evidence.

They further stated in the same affidavit that they knew of no other witnesses by whom the same facts could be proven, except John Long, Aaron

Long Judge Fox, and Henry Adams, of St. Louis, Mo. The three first named afterwards became widely known from being the murderers of Col. Davenport. These witnesses it is stated in the affidavit, were at Nauvoo on the night of the murder, and they could procure their evidence by next term. This application was properly overruled by the Court, and we recite the names in the affidavit for the purpose of showing who were the confederates of the Hodges, and connected with the old Mormon Banditti and Danite Band. Robberies still continued all over the country, one of the largest was that of the law office of Knox & Dewey, at Rock Island, whose safe was broken open and robbed of $640.

The murder of Col. Davenport on the 4th of July, 1845, at Rock Island, at his home, in broad day light, was the boldest and most daring yet committed by the old Mormon Banditti, and startled the whole country as the echoes and reverberations of a fire bell in the night.

Col. Davenport was an aged and feeble man; a prominent and deservedly popular citizen, and an old settler, universally respected and loved for his many virtues by the entire community.

His family were absent, taking part in the celebration of our national independence. He was quietly reading a newspaper when, hearing a noise, his attention was called away to ascertain its cause. Rising from his seat he started to the door, which was suddenly pushed open and three men entered.— Instantly, and without a word of warning, the foremost one discharged his pistol, the ball passing through the Colonels left thigh. As he attempted to seize his cain which stood near, he was seized, blind-folded, and his arms and legs tied securely with hickory bark. He was then seized by the hair and shirt colar and dragged into the hall and then up a flight of a stairs to a closet containing an iron safe, which they compelled him to open. Taking out the contents, they dragged him into another room, put him on a bed and demanded his money. He pointed his hand to the drawer of a dressing table. Twice they made a mistake in searching for the money, each time opening the wrong drawer. Each time, supposing he was deceiving them, they beat and threatened him till he fell back exhausted and insensible. They dashed cold water in his face, but he was now speechless. Making another search, they found seven hundred dollars in money and a gold watch and chain, a double barrel shotgun and pistol, which they appropriated, and hearing noise outside, took the alarm and precipitately fled. Shortly afterwards he revived and cried murder! murder!! as loud as his feeble voice could utter the words. Fortunately a Mr. Cole and two other men from Moline were passing in a skiff, and heard his cries, stopped, and landing, rushed to his house, by the front door found blood spattered upon the wall and in the hall, and heard his feeble moans up stairs, where they found him as he was left on the bed still tied, and covered with blood.

Surgical aid was at once procured, a Dr. Brown, who was on the Island at the time with a pic-nic excursion, was hurried to his aid. He was revived sufficiently by restoratives to be able to describe the murderers, and all the circumstances of their attack upon him, but was in great agony, and from his advanced age and feeble condition, from the loss of blood, continued to fail till he finally sunk in a comatose condition, his heavy and suppressed breathing only showing that he still lived; his breathing grew fainter and fainter while his friends and relatives stood around his bed side. A deathlike stillness filled the room only relieved by the ticking of a clock in the next room. The surgeon held his right hand and felt his pulse, which grew weaker and weaker till about ten o'clock that night, when it commenced beating rapidly, like the last flickerings of an expiring lamp "blown out by a gust of wind from the casement" when it ceased to beat, and Col. Davenport was dead!

A reward of fifteen hundred dollars was offered by his family, which was afterwards increased. Hand bills described the watch, shot gun, pistol, and part of the money, and the murderers, as near as could be from the Colonels personal description. The murderers who had met at the hotel of one Loomis in Nauvoo, before they went to Davenport, asked Judge Edmunds who was going over to Montrose, to take a note to Bonney. On the way to the ferry he met Bonney and delivered the note. Afterwards they were seen up at Fort Madison waiting for a steamer for up the river. It was their intention on the route to rob Daniel McConn, the general steamboat agent, when he visited the boat as was his habit after night as he generally carried a large amount of money. It is said that they were only deterred from this by the fact that on this occasion on his visit to the upward bound steamer, he was accompanied by another man. They proceeded on the boat up the river. Several old citizens of Fort Madison recognized them among the rest John G. Kennedy. Bonney was at West Point when the hand bills offering the reward reached there, and according to his own story at once recognized John Long and Judge Fox from the description as two of them, and going to Sheriff Estes got him to write to George L. Davenport, offering his services to assist in arresting them. Sheriff Estes wrote the letter and recommended him as having been active as an employe of the authorities of Lee county, in arresting the Hodges. To this letter Bonney added a postscript, and he was sent for and employed. Judge Edmunds saw him on a steamboat after he had got one of the hand bills, offering the reward, on the eve of the Judge's departure for New York, when he said to him he was satisfied he knew the parties who murdered Col. Davenport, and intended to capture them. Employed to catch the murderers and stimulated by the hope of the reward offered, he went to work to ferret them out. Consulting with Joseph Knox, Esq., a prominent attorney of Rock Island, Ill., he was shown a letter from Anson S. Miller, Esq., of Rock Island, Ill., an old and prominent citizen, who is still living at Rockford, and has written an interesting history of Winnebago county, from which he came, to the conclusion that one Birch, a daring desperado, connected with the Danite Band, was the man who shot Col. Davenport. He had been suspected of robbery and murder since he was fifteen years of age, and was an adroit villain of good personal appearance, being well made with a broad chest, light complexion, and large blue eyes, and went fashionably dressed, playing the bar room dandy to perfection. In traveling through the country he went by different aliases, that of Brown Birch, Harris, and others. After the robbery of Mulford in Winnebago county, he changed the theatre of his operations to the Mississippi valley where he committed many other robberies. Old Grant Reddins, about six miles from Montrose, and eight or nine miles from Fort Madison, up near the bluffs in Devil Creek bottom, was the favorite of these Mormon murderers and thieves, as he harbored them all.

It was at his house that Granville Young was convicted and hung for the murder of Col. Davenport, as accessory before the fact, was captured. Dr. D. H. Rousseau, of Fort Madison, had an extensive practice at that day in Devil Creek bottom. In the border of a pond which had partly dried, a boy, the son of one of his patients, found a pistol and shot gun, and showed them to the doctor, who having seen the description, suspected them to be those taken from Col. Davenport, when he was murdered.

He procured the pistol, took it to sheriff Estes, and it was identified, which led to a raid by the sheriff and posse upon the house of Old Grant Reddin, where Granville Young was stopping, and where he was captured one Sunday morning and brought to Fort Madison and lodged in the penitentiary for safe keeping till a steamer came up to take him to Rock Island. He employed Miller & Williams, the late [Attorney General, to defend him, and Williams went up to Burlington on horseback; got the writ, and the sheriff started up on a boat with the prisoner.

As the evidence against Young was only circumstantial, and his conviction finally resulted from his confession as sworn to by Bonney on the trial, he would doubtless have been discharged. But Armstrong Walker, post master at Fort Madison, resolved to circumvent this, and he and a party of outsiders, accompanied the sheriff on the boat while Williams proceeded again to Burlington on horseback, and as he went in a gallop riding a pony, his long legs reaching nearly to the ground, with his long chin and hair streaming in the wind, he made a fit picture for Hogarth. At Burlington, when the stage plank was put out for the boat to land, in pursuance of his programme previously concocted, in which it is alleged, but never established, that the sheriff was a party. Sheriff Estes was shoved off of the boat, leaving the prisoner aboard, when the steamer proceeded on its way to Rock Island, leaving the sheriff at Burlington, where the late Senator Grimes, who was consulted by Estes, advised him what return to make to the writ.

Williams was compelled to return to Fort Madison without accomplishing anything, and found when he got there that a yoke of oxen he had taken from old Grant Redden for his fees, had been replevied by another Mormon.

Young was afterwards hung, and if not clearly proved to be guilty of this offense, no doubt deserved to be hung on general principles, the same as the horse thieves found hanging to a tree near Council Bluffs, who were disposed of by a vigilance committee, on whose breasts a paper was found pinned, on which was written "hung for rascality generally." John Long and Aaron Long were hung also on the 19th of Oct., 1845, Birch, their confederate, having turned states evidence. Aaron Long was arrested by Bonney and Jo Johnson at the house of his father, at Sand Prairie, nine miles from Galena. John

Long, or the captain, as he was called, was arrested in Indiana. Fox, who was also arrested near Connersville, was put in charge of old Tom Johnson, once U. S. Marshal for Iowa Territory, who let him escape, and as the father of Fox had money, it was always supposed that he and old Tom had an understanding. He was never afterwards heard from. From information given by Birch, the money taken was burried on the Des Moines river, in Lee county, Iowa. A search for it revealed the spot to sheriff Estes, but no money was found, and it had no doubt been taken away by Fox.

We have thus given a short account of the murder of Col. Davenport, and the leading parties concerned in it, leaving out necessarily many of the details.

Great excitement grew out of these murders and robberies, and an indignation meeting was held at Montrose, which was largely attended, Judge Edward Johnstone making the leading speech. The result was the subsequent nomination by a mass meeting at Fort Madison of an Anti-Mormon ticket, an address to the people of the county by a committee appointed for the purpose, and a resolution to expel the Mormons. As no copies of the proceedings of this meeting are extant, we publish it to show the feeling that then existed.

LEE COUNTY ANTI-MORMON MEETING.

In pursuance of public notice the Anti-Mormon citizens of Lee county, without distinction of party, met at the Court House in Fort Madison, on Thursday evening, 16th October, for the purpose of nominating candidates to represent said county in the next legislature.

EDWIN GUTHRIE, Esq., was chosen President, WM. PERDEW, and CAPT. SAMUEL VANCE as Vice Presidents, and D A. LAYMAN, and I. G. WICKERSHAM, Esq., Secretaries.

T. A. Walker being called on stated briefly the object of the meeting, and submitted the following preamble and resolutions which were unanimously adopted:

Whereas the late difficulties between the old settlers in Illinois and the Mormons, and the numerous offences committed in this county by persons professing to belong to the "Church of the Latter Day Saints," has caused great excitement among our citizens, and whereas it is firmly believed that the Mormons and others who do not belong to their peculiar faith cannot reside together in peace, and whereas for the purpose of preventing further violence it is thought advisable that the Mormons and citizens of Lee county should no longer remain together, therefore,

Resolved, That it is the opinion of this meeting that the public welfare requires that the Mormons should depart from this county at as early a day as practicable.

Resolved, That this meeting deprecates all acts of violence, but stamps with contempt the conduct of those sympathizing individuals who prate about the *"cruelties of Anti-Mormonism."*

Resolved, That two Anti-Mormon candidates to represent Lee county in the next legislature be nominated by this meeting, whose election may fully ascertain and express public sentiment on the subject of the Mormons leaving this county.

Resolved, That a committee of ten persons be appointed by the chairman to present the names of two suitable persons as candidates, and report forthwith.

Resolved, That a committee of ten persons be appointed by the chair to draft an address to the citizens of the county, in furtherance of the object of this meeting.

The following gentlemen were appointed by the chair as the committee to select and report the names of candidates to the meeting, viz.: T. A. Walker, David Galland, Esq., Samuel B. Ayres, Joseph A. Clark, Esq., Absolem Anderson, Esq., Samuel E. Jack, John Milliken, Esq., Isaac A. Lefevre, Hawkins Taylor and Samuel T. Marshall, Esq..

The committee after being absent for a short time returned, and reported as suitable persons to be supported as Anti-Mormon candidates for the Legislature, the names of Col. William Patterson and General Jessie B. Browne.

On motion, these nominations were confirmed unanimously by the meeting.

The president then proceeded to appoint as a committee to draft an address to the people of Lee county the following persons, to wit:

Wm. Stotts, Jesse O'Neil, Adam Hine, Lewis R. Reeves, John Burns and Henry Cattermole.

During the evening the meeting was addressed by J. C. Hall, Esq., of Burlington; Col. H. T. Reid, T. A. Walker, Ed. Johnstone, Esq., Hawkins Taylor, and H. E. Vrooman, Esq.

On motion of Ed. Johnstone, Esq., it was unanimously

Resolved, That the members of this meeting hereby pledge themselves to use all honorable means to secure the election of the candidates nominated this evening.

On motion of H. E. Vrooman, Esq.,

Resolved, That the proceedings of this meeting be published in the newspapers at Burlington, and the Warsaw "Signal."

Whereupon the meeting adjourned without day.

EDWIN GUTHRIE, President.

WM. PERDEW, } Vice Pre's.
SAM'L VANCE,

D. A. LAYMAN, } Sec's.
I. G. WICKERSHAM,

ADDRESS TO THE VOTERS AND TAX-PAYERS OF LEE COUNTY, IOWA.

A very large and respectable meeting of citizens, favorable to the departure of the Mormons from Lee county, was held at the Court House in Fort Madison on Thursday evening the 16th inst. Two Anti-Mormon candidates for the legislature were nominated at that time, and the undersigned were appointed a committee to address you in furtherance of the objects of said meeting.

The next election for members for the Legislative Assembly will take place on the 1st Saturday of November next, and the meeting presented for your suffrages as an

ANTI-MORMON TICKET.

Col. WM. PATTERSON,
Gen. JESSE B. BROWNE.

These gentlemen are among the "oldest settlers" of Lee county and known to every legal voter in it. They are esteemed as men of intelligence, and tried legislators, and no one doubts their entire willingness and ability to do, in a legislative capacity, full justice to the different interests of our citizens. The meeting referred to was composed of men of both political parties, the officers and committees were equallly divided in their political and local preferences, and it was hoped that in the selection of candidates, every man who felt disposed to aid in expressing public opinion on the subject of the departure of the Mormons, might do so without conceding his party predilictions. It was considered that it was the duty of every citizen to unite in inducing by moral means the "Latter Day Saints" from longer abiding among us. This question is now superior in importance to all others, and a truce was therefore declared by the two political parties, and such an union we believe is accomplished, as will show, at the next election, and expression of popular sentiment on this subject not to be mistaken. One of the Anti-Mormon candidates is a whig, the other a democrat, and are both prominent in the several parties to which they belong. In regard to the many sectional interests which have divided this county, the candidates hold different opinions, but it is understood that all local questions, as well as politics, are merged in the necessary and important movement of Anti-Mormonism.

It is due to you to say why an Anti-Mormon ticket was selected. We shall do so briefly. The progress of the Latter Day Saints is well known and their frequent strifes with the citizens of Ohio, Missouri and Illinois are matters of history. Wherever they go and *grow strong*, there springs up dissensions and violence between them and other citizens. The crimes charged upon them are without number. It is scarcely necessary to recount those which have been committed in this county. The old German preacher, Miller, was shot down in his own house, and his son-in-law, Leiza, was cut to pieces in defending his family. Where did this occur? In the very heart of Lee County. By whom was this outrage committed? By a band of Mormon brothers, some of whom were expounders and teachers of the faith of the Latter Day Saints. *Tax payers* what did this midnight murder cost you? The expenses paid by the county growing out of this nefarious butchery amounted to upwards of $2,800.

The Reddings living a few miles from Montrose, openly and knowingly entertained the murderers of Col. Davenport, and when they, and one of them who shot him, were arrested, an attempt was made by some of the leading Mormons and their sympathizers to have them turned loose on the community by a writ of *habeas corpus*, and the persons arresting them indicted for kidnap-

THE OLD SETTLERS.

ping! It would be impossible to enumerate Mormon theft and offences in this county alone. A few will suffice. They are obtained from the records of the District Court.

List of Mormon thieves, etc., who have escaped from justice in Lee county, Iowa, by forfeiting their recognizances, and with their securities running away to Nauvoo:

United States, vs. Jeremiah Plumb,	Larceny.
Same, vs. Mark A. Childs and E. C. Richardson.	Buying and receiving stolen goods.
Same, vs. Nathaniel Eames,	Bogus making.
Same, vs. Wm. A. Hickman.	Larceny.
Same, vs. Philander Avery.	Larceny.
Same, vs. Levi Wickerson.	Stealing nails.
Same, vs. Jonathan Barlow.	Horse stealing.
Same, vs. Jefferson Bradly & Alvin Sanford.	Larceny.
Same, vs. Jedediah Owens.	Larceny.
Same, vs. Sam'l Musick.	Larceny.
Same, vs. Nelson Benton.	Larceny.
Same, vs. Robert Owen & Sam'l Avery.	Larceny.
Same, vs. Sylvester Jackson.	Counterfeiting.
Same, vs. Ethaw Pettit.	Assault with intent to kill.

It is a remarkable fact, fellow citizens, that the only Mormon ever convicted in this county was one Davius Gibb, indicted for burglary, and proven to be guilty by Mormon witnesses. Time explained this mystery, for it was afterwards discovered that Gibb was a renegade from the church of Latter Day Saints. In many of the foregoing cases the cost paid by the county amounted to $150, and upon a computation made by some of the county officers, it appears that Mormon offenders, have since their coming here in 1839, cost the county the round sum of $5,000 or $6,000. Tax-payers, what say you to keeping up the Mormon organization in your county at the rate of $1,000 per annum.

Such is the startling array of facts, fellow citizens, presented to you from a cursory examination of the record of our court. And yet you are told by a newspaper published in your midst, dated on the 20th of the last month, that *"what few Mormons there are in this county conduct themselves as good citizens!"* We have the same high authority, on the 11th inst., canting about the "absurdities of Mormonism, and the cruelties of Anti-Mormonism."

When the citizens of Lee county, exercising a constitutional right, assemble, entertaining no feelings of personal hostility towards "Mormons" individually, but for the sake of future peace, earnestly recommending and requesting those residing in this county, to make preparations to remove therefrom as soon as practicable. Such request is placed under the head of the "cruelties of Anti-Mormonism." When the citizens are requested to aid by exchange of property or otherwise the departure of any Mormon or Mormons who may desire to leave the county, it is charged as among the cruelties of Anti-Mormonism. But when the Hodges and their accomplices waken from their repose by the blows of their bludgeons, a sleeping and peaceful family; when the father dies at his own door, and the son falls, bathed in blood, mortally wounded, it is only one of the "absurdities of Mormonism." When those who had shot and choked to death an old soldier on the day of liberty, in his own house, came with their hands red with murder, and were entertained and comforted by their "saintly" accessories in this county, it was only another of the "absurdities of Mormonism." When the Mormon burglars broke into and robbed the house of Smith, near Franklin, it was only another "absurdity!" When Amos Hodges and his fellow "saints' plundered the Norwegian family on the "tract," it was not "cruelty" but only an "absurdity!" Childs, Richardson, Eames, Hickman, Avery, Nickerson, Barlow, Bradley, Sandford. Owens, Musick, Burton, Jackson, Pettit, all Mormons, and a host of others were guilty of similar absurdities! "Cruelties" is the term applied to the peaceful movement of Anti-Mormonism, and the tender epithet of "absurdities" to the midnight murders and felonies of the Mormons.

A system of petty Mormon thieving is extensively carried on in this county, that our citizens can scarcely any longer exercise a peaceful forbearance. Every old settler has lost something. No one feels secure. Each man before he retires to rest, bolts and barricades his house, and hospitality reluctantly opens the door after nightfall, fearing it might let in the cut-throat and thief, instead of the stranger seeking a shelter. All good men reprobate violence, and therefore the "Latter Day Saints" have been solicited to depart from among us. This request was made at a meeting of our fellow citizens on the 1st inst., at the town of Montrose. It was thought prudent to give further force to that expression of public sentiment. No means appeared so effective for this purpose as the ballot box, and the ticket above referred to was therefore presented for your consideration. It is hoped that the vote given for it will be so decided as will leave no doubt of the wishes of the people in regard to the Mormons leaving the county, and when you cast your suffrages for the Anti-Mormon candidates remember that you are thus exercising your moral power to induce the deluded people called the "Latter Day Saints" to depart in peace. Remember that your are doing an act which will save you county from future scenes of violence, and the tax-paying community from burdensome levies upon them.

The meeting which nominated the ticket above presented, desire to lay aside at the coming election all questions political and local, and present the issue of Anti-Mormonism and Mormonism alone, and none others. Men of both parties, men differing upon all local questions, were in attendance, and all agree as to the present paramount importance of inducing the Mormons to leave the county. It is not expected that they will permit the Anti-Mormon candidates to be elected without opposition. They number many votes themselves and they have many sympathizers. They and their coadjutors *dare not* meet the issue fairly, but will strive to avoid it. They will get up tickets and denominate them as the "*Peoples*," "*Settlers*," "*American*," or by some other attractive or delusive title. But by this many cannot be deceived. . A cry, too will be raised against the Anti-Mormon ticket by disappointed office seekers, hoping thereby hereafter to procure Mormon support. The designs of all such politicians are too transparent to blind any one but themselves. An attempt will be made to rouse up local prejudices by the Mormons and Jack Mormons. This, too, must fail, for the committee are authorized to say that the Anti-Mormon candidates are pledged to move, if elected, no sectional question of any kind in the legislature. They desire to run free from all trammels, and will esteem their election as expressing in a manner not to be misunderstood, the opinion of the people of Lee county on the subject of Mormon emigration therefrom. An attempt will be made to draw aside public attention during the canvass by abuse heaped upon individuals not before the people. Such assaults will only recoil upon the heads of the calumniators themselves, and cover them with shame and confusion. An attempt will be made by the Mormons to assail Anti-Mormon candidates, because at one time they may have expressed sympathy for their sufferings. This cannot avail anything. General sympathy and kindness were extended, to these people when they came poor and needy among us, but since the true character of many of them is truly developed, the desire for their immediate and peaceful departure is universal. Every honest citizen will cheerfully assist a worthy fellow-man in distress, but withdraws his support when the object of his compassion proves to be a thief or a cut-throat. Other individuals are indifferent to suffering, when clothed in the garb of integrity, but so soon as the object of charity is suspected as a felon they seek his society.

Fellow Tax-payers, we appeal to you to aid us in getting rid of an abundant source of taxation. Fellow voters, we call upon you to exercise your moral influence at the ballot-box, and induce the Mormons to seek another place of abode. Fellow citizens, without distinction of party, vote for the Anti-Mormon ticket, and prevent those days of violence, which the future may have in store for our county. The true issue may be evaded, Mormon and Jack Mormon abuse will flow freely; demagogues will squirm and writhe, every effort will be made by a few expiring place hunters, but let every citizen do his duty, and all their denunciations and struggles will be in vain.

On the first Saturday of next month, let every man come to the polls, and let every one who desires future peace, prosperity and a healthy state of society in the "Empire county," cast their suffrages for Browne and for Patterson.

Your fellow citizens,

JOHN BURNS,
WM. STOTTS,
A. HINE,
L. R. REEVES,
JESSE O'NEAL.

October 16th, 1845.

The following communication was handed to Judge Mason during the present sitting of the Lee county District Court. He felt authorized by the unanimous request of the Grand Jury to excuse from further attendance the persons therein named, Rev. Wm. O. Clark and Dr. John Patten, as two of the most prominent Mormons in Lee county.

GRAND JURY ROOM,
Oct. 14th, 1845.

To the Hon. Charles Mason, Judge of the District Court of Lee county:

The undersigned Grand Jurors for the county of Lee respectfully represent to your Honor: that there are now upon the Grand Jury, two Mormons, to-wit: William O. Clark and John Patten; that owing to the many crimes with which the Mormons have been charged in this county, the Grand Jury will undoubtedly be called upon to investigate said charges, and particularly to ferret out, if possible, a company of Mormons whom the Grand Jury believe to be engaged at this time manufacturing spurious coin. And apprehensive as we are, that the said Mormons upon the Grand Jury will not be disposed in consequence of their intimate relations with said company to co-operate with us in said investigation; we, therefore, most respectfully and unanimously, ask your Honor to excuse said jurors from further attendance upon the Grand Jury.

1. J. A. Clark,
2. Theopilus Bullard,
3. D. M. Sherman,
4. Joshua Owen,
5. Wm. Steele,
6. Salmon Cowles,
7. Isaac May,
8. John E. Leeper,
9. Wm. L. Matthews,
10. Campbell Wright,
11. Samuel Davis,
12. Alex. R. Wheat,
13. Wm. Howard,
14. Luke Shepley,
15. Joel W. Hiatt,
16. John Houston,
17. A. N. Deming,
18. Richard Pritchett,
19. John H. Lines,
20. James McAlenny,
21. Robert Henry.

THE OLD SETTLERS.

The Anti-Mormon ticket was triumphantly elected by a large majority, and all the Mormons able to travel were expelled from the county. The old Mormons having left the country, the mormon element still survived, not in midnight assassinations, but in horse stealing, petit larceny, and in other thievery. Counterfeiters of coin and paper money succeeded them with their headquarters at Nauvoo. Old Ben Brooks, and his sons, ran the horse thief ferry to Montrose, with Brooks' son-in law, John Hine and old Dave Vrooman. A store in Montrose was burglarized by them and a lot of horses stolen, which were found in their possession. They were arrested, and bound over by Squire Conlee, of Jefferson township, and all but Vrooman committed. They sued out a writ of habeas corpus before Judge Williams and C. J. McFarland, Lyman E. Johnson and Jim Woods (old timber) appeared as their attorneys in the burglary case, and they were discharged, as they produced a host of perjured witnesses, dressed as farmers and laboring men, who were strangers to the court, and proved an alibi. They were again arrested, and this time by the aid of outside confederates broke jail at Fort Madison, leaving as a parting salute the following note written with charcoal on the plastering: "Farewell! a long farewell to this d—d hoal." They did not leave the country. A part of the gang, Whitcomb and one Collins, robbed John Wright on the bluff near Devil Creek, in the neighborhood of Jim Bullards, entering his house at midnight, masking their faces, covered with handkerchiefs, with holes cut out for their eyes, getting near a hundred dollars in gold. Collins escaped, but Whitcomb, who was then under arrest for horse stealing, was tried, convicted, and sent to the penitentiary for three years. He had been confined but a short time when one dark night old Vrooman and others came from Nauvoo, and by some means secured his escape. The alarm was given and Vrooman found with two skiffs waiting to take him across the river and arrested. As there was no evidence against him he was released and then taken down where Atlee & Sons mill now stands and severely whipped, and given his orders never to return.

Judge McFarland was then prosecuting attorney. Vrooman showed him his back, with the marks of the lashes still upon it, at Montrose. Next week afterwards Me organized a crowd of his retainers at Montrose, and armed with long cowhides took the Brooks family, one Conn, John Hine, and others, out of their beds at night, and rowing to the Island between Montrose and Nauvoo, whipped them severely, and putting them in their own skiffs, without oars, shoved them off in the river to float over the rapids, with orders never to return. The Brooks family went to the Missouri river, Vrooman to the interior of Ill., where he was afterward murdered by his own son.

None of them ever got back.

During the time this gang lived at Nauvoo they frequently stole waggons, buggies, harness, and small articles, in Fort Madison. On one occasion they stole the buggy of Dr. Rinehart of that place, which was found sunk in a slough on the opposite side of the river. Waggons were frequently found sunk in the river, and kept down by weights, to be taken up and painted over after search had been made for them by the owners.

When the Brooks family and their hangers on were driven away these petty depredations ceased. During the reign of the Danite Band its victims in

Iowa were often arrested at their houses by these masked marauders, taken from their beds and put on horseback, tied securely, behind some one of the band, and when crossing the horse thief ferry at Montrose, those against whom death was decreed were killed, their bowels ripped open and entrails taken out, and their bodies with weights attached, sunk in the river.

CAPTAIN GEORGE C. ANDERSON, THE COMMANDER OF THE BULLY OSPREY—THE EMINENT BANKER.

George C. Anderson came to Keokuk in 1846, and engaged in the grocery trade, and selling exchange, and afterwards, till up to his death, December 4th, 1867, was the most prominent and wealthy banker in the city, being the first to engage regularly in that business. He was a native of Scotland, was born in Bauffshire, 20th March, 1807. Previous to coming to Keokuk he was a member of the firm of Anderson & Thompson, commission merchants of St. Louis, and owned the steamer Osprey, of which he was captain, and Thomas F. Anderson, his brother, clerk. This steamer was known as the "Bully Osprey," and the captain, who had an eye to business, kept on good terms with the Mormons, then flourishing at Nauvoo, for the purpose of making money out of them, and his boat was much of a favorite with them, and called the Nauvoo powder packet, as he was charged with taking powder to Nauvoo as freight during the Mormon disturbance, while Joe Smith was still living, in 1844. In June of that year, when Governor Ford was at Carthage, it was reported that the Osprey was on its way to Nauvoo, freighted with powder.

The Governor at once ordered Captain Mark Aldrich with his militia company, to go to Warsaw and intercept, and search the boat. Judge Thomas C. Sharp, who was then the editor of the Warsaw *Signal*, in which, at the risk of his life, which was frequently threatened, he handled the Mormons without gloves, tells the story of stopping the boat, which was hailed, but at first refused to land. It finally landed, but the captain refused to allow it to be searched.— The argument to make the boat land was a twelve pounder cannon, which was trailed on the boat which was loaded with passengers, many of them women and children. When Anderson first refused to allow the boat to be searched, the cannon was pointed towards it, loaded with grape and cannister, and a drunken Irishman of Aldrich's company was in the very act of touching off the cannon, when he reluctantly consented to have the boat searched. The search went on but no powder was found; it was concealed in the after part of

THE OLD SETTLERS. 55

the hold. Had the cannon been fired it would have caused great loss of life.— Captain Anderson was full of fun, played the flute, and told many good stories, and delighted in getting a joke on some one. He had a keen sense of the ridiculous, and to illustrate one of his many "sells," on one occasion he saw a prominent citizen, who was very indolent and wanting in snap, who walked along at a snails canter; as he passed by the bank one day, at his usual gait, Anderson stopped him, and in a very confidential manner said to him: "Did you ever see a snail?" "Yes," said the party addressed, looking up with surprise. "Did you ever pass one?" said Anderson. His friend saw the point, flew in a passion, and muttering cuss words, walked off rapidly, while Anderson and his friend roared with laughter, and the snail story became the town talk and was carried every where and repeated.

When the financial panic of 1857 took place, in consequence of the failure of The Ohio Life and Trust Company, the Bankers of Keokuk were all frightened. A run was made upon them by depositors; some of them after a short time suspended, others closed their doors and never resumed, and the city was full of depreciated or Wild Cat Bank paper and depreciated city scrip, circulating as money.

Mr. A., a prominent banker of Des Moines, had issued a lot of Wild Cat currency, the bank bills purporting to be from Florence, Nebraska, a village in that territory. On one corner of the bills was the picture of the bankers wife, and when this money depreciated, the holders of some of it got revenge by punching out one of the eyes of his wife's picture on the bills, much to the bankers disgust.

"Old George" was believed to have plenty of gold, and the people had confidence in him. The foreign part of the population who did most of their business with him swore by him. When the panic came, as he said afterwards, he did not have much gold, but he had friends who had. So he kept up his courage, borrowed all the gold and silver he could get, and piled it up on his shelves behind the counter, to make a show.

He had others come and deposit, and opened earlier and kept open an hour later than any other bank. When a depositer withdrew his funds from his bank, and after the scare had somewhat subsided, he would sometimes come to re-deposit it, but he would invariably refuse to receive it. Thus by standing up and making a square fight, he bluffed off the run upon his bank, stopped the panic, and gained the confidence of the people forever thereafter.

He liked a drink, a cheap drink, and took many of them with his customers, generally making them treat, and when he had to do the treating he would not pay over five cents a drink. But no matter how much he took, he could always attend to business, and was harder to make a bargain with then than any other time, unless it was in his favor. For several months before he died, he touched nothing in the way of spirituous liquors, and his death was caused by chronic enlargement of the liver. A shrewd financier, he made a close bargain in his own favor, but socially he was generous with his friends, and never felt better than when he was telling a story, or singing "John Anderson, my Jo John!" at one of the annual festivals of the St. Andrews Society.

We give you the old song of the "Bully Osprey," written, it is said, by W. C. Rentgen, of which Mr. Anderson was the hero:

THE "BULLY OSPREY."

1

My song tells of the ancient time,
  Of the "Bully Osprey's" prime.
When the NAUVOO POWDER PACKET ran
  In the good and olden time;
When her brave and scarred old captain
  Walked a hero on her roof,
And swore the "BULLY OSPREY" was
  Both GUN and BULLET proof.
    My song is of the "Bully Osprey"
    That ran up Sucker Chute—
    Her oaken keel played on the rocks
    While the Captain played his FLUTE.

2

This land owes Scotia such a debt
  We never can repay;
She sent her gallant Captain here
  To cleave our inland spray;
For what would have become of us,
  And what become of you,
If Scotland had not sent her son
  To run up to Nauvoo,
    With his " BULLY OSPREY " steamer
    And his trans-atlantic crew,
    Who ran in the good and olden time,
    And *touching* at Nauvoo.

3

Old Rome has had her heroes brave,
  And Greece her men of might;
Old Tamerlane was *"pumpkins"* on
  The gory field of fight.
O! tell me not of Austerlitz,
  Or bloody Waterloo,

But bid the minstrel tune his lyre
  To "*Osprey*" and Nauvoo.
    Then strike up "*Bully Osprey*," boys,
      Her brave and gallant crew,
    Who went with *gin* and *leather guns*,
      And took far-famed Nauvoo.

4

Sebastopol was hard to take,
  With all their battering-rains,
And tons of powder were consumed
  With any amount of d—ns;
And Vera Cruz held out some days
  With Gen'l Scott to fight,
But Nauvoo, with her *arms* and *legs*,
  Surrendered in a night.
    To the "*Bully Osprey*" packet
      And her trans-atlantic crew,
    Who took the *Mormon hostages*,
      And saved their powder too.

5

Old England boasts of NAVAL feats,
  Trafalgar and Nile;
And history names the Guerriere,
  At which all Yankees smile;
Decatur taught the Algerines
  A fearful lesson, too,
But nothing like the Osprey boys
  Taught fortified Nauvoo,
    With their *gin* and *leather swivels*
      They met in bloodless fray,
    And Nauvoo hauled her colors down,
      Before the break of day.

6

Her temple lies in ruins gray.
  The owl hoots on her walls;
The *fennel* now her plaza decks,
  The wind sighs through her halls;
The mouldering hand of Time has touched
  Her towers, and they decay—
But the glory of the Captain's deeds
  Can never pass away.
    The deathless page will still preserve
      The meed of Scotia's few,
    Who in one night, with leather guns,
      Took fortified Nauvoo.

CHAPTER IV.

Keokuk and its Old Settlers.—Its Oldest Merchants, A. B. Chittenden, W. S McGavic, C. F. Davis, J. C. Ainsworth & Co., Ross B. Hughes, Devil Creek Bill Clark, Cock-Eyed Brooks, Lloyd B. Gall, Daniel and Adam Hine, Bucket Campbell, Old Rouser, Captain Holliday.—The Ship of Zion—Hold Him Shores.—Marrying a Jug—The State Penitentiary.—Old Jack, the Indian, and Mayhew, of Fort Madison.—A French Half-Breed Deposits in a Faro Bank.—Antoine LeClaire Burns a Lot of Wool.—Capt Israel Anderson and Others Treed by the Wild Hogs.—The First Telegraph.—Col. Crocket Cutting Down the Mast, etc., etc.

From 1837 to 1848, when the city was organized under the act of incorporation, as the population was sparse, no great events took place, though many things of interest to us happened in those days.

Our city took its name from the old Indian chief "Keokuk" who had white blood in his veins. Before this it was known by the whites and called "The Point," from its high, bold-looking bluff extending like a promontory into the ocean, which could be seen at a great distance, and has the appearance of a "Point" before you reach it.

This was a favorite spot with the old traders and Indians.

The Indian name for Keokuk was Puc-e-che-tuck. This means in their expressive language the place where the water stops. We call it the foot of the Rapids.

The lower rapids of the Mississippi river, since they have borne any name at all, have been called the "Des Moines Rapids." This name probably originated from the name given old Fort "Des Moines" which we for convenience have all along called Montrose, its present name at the head of the rapids.

Keokuk was laid out as you see it on the original map, one mile square, the sinuous windings of the river in front, only preventing it from being square. It was laid off upon a scale of grandure and magnificence, with great broad streets and public squares; Main street, to-day, being the most beautiful street on account of its width and length to be found in the Union, outside of the city of magnificent distances, Washington; no city in the country can compare with it in this particular except Savannah, Georgia, which was laid out by General Oglethorpe before the American revolution. Great Broad street in Savannah is two hundred feet in width, its sidewalks and an avenue or walk in the center, being shaded by evergreen live oaks, China trees, and crape myrtles, blooming with beautiful flowers and perrennial in foliage.

It is to be regretted, for all time, that our public squares, as originally laid out, could not have been set apart for the use of the public forever, instead of being divided amongst the different claimants under the decree title to whom it was allotted, and sold by them to others for private uses. The New York

Company, who laid it out as a city, had no right to take the private property of others for public uses, without compensation, which they very well knew, but should then, at that early day, have taken the initiative and donated such parts of our public squares which fell to them, to the city, thus inducing others when lots were not valuable, to follow their example. But the New York company and a large number of the original owners of lots here were non-residents, and these non-residents were like soulless corporations. They have sold at high prices, computed interest on deferred payments on property, which in time grew valuable through the improvements made by residents who have built our city, improved its streets and highways, and created its trade and commerce.

Chittenden & McGavic were our oldest and first merchants, and commenced business on the levee in 1841, the year Wm. S. McGavic came here. Abraham B. Chittenden came first in 1840, in a sail boat with his father from Fort Edwards, which we shall call Warsaw, its present name, and they sat down by a spring on Main street, gushing from the hillside, and ate their lunch, and while partaking of this picnic dinner in the woods, Mr. Chittenden declared his intention of locating here on the river, being then a resident of Galena. This firm continued in business, trading in dry goods, groceries, clothing, and produce for over twenty years amassing a fortune.

For the last few years of its existence C. F. Davis, Esq., was a member of the firm, and Lee McGavic till his death. Both of the McGavic's are now dead. W. S. McGavic was the active member, traveling in the country, and was said to be the best collector who ever went out of Keokuk, excepting always Col. Shelley.

J. C. Ainsworth & Co. started business afterwards, and Ross B. Hughes a merchant, ran a cooper shop and almost everything else. Daniel and Adam Hine did an extensive business towing boats over the rapids; besides others, there was a firm bearing the noted names of *Death & Haight*, (hate.) Ainsworth was at one time a noted steamboat captain, and is now President of the Steamship Navigation Company, at Portland, Oregon, and said to be the wealthiest man in that state.

Citizen Brown kept a commission house; Cock-eyed Brooks and Tom Crooks, saloons, Joe A. Clark was Justice of the Peace, kept no docket, but carried his papers in his hat. "Rouser" Holliday and Lloyd B. Goll were steamboat pilots; Lyman E. Johnson and Liberty Elisha Holmes Houghton were lawyers; General Jesse B. Browne was a member of the legislature and politician; T. Davis was a druggist on the levee, and A. Hamlin on the hill; besides there was R. M. G. Patterson, Harry Fulton, Moses Gray, the Meeker family, M. D. Springer, "Doublehead" Hillis and a host of others we could name, and last but not least was Devil Creek Bill Clark, a brother of "Joe" and "Bob," the Clarks being merchants, the partners of Ainsworth.

When strangers used to ask "Devil Creek Bill" how long he had been here, he would answer "ever since the Mississippi was a spring branch." Some of these parties were always getting up jokes or playing pranks on some one. Those who have a noted history in this way were "Devil Creek Bill" Clark, Old Rouser, General Browne, Daniel Hine, James Mackley, Charley Moore, Cock-Eyed Brooks, Lyman E. Johnson and Bucket Campbell, who had a farm in the country, would come to town to get a plow sharpened and stay a week at a time. It was their special delight to worry the crabbed old druggist Hamlin and have old Joe Doan (Squire Van Fossen) in hot water. A word about "Cock-Eyed Brooks" or "Brooksie," as he was sometimes affectionately styled. Speaking of his eyes, Alf Roberts tells the story that he was in the habit of stopping at "Brooksie's" eating house for breakfast, when he came over the rapids on a lighter or tow-boat from Montrose. One morning he was on the outside, waiting breakfast call, some other parties were standing there also. Brooks came out and looking towards him addressed him, "do you want breakfast, sir?"

Roberts never moved.

Brooks spoke to him the second time, and then, as he still stood motionless came up and tapped him on the shoulder, and said again, "do you want any breakfast, sir?"

Roberts declared that he thought all the time he was looking at some one else, though he was gazing directly at him.

He was not a christian, but it was said he was always looking two ways for Sunday in the middle of the week. He was full of originality and wit.

A traveling occulist came to him one day and proposed to operate on his eyes for strabismus. He told him that for fifty dollars he would fix his eyes so he would look as straight as any one.

"No!" replied Brooks, "you can't do it, sir!"

"Why?" said the occulist, anxious for a job. "I wouldn't have it done if you would do it for nothing, for then I'd have to make a thousand new acquaintances!"

He was coming from Montrose one cold day with Lloyd B. Goll, and on the way they stopped at a house to warm. A lady at the house was making ley hominy which those who are familiar with, know is made out of whole grains of corn. Brooks was eating the hominy as Gall came in and requested him to give him some; Goll held out his hands as he spoke. Brooks, who had been anticipating this, had a tin dipper full of hot hominy and dropped it in his hands. He screamed with pain, let it fall, and with an oath seized Brooks and tore his clothes badly before he could escape, which he managed to do laughing at Goll.

Tricks upon travelers were frequent, and our gay, reckless young fellows delighted in laughing at their calamities and mocked when their fear came.

A stranger landed from a steamboat, a hungry deck passenger, and went up to the counter of the "Ship of Zion" wharf boat and called for sausage. They were out of sausage. "Wharf Rat" called out to one Fred Breitenstein, "see here, Fred, didn't I tell you we were out of sausage! Go and get some more cats!" The stranger walked off in disgust. Fred ever after went by the name of *sausage*.

Sometimes they took a new man *sniping* over the river or in the brush. The verdant traveler was anxious to get game and would be set to hold the mouth of a gunny sack open, expecting the snipes to run into it. They would then go off and leave him. He would perhaps hold it open all night expecting the snipes, before he discovered his mistake.

THE OLD SETTLERS. 61

On another occasion Old Bucket and his party had been followed all day by a new man, who was a great talker, from one saloon to another, till at last they got very tired of him, as he kept talking and laughing and telling stories but did not spend any money. The day was very cold and the stranger wore a pair of big legged blue jeans trowsers with great pockets at the sides. Bucket fortified himself with some warm water, and taking him out to one side very confidentially to talk to him, while he was listening intently, poured the water into one of his pockets. Clapping his hand on his pocket in amazement, he exclaimed, what is this? What does this mean? Oh! replied Old Bucket, this is nothing, but just a way we have in this country of getting better acquainted, and walked off, his blue jeans pantloons friend looking astonished while the cold was freezing his pant-legs stiff.

We used to hear some of these parties using the words *"hold him Shores!"* which appeared to create a good deal of amusement.

"Old Shores" as he was called by every one, kept a livery stable and drove a ball-faced sorel horse to a bugy. One day he got in the buggy in front of the Laclede Hotel, which had a hair-lipped porter, who, when he spoke, talked through his nose. "Devil Creek" came along just as Shores had got in his buggy, and putting a thistle under the horse's tail gave him a severe cut with a whip. The horse commenced running away up the hill as fast as his legs would carry him. Devil Creek cried out at the top of his voice, Hold him Shores! Hold him Shores! Chapman was excited and called out as loud as he could yell—through his nose—Hold him Shores! Every one ran out on the street to see the race; the horse tore up the street flying like John Gilpin's charger, plunging and kicking till he landed with his head in the window of a drug store, and planted his driver on his back in the dusty street. He went off to hunt a shot-gun but never used it. When he went on the streets for a long time afterwards his ears were saluted by every little mischievous urchin as he passed with, "Hold him Shores!"

General Browne and Norton Munger, a lawyer, one day got on a spree and resolved to take a buggy ride out in the country about four miles, to the house of an old settler Alexander Kerr. Just before they got there, Browne saw a cow in the road. He was driving, and giving the horse a severe and sudden whipping up, horse and buggy went headlong over the cow. Munger and Browne were spilled out, the horse ran off, tearing the buggy to atoms, and our adventurous larks had to make their way home on foot as best they could.

Cock-eyed Brooks, Tom Crooks and General Browne, took another ride, this time in a buggy belonging to some man who came in from the country and left his horse tied to a post. They had that day all been enjoying themselves in their way, and Browne at such times was reckless. He seized the horse and made them both get in the buggy and took a drive till they came to a steep hill, down which the road led across a deep ravine, over it spanned by a codoroy bridge, across one end of which and the wagon track was a pole to collect toll or for some other purpose, it matters not what. Just when they came to the top of the hill, Browne drew out his big bowie knife, which he always carried, cut off both lines, and striking the horse with his whip furiously, gave a loud, ferocious Indian yell, which could be heard half a mile; the horse dashed forward striking his chest against the pole, the shock killing him instantly. The hilarious party were thrown over one side of the bridge in mud and water of the ravine, one piled up upon the other, and when they got out and came down street with their hair and faces covered with yellow clay, they were as folorn a looking set as ever came back defeated in a pitched battle from Donnybrook Fair. Just such transactions were of weekly and often of daily occurrence.

A story is told on a Miss Snubs, we shall call her, who long since lived out in Muddy Lane, in a frame house beyond Lu Collins The Snubs family many years ago went to California; the brothers of Miss Snubs used to run horses and bet on their speed, and the sister was a great dancer and brim full of fun. She was engaged to be married to one *Wash Fuget*, we shall call him, from the shady groves of Sugar Creek Bottom. He had courted her for some time and the day was fixed for the wedding. Wash got his license; she had found out in the meantime that he was a very worthless, drunken fellow, and made up her mind not to marry him, but did not tell him so. At the appointed time he took a Justice of the peace to tie the knot, and went out in a buggy; this day he however was duly sober. He drove up in front of the door and Miss Snubs came to greet him with a smiling face and invited him in. He went into a side room and soon our Betsy Ann came out holding a jug.

He stood up to be married, she stood the jug by him on the floor, saying as she did so, Wash, here, you can marry the jug. Wash looked crestfallen; the "jug" was a two gallon one, filled with the best Bateman's drops from Montrose. He seized the handle as if it were the hand of an old and dear friend, and sought consolation and sweet oblivion of the past; turned on the heels of his new boots and left Betsy Ann to go to a certain warm country not spelled like California.

Wash took the jug, there was no help for it, for the hard-hearted Betsy Ann Snubs had put her foot down and that ended it, and swearing and drinking made his way back to Sugar Creek, and Betsy Ann next week married another "feller." The story went the rounds and Wash was the butt of every crowd till he married another girl.

The vigilance committee was organized in 1843, in the days when the Mormons flourished at Nauvoo, and Joe Smith, the Mormon prophet, was at the height of his power and the meridian halo of his glory. He ruled the Mormons with a rod of iron, and had but to command to be obeyed without question.

The Mississippi river and its borders was then infested with reckless traveling thieves, vagabonds, counterfeiters, burglars and murderers from St. Louis to Galena. From this time till the death of Joe Smith, 27th of June, 1844, and till the final expulsion of the Mormons in 1846 and 1847, was the darkest and bloodiest period in our history.

Porter Rockwell and Bill Hickman, two noted desperadoes, led the "destroying angels" of the "Danite Band," bound by secret grips and signs as alleged, and "held together by the cohesive power of public plunder," who were under the immediate direction of the Mormon prophet, whose bloody mandates they executed without question. A state of lawlessness reigned supreme in Southern Iowa, particularly on the half-breed tract, and thither counterfeiters, horse thieves and other felons flocked. While Nauvoo furnished them a safe resting place, they could commit their depredations, flee there and be secure.

If arrested on this side it was little better, for if tried, they found swift witnesses to prove an alibi in nearly every case. If convicted, as rarely happened, there was no certainty of punishment. The public jails were very insecure, and with the aid of their friends from the outside, it was no trick at all to break jail. Sometimes there was a general jail delivery, and we have known as many as five horse thieves to escape at one time.

The State penitentiary was more insecure for a long time than the jails. We have known wardens of that institution to eat with and associate with the convicts, and in that day, as they had no uniform of striped clothes, if one did not know the warden, personally, he might take him for a convict, as some of the convicts looked much better then some of the early wardens. When convicts, who were also taken out of prison to work, got dissatisfied, they would run away.

On one occasion he had two Mormons up on the hill in the woods who had got tired and wanted to leave. They threw the Warden down, tied him loosely and gagged him by putting a dirty woolen sock in his mouth, and cleared out. It was said at the time that he had been bribed, but the case was never investigated, and he served out his full term as Warden. He had an Indian prisoner sent there for life, confined for being engaged in the great massacre in Minnesota, whose name for short was called "Jack."

Jack used to run about town and go where he pleased, and was known by every one, but never attempted to run away. Sometimes he worked at light work, such as blowing the bellows in a blacksmith shop for one Fridley. In the same town there was an old man named Mayhew. Jack was a Chippewa or Sioux Indian, we don't remember which. Mayhew claimed to be part Spanish, and was of a dark color, darker than the copper colored Jack. Many called him an Indian, and when they did so he got very indignant and flew into a rage. One day he passed up front street, and in doing so went by the shop where Jack was at work. Jack saw him and rushed to the door, and puckering up his lips, so as to show his white evenly set Indian teeth, with a demoniac expression on his face, hissed out at Mayhew through his teeth the words S-a-u-kee! S-a-u-kee!! a name designating a tribe hated by his nation. Mayhew heard him, and turned about, and as he shook his fist defiantly at Jack cried out: It's a d—d lie! I'm no more an "injin" than you are!

The vigilance committee was organized here for the same reason vigilance committees were subsequently organized in California and the territories; because the courts were too slow and rarely convicted criminals, though guilty.

We give these anecdotes of penitentiary convicts as an illustration of the very lenient manner in which convicted criminals were treated, and to show, that though nominally deprived of their freedom by the sentence of the court, still to a certain extent they were free, many of them, as they were trusted outside with a guard, or alone without a guard. Except a little surveilance they were not under one half as strict discipline as soldiers in the regular army. They slept in cells in which the Warden went through the form of locking some of them, or may be sent another convict to lock in his comrades for the night, and then went himself and sat at supper at the same table with the Warden. They were awakened at a certain hour and retired at a certain hour. So any country school has its discipline and its rules, and bad boys sometimes think they are severe.

Prisoners in the Fort Madison penitentiary were well fed and well clothed, and lived better, no doubt, than people in their condition and circumstances in life had been in the habit of living at home before conviction.

True, this was the fault of the State and the State authorities, but it was nevertheless a fault of which the people who knew the fact and complained that confinement in the penitentiary was no punishment. Hence criminals were reckless and defiant, and with a bold effrontery sought to mingle in matters of public business, to manipulate the workings of the court till an honest people became disgusted and toleration towards them ceased longer to be a virtue.

In the language of the late Judge Clagett, which we fully indorse, we had fell upon a time when there was wanted a little "hell whipping and hanging."

No one man could attack these desperadoes alone without danger to his life, or destruction of his property. He might be shot from under cover of the brush by some one lying in wait when he least expected it, his horses or cattle might be spirited away by night, his store or dwelling might be entered, and robbed, or a fire set going by the torch of the incendiary, startling himself and family from their sleep, to find their dwelling burning down over their heads.

This became unbearable, and one night the residence of Pompey, (Fleak,) was burglarized and robbed, and he offered a hundred dollars reward for the arrest, trial and conviction of the thief or thieves before the court of Judge Lynch. He had hand bills printed and posted up to this effect and signed his name to them. This was a daring thing to do, but nevertheless he did it and was indicted by a grand jury for it, part of whom no doubt sympathized with the outlaws, but he, too, had friends at court, and was never arrested or tried on the indictment.

This proclamation or hand bill of Fleak's first led to the organization of the vigilance committee.

Thus on the Mormon side of the river, at Nauvoo, there was the "Danite Band" organized for bloody and criminal purposes, and now on this side to counteract its influence, the vigilance committee of regulators was organized here, the intention of its originators being to punish criminals and prevent the commission of crime. It had a president, and a great many members, and Devil Creek Bill Clark was at one time president, and always active as a member and reckless, dare devil as he was, he hated thieves and their associates.

We will tell you now something in a general way about the half-breed tract and a French half-breed and his adventures after selling out his interest; also about Antoine LeClaire, who, not only on account of his immense size, but from his position occupied a prominent place in our early history, and only died a few years ago. Peter W. Potter was his agent and bought out his landed

THE OLD SETTLERS.

interest. General S. R. Curtis bought the interest of Major Crossman. The title to lands on which Keokuk stands originated under a reservation in the treaty of August 4th, 1824, between the United States and the Sac and Fox Indians, by which the half-breed tract was reserved for the use of the half-breeds belonging to the Sac and Fox Indians. It was granted to the half-breeds to hold by the same title as other Indian lands are held, the reversionary interest being in the United States, but an act of Congress, passed on June 30, 1834, relinquished the reversionary interest of the United States, and vested it in the said half-breeds of the Sac and Fox tribe or nation of Indians, who, at the passage of this act, were under the reservation in said treaty, entitled to the Indian title, "with full power and authority to transfer their portions thereof, by sale, devise or descent," &c.

During the long residence of the traders and other whites among these Indians, many of them had married Indian women, or squaws, such as Dr. Muir, Bill Price, Antoine LeClaire, Augustus Gonville, Otis Reynolds, etc.

The first sale of lots in Keokuk was in June, 1837, which was extensively advertised, the New York Land Company, and a St. Louis Land Company, who had been purchasing lands of the half-breeds, being rival companies.— Only a few lots were sold, one corner lot bringing $1,500.

A steamer from St. Louis brought up a load of people to the sale, and there was great excitement, but no blood shed.

In the short space of time between the passage of the act of 1834, permitting the half-breeds to sell their interest in the lands, most of them had sold and many had died ; in some instances they sold for a nominal consideration, and principally in cases where they sold for a valuable consideration in money, the half breed was not satisfied till he deposited it in a faro bank, considering that the safest and surest investment. Long after this, and long after the decree of partition had been made in 1841, and the rights and interests of all the parties to the decree in these lands were specifically set apart and stated, so it could be known by the records what each party who drew under the decree was selling, in lands and town lots, we saw a half-breed named Powers, from Prairie du Chien, at Montrose. This Powers, we think, was one of the children by a second husband, of Mrs. Antaya, but this is no matter, he was a half-breed, and we want to show how these terribly cheated half-breeds, for whom so much maudlin sympathy has been wasted, were taken in, and what they did with their money. He had just sold out to some one in Keokuk, and had received his money, thirty-five hundred dollars in gold coin, and had it there carrying it about with him in a red silk handkerchief. The little pock-marked French half-breed felt uneasy, and out of his element,. This was more money than he had ever had at once, and he did not know what to do with it. He was asking advice, and found plenty of advisers. Some of them wanted him to buy an interest in a steamboat, it would just take thirty-five hundred dollars to get in, and he had the money; it would make him rich.— "Don't want any steamboat—ride on him, but no buy him," said Powers. Then buy a saloon! "Don't want any saloon—want whisky—I buy him and drink him!" Nothing that was for sale suited him; not even a steamboat or saloon; but he bought some ruffled shirts and red neck-ties, and many other fancy and gaudy articles of dress, but still had plenty of money, carrying it about with him in that red silk handkerchief.

We watched to see what this fellow would do with the money, as we were waiting there also to go up on a steamer. First, he went into a barber shop, and got shaved and his curly hair greased; after taking a bath, came out with his ruffled shirt and his new suit of ready-made clothing; he looked pretty respectable for a pock marked half-breed, as he stood on the door steps; his stove pipe hat was cocked jauntily on one side of his head, he lit a cigar and stood as if in deep meditation. He heard the well known click, click, click, of billiard balls. That was music he understood: it was like it was in the far north, in the towns near the pineries of Wisconsin. Just then a load of passengers came up in a hack, and amongst them were two of his old friends from Prairie du Chien. They had been to St. Louis and sold out their raft of lumber, and were flush with plenty of gold, and felt good. Powers shook hands with them, and they greeted each other in French. He showed them his handkerchief full of gold; they looked better pleased, and shook hands again, gesticulated and talked French, and adjourned up stairs to take a drink and play a game of billiards. They played one game, Powers paid for it, and they took another drink. A Faro bank, at which a slender, sleek, cleanly shaved, fancy looking young man stood playing with the ivory chips which he was transferring from one hand to the other, while he cast longing eyes on the new party, now attracted their attention. He very politely asked them to come and amuse themselves. The boat for above was at the foot of the rapids, Neil Faulkner the pilot, who just dropped in, said it would not be up for five hours. He volunteered to help amuse them for the time at cards or faro, as he was waiting for the boat, and had nothing else to do. He invited them and they all took another drink. Powers and his friends bought ten dollars worth of the ivory chips, and Faulkner bought ten dollars worth of chips also. The sleek young man and Faulkner looked smilingly at each other. The game commenced and progressed slowly for a while, till Powers and his friends commenced winning, and got very much excited, so much so that they could hardly stop to take their drinks. They talked French, talked fast; their eyes flashed with excitement. Powers had found the business now to suit him; he saw the way to wealth if not to fame. The stakes were doubled, and they kept winning, and the gold was piled in heaps on the table. Soon fortune, that fickle dame which smiles upon you sometimes so deceitfully, to woo you on to destruction and financial ruin, was changed—it forsook them. Powers and his friends commenced losing, but kept doubling the stakes. The gold was now piled up on the corner of the table. The steamboat came; Powers and his northern friends were too much interested just then to leave. But when we left, half the gold in that red silk handkerchief, for which that Half-Breed had sold his interest in lands on the noted Half-Breed tract, was deposited in that faro bank, and he was betting still, resolved to have it all back or lose his last dollar. Whether he lost or won, personally, we cannot tell. But one thing we do know, though we do not claim to know any thing about faro, that it is a game where you buy your little white and red ivory chips, put down your money to the banker, as he is called, and if you win he deducts an enormous

THE OLD SETTLERS.

per centage in favor of the bank, but you keep on losing, doubling your bets, hoping to break the bank, and keep putting down your money, and he keeps picking it up. We have no doubt Powers deposited all his money in the faro bank, and went home no richer than when he came.

It is said that the old half-breed land speculators traded showy blankets and beads, shot guns, and now and then some pork and whisky, and a barrel of flour, to the half-breeds for their interests.

It made little difference to the half-breeds, at the time, who sold, as the land was not then very valuable. The long continued squabble in the courts, and on the outside of the courts, about the titles to the half-breed lands, was like all political fights between the "outs" and the "ins."

If the half-breeds were cheated, the hero of the border brigade who discovered the lost art of emptying a demijohn into a vial, was only traveling in the footsteps of his illustrious predecessors, when he distributed half blankets for whole ones, to full grown Teton Sioux, tearing a government blanket into two parts, he gave quarter blankets to the little naked diggers. Probably the government made a great mistake in giving them anything, as it goes in such cases to traders and agents, and gets around to Sitting Bull at last.

Antoine LeClaire called himself French; he was part Indian, and married a half-breed Sac and Fox woman, through whom he drew an interest in the half-breed lands, under the decree. He was a remarkable man, weighing about three hundred or upwards when we saw him, a great talker, enjoyed fun, and a joke at his own expense, and used to tell many good things on himself. He was for a long time interpreter for the United States, much trusted by the Indians, knew them all and much of their history, and many of their traditions. He was very dark, and showed his Indian blood most unmistakably by the color of his skin, his hair and eyes, and his high cheek bones were hid by the fat. He was as corpulent and waddled about, though very active, as the dancing refugee emigree French king and the princes did, on their return from exile, from teaching dancing schools through Europe, at the fall of the great Napoleon.

Dark skinned as he was, it used to be a standing joke, a saying of LeClaires, that he was the *first white* man that ever crossed the Mississippi river. LeClaire is the best authority, no doubt, as to how our State came to be named "Iowa." His version is this, that a band of Sac and Fox Indians crossed the river in their birch canoes at Rock Island, struck the shore on the west side of the Mississipper river, and finding a place they admired, cried out Iowa! Iowa!! Iowa!!! this is the place! Many other versions are given of how Iowa came to be named, but as LeClaire was familiar with the language which he spoke, of the Sacs and Foxes, knew all the chiefs and head men intimately, witnessed their treaties, and had the best opportunity to know the facts. His story is no doubt true, the other theories based upon hypothesis; and it is not worth while to take up your time discussing them. Like the pre-historic remains of the glacial period, and how the first inhabitants came to America, is of no interest to any one except some old fossil antiquarian, it resolves itself into the Scotchman's definition of a metaphysician, one fool trying to explain to another what he don't understand himself. A good story is told of LeClaire, the truth of which is vouched for by George L. Davenport, who told Mr. Edward Kilbourne to get LeClaire to tell him the story, and he told it to him, about burning a lot of wool.

A gentleman had a large drove of sheep, twenty-five hundred altogether, which he was driving up north, the sheep got tired and required rest, and he came to the conclusion he would stop a few weeks and pasture them, and get them recruited up so as to renew his journey. LeClaire was then a prominent citizen and wealthy man for that day, living at Rock Island, with a good comfortable house and out houses, very hospitable and kind towards strangers, and often kept them for weeks at a time, entertaining them with the best he had, an open hearted generous hospitality, a marked feature and redeeming quality of the old frontiersman, of which he was a noble representative, never making any charge; to offer to pay him would be considered an insult.

Our sheep herder asked to stop with him and was granted permission.— Time flew by, the sheep were in good condition, but their wool was long and it was also warm weather, and before proceeding on his journey he resolved to shear off their wool, which he did, this occupying several days. The fleeces were all rolled up and put away in an empty corn crib, and our sheep man was then ready to go on his journey northward. He bade a last adieu to LeClaire, and thanked him for his hospitality, but before his final departure told him as he had been so very kind to him he wanted to make him a present of the twenty-five hundred fleeces of wool. LeClaire, as he said afterwards to Mr. Kilbourne, was glad to get rid of him and his sheep, for the latter annoyed the life out of him. They ran all over his place blating, and got under his house, under his cribs, and everywhere, the last thing he heard at night was the blating of sheep, and it was the first thing when he awoke in the morning. They serenaded him all the time, till he was sick and tired of hearing them. When they left he slept soundly, and awoke in the morning feeling like a new man, and congratulated himself that it was so.

Warmer weather came on, the July and August sun streamed down on the corn crib containing the fleeces, and the odor came to the olfactory nerves of the fastidious old French Indian at his house, but at first he could not conceive what it was. Finally he discovered this nauseous smell came from the corn crib containing the fleeces of wool. He could stand it no longer. The stench was bad enough, and loud enough, for a hundred men, and he had to smell it all himself. He thought the fleeces were certainly spoiling, and so certain was he of this that he ordered them taken out and burnt, sending a lot of young men in his employ to execute his order.

The fleeces were accordingly all taken out and put in one big pile, looking like a hay stack, and set on fire and burnt to ashes. It took a long time to burn up this wool, and the smouldering remnants of the fire with the smoke issuing from it, was seen in the day time, and the fire at night, for at least a week. Mr. Davenport saw it burning, made inquiry what it was, and LeClaire then told him the story of the spoiled wool, which he had ordered burned up, as he thought it was of no value. What was his astonishment when he ascertained it was worth several thousand dollars.

Years afterwards, when LeClaire knew better the value of wool he used to tell this story on himself, and laugh at it till his fat sides shook and quaked, and say like the school boy, "he would never do it again," but it is not supposed he ever got another chance but this once in his life time to burn up five-thousand dollars worth of wool.

Major George H. Crossman in 1834, stationed at Fort Des Moines, now Montrose, bought an interest in the half-breed lands, and used to be frequently here. He served in the Mexican War, and rose to the rank of Major General in the late war of 1861-5, serving in the Quarter Master's Department, principally in the city of Philadelphia, his present residence of living. He was a large, corpulant, good natured gentleman, a good talker, and told a story well. While on a little steamer, in the Gulf of Mexico, during the Mexican War, we cannot now recollect the steamer, an explosion took place from the boiler being bursted, and many were killed by being scalded to death or drowned after being thrown into the water. Crossman miraculously escaped with his life, suffering no serious injury. It was amusing to hear him tell his experience, and how he felt when he first became conscious. He was bruised and black and blue for a month, but he took it as cooly as if it was a mere scratch. Crossman was acting as Quarter Master at Fort Des Moines, and built the barracks there. He was still in the army in the late war; became a General in the Quarter Master's Department, his head quarters being at Philadelphia, and is reported insane.

TREED BY THE WILD HOGS.—ADVENTURES OF CAPTAIN ISRAEL ANDERSON, (OLD BLACK HAWK.)

He was twice sheriff of Lee county, once before and again during the war of 1861, in which he was a Captain in Company C, of the 3d Iowa Cavalry, and was engaged in the battle of Pea Ridge. The company was marching by columns of four. The rebels were coming from the right. The captain looked about and cried out, where is the Colonel? (Lieutenant-Colonel Trimble had been severely wounded and compelled to leave the field.) Not seeing the Colonel or Major Perry, he gave out the following order, not found in cavalry tactics, in his loud, deep, determined voice, "Fours right ! *Draw revolvers and give them hell, boys !*" The order was promptly obeyed. One of General Pike's Indians just then fired at him from where he was lying on the ground in ambush, the ball missed the captain but struck his horse in the breast and passing through his body, its full length, emerged at his rear. His horse quivered like an aspen leaf. The captain perceiving this and knowing his horse was hit, saw the Indian, fired at him with his revolver, and called to one of his men to shoot that scoundrel. His cavalry were repulsed, the company moved to another part of the field and in half a mile from where the Captain's horse was shot he dropped down dead, and he immediately remounted another. Next day, on looking over the field, several of General Pike's dead Indians were found piled up on the very spot from whence his horse was fired upon and killed. He was subsequently wounded at Batesville, Arkansas, in 1862. Tall and straight, six feet and two inches in height, with a dark complexion, and keen piercing eye, he is generally known as old "Black Hawk," with which chief and Keokuk and leading Indian chiefs he was well acquainted, as he settled first in Van Buren county in 1837, and when he first voted in Keokuk the whole vote polled was only seventeen, and he was from the country then as every one voted in any township he pleased to in the county. He tells many interesting stories of the old settlers, and one of "Trigger Leg" Washburn, who climbed up a tree for a coon, got fast in a fork of the tree, and his feet froze before he was discovered and rescued, but his legs were ever after that crooked, hence he was called trigger leg Washburn, and used to pettyfog before Justices of the Peace in the country.

On one occasion Captain Anderson, Bill Jackson and one John Smith, of Keokuk, went down on Nassau Island to hunt, taking with them a lot of dogs. At that early day, 1840, the island was full of game of all kinds, as well as of wild hogs, which latter are the avowed and traditional enemy of all dogs. The hogs on Nassau Island were of the long, lean, slab-sided, ferocious kind, with long snouts, great curved and curling tusks and tushes, long bristles and long legs, and could run equal to any race horse or stand with their hind legs on the ground and peel the bark from an elm tree eleven feet up its trunk, or reach their snouts through the cracks of a fence and eat the corn off of the fourth row without an effort.

Such were the wild beasts, the hogs of that day, as blood-thirsty and ferocious as the wild boars of the Hartz Mountains of Germany, or those of the King's forest in Britain, hunted by the feudal barons in the days of Warwick, the King Maker, and his sovereign, making royal sport for them and their vassals.

Bill Jackson was a large fleshy man, weighing full three hundred pounds, and had a sweet tooth for pork, as he was killed afterwards on Sny Island, as supposed, by a party of men, the owners of hogs upon whose property, it was alleged he was raiding, but his murderers were never ferreted out.

John Smith was a short but active man.

The dogs were running about in the woods, and after dark the hunters had their camp fires lighted and were fixing for supper, when the dogs came rushing into camp bounding furiously, the first arrivals lying down at the feet of their masters to seek their protection, whining piteously. There was little time for consultation, the rushing of feet and the clashing of teeth was heard at no great distance either, coming through the thick underbrush in mad pursuit. Our hunters smelt war in the atmosphere and knew what was coming, and rushed for a tree, the under branches of which reached near the ground. With great effort Anderson and Smith assisted the lubberly Jackson to climb, boosting him up into the branches, where he was now safe, and they had barely time to save themselves by following him up into his retreat. The old catechisms used to say,

"Zacheus he did climb a tree,
His Lord and Savior for to see,"
but our hunters went up the tree for a different purpose, just in time to "save their bacon."

The dogs escaped by flight, and the wild hogs scenting their masters up the tree, with their mouths full of foam and froth, gnashing their teeth, dashed at the tree, peeling off the bark with their teeth, while they made desperate efforts to gnaw it down. Till daylight they raided in their fury about it, foaming at the mouth, groaning and grunting furiously, a ferocious herd of at least thirty, while our hunters from their perch surveyed them by moonlight.

Captain Anderson, who had the only gun in the party, fired on them till he exhausted his amunition and bullets, killing seven, which fell down bleeding, to be devoured by their companions of the herd, who pounced upon them as they fell, and ate them up as hungry wolves devour the bleeding and exhausted stag before it is dead.

THE FIRST TELEGRAPH WIRES.

The first telegraph wires were run here in 1851 or 1852.

At Fort Madison old Isaac Johnson attached a string to the wire and tied an Irish potato to it, and under the potato,filled with water, he put a bucket, thinking, no doubt, as he said, that he would catch the news as the messages whizzed over the wires, and the potato at the end of the string bobbed up and down, but not a word of news did he get. On the hill or bluff at the highest point, where High street approaches the river, a tall telegraph mast was put, from the top of which the wires communicated messages over the river to Illinois, and it kept up an eternal buzzing and whizzing day and night. It was near the residence of Col. Crocket, a Tennesseean, a fidgity, nervous old fellow, who had been for a long time a bachelor, and finally married the daughter of old Joe Doan, Squire Van Fossen. The noise at night disturbed him so he could not sleep. In the daytime it never troubled him as he was out in town, some said playing poker.

We do not pretend to know whether this was true or not, one thing we do know, he was a cranky, old blue face, dissatisfied with the world and "the rest of mankind," but satisfied supremely with himself.

The country, with him, like disappointed politicians, was all gone to the devil, or some other sea port. Consequently, he was mad, he lost money on his property, his wife failed to have twins, and this made him still more cranky, and he was at outs with the telegraph company and swore vengeance against it—it disturbed his sleep and his dreams. Therefore he swore deep vengeance, upon it.

One very dark night, when the winds blew and the storms raged, he took his axe and ventured out while all was still except the whistling winds, resolved to settle with the telegraph company. He looked all about him, carrying with him Tennessee's favorite weapon of war, a double-barrelled shot-gun loaded with buck shot.

He listened, but heard no one, and at that hour of midnight, amid darkness, with the blood of Crocket, the hero of Alamo, in his veins, coming from the land of Old Hickory and the Hermitage, no policeman and two bulldogs could make him afraid. Courage, Stephano! He had plenty of it and two drinks ahead to make him brave. Feeling his axe and looking about him in the darkness, he saw no enemy, and he was oraver than the lions which did not eat Daniel, because they had been to dinner and wanted an afternoon siesta. Bully for Crocket! a corporation has no soul, no troops on guard, and he ventured up to the tall telegraph mast and commenced chopping.

It was the first work he had done, as an old lady friend of ours said to us once, "since Bruce was born?" Whacking away, with tiger ferocity and bulldog tenacity, for two hours, stopping occasionally to listen for for the enemy, but no enemy came, down came the telegraph mast, and Crocket, the immortal Crocket, was a hero, greater than the hero of the Alamo in his own estimation! The telegraph mast fell, to rise no more forever, and Colonel Crocket went home and toasted his toes by the fire, and then to bed, dreaming he was the greatest man in America if he dared to tell it.

CHAPTER V.

Poem—Invitation to the Grand Fancy Ball, by Kate Hughes, Afterwards Mrs. Attorney-General Williams—The Spiritualist.—Trial of Mary Margrave and Parson Hummer—The Kiddship and the Margrave Family.—The Candidates for Mayor and the Poem of Hiawatha. Hugh W. Sample.—Brother Dull's Colored Sermon.—The Ku Kluk Skare and Sugar Lips.—"Compromise" Robert's Dream —Dr. Galland and the Devil with his Hot Metal Boots.

INVITATION TO THE GRAND FANCY BALL.

Oh yes! oh yes! oh yes! Come one, come all,
On Tuesday, the 20th, is the Grand Fancy Ball,
Where grades of distinction will never be known,
'Twixt gentry of country and loafers of town.

Come hie to the mansion, for there it will be
The most splendid sight that you ever did see.
The mansion is kept by a Methodist priest,
Who of sins the most common, thinks dancing the least.

THE OLD SETTLERS.

Of the grades of society which will be there,
I'll give a description of all but the *fair*,
The first I will speak of is the Cheap Firm's man, John,
Who has been quite active in what has been done.

When he's drest for the ball you then will discover
His raiment is plaid, in his cap is a feather;
His clerk's and his agent's, to show him good will,
Have agreed to attend if he'll settle the bill.
And before he'd consent the ball should fall thro',
He'd spend his whole fortune to the very last *sous*.

And next comes "Long Jacket," so gay and so fine,
With an apron in front and a square and a line.
He is slim in his figure, in his form he is tall,
He would wish to be tho't the prince of the ball.
Though a cutter of tape from a far eastern city,
He has the assurance to think himself witty.
To the natives and strangers he'll make a display,
And will do the thing nicely in just his own way.

The next I will speak of is a dealer in pukes,
His trade it is easily known by his looks.
If you hate to take physic or part with your pelf,
You will puke just as much if you look at himself.
The garb he will shine in belongs to the water,
And suits him much better than that of a doctor.
To attend at the ball and appear along shore,
A present, his dress, from a large firm's store.

A stage agent of late, 'twill next be my care,
To show to advantage, so bright and so fair,
His frock is from Scotland, his cap from Nauvoo,
And is plaided with ribbons of red and of blue.
At the ball he will shine in his lively costume
By his side is a sword, in his cap is a plume,
With breeches quite short, and stockings so neat,
How nicely he's dress'd from his head to his feet.

A brave noted warrior from Churchville, Missouri,
When call'd into action he'll fight like a fury.
He is small in his person, in statue, quite low,
From Keokuk to Churchville this warrior did go.
In his exercise dress he oft does appear,
To encourage the natives when danger is near.
This evening in costume he'll show very well,—
Of his deeds in the war let all history tell.

A limb of the law will engage my attention,
He will act his part well without defalcation.
In the dance you will see, and all surely must feel
That light are his movements and heavy his heel,
His dress well becomes him, and all persons say,
In the figure he cuts he makes a display.
The old honest Quaker he will show to a fraction,
In thought and in deed, in word and in action.

And now I'll inform you, all those who come there,
That they must be attended by one of the fair.
No one at the ball will be admitted an actor,
Unless they can show a respectable character.
The tickets you'll find, so the managers say,
At the bar of the Mansion, three dollars to pay.
The music is good, and the supper will be
As good for the kind as you generally see.

ARIEL.

The Grand Fancy Ball was a ball given at the old Mansion House, now the Depot House, the oldest hotel left standing, occupied as such, west of the Mississippi River in Iowa.

The keeper of the hotel was a Methodist preacher, named Welch.

Cheap Firmsman John was Capt. John C. Ainsworth.

Long Jacket was a fancy clerk, named Crossby.

The doctor was Birdsell; the "Warrior" Dearduff; the Stage Agent Justin J. Johnson, "Jet." The lawyer who danced on his heels, Lyman E. Johnson.

Several ladies now residing in Keokuk, were at this grand party, which was the great ball of the season.

Kate Hughes, afterwards wife of Attorney-General Williams, wrote the poem signed "Ariel."

THE SPIRITUALISTS.

Dr. Margrave at an early day, 1851, was one of the first spiritualists who flourished in Keokuk, and his sister, Mary Margrave, was a medium.

He was a tall, slender, pale-faced, hungry, dispeptic looking man, a lean Cassius, whose digestion was bad, which enabled him to dream dreams and see visions. He was an herb or steam doctor of the Thompsonian or dog fennel order, with dark hair and pale furtive blue eyes. His sister, Mary, the medium, was a brunette, tall, slender, dark hair and black eyes, with a long face and rather thin visage, she was not pretty nor young and tender. A voluptuary in admiration of the female form would not select her as a model for statuary; she had not the classic outlines of the Greek slave whose faultless figure has won the admiration of the world. Wanting the beauty of De Medici, she had the talent for intrigue of the wily Italian, and as a first-class impostor was a marked success. Keokuk was then becoming noted as a fast place, the price of property was increasing, and sales of lots were readily made and buildings of all kinds went up rapidly. Michael Hummer, a noted Presbyterian minister, of Iowa City, a man of much talent and force, came to Keokuk, and about the same time General Ralph P. Lowe came from Muscatine, where he had been practicing law, and located here.

Lowe and Hummer, both Presbyterians, purchased an interest of the heirs at law of Nathaniel Knapp, of Fort Madison, who drew an interest in the decree of partition in the half-breed tract, in which was included lots in Keokuk.

Rev. Hummer came to preach the gospel, General Lowe, afterwards Judge of the District Court, Governor, Supreme Judge and Chief Justice, came to practice law, and at that time were both good friends, and expected to make money by selling their land purchases at a large profit.

The Margraves were needy adventurers, spiritualism was new and strange, and as a consequence first attracted attention and soon after made its converts. Mary held frequent seances, and got monied contributions on which the Margrave's lived, it was their only source of revenue, as Dr. Margrave had no property, except a little frame house which was not paid for, his practice as a dog fennel doctor being small and among the lower classes, yielding him little. But their fame spread, at least Mary's did, and she went on swimmingly—it was the town talk on the street corners and at the family fireside, and in all the hotels and places of public resort. Converts and devotees to Spiritualism increased at home and abroad, and tipping tables, holding spiritual communications with deceased friends in the spirit land, was the order of the day. As the rich man in torment lifted up his eyes to Lazarus in Abraham's bosom, and the followers of the cross turn theirs to the blue-eyed Madonna above the altar, the wondering eyes of all those ready to believe in any new and strange doctrine, no matter how absurd, were upturned towards this Mary, and came as the followers of Mahomed to the shrine of Mecca, first doubting and went away believing in the doctrines of spiritualism.

The Rev. Michael Hummer and General Lowe were numbered among her converts, and were destined to be her victims. The Margraves were coming up in the world, and the trumpet of fame sounded their advance. They got all their revelations from Mary Margrave. They resolved to build a house together, the minister and the lawyer, where brethren could dwell together in unity. The place was selected, a lot on Concert street, between Second and Third, now a populous part of the city. They did build it, and it stands there to-day, and though not haunted by the spirits of the dead returned to earth to hold communications with their friends in the flesh, is a lasting monument of their folly, and those who look at it and wonder at its strange appearance, if they are not strangers to its history, will not think for a moment it was built by revelation.

Before it was commenced they consulted Mary Margrave. Mary consulted the spirits, and the spirits told her they should build it of brick, and they commenced it and built one story brick. Mary had another revelation; it was to be completed with wood, and they went on under her inspirations, and the carpenters carried out their instructions, adding two stories in wood, when Mary communicated with the "spirits of just men made perfect" who told her it was to be completed with a steamboat roof and attic like a Texas, with windows to open and shut that the spirits and angels might at their pleasure fly in and out. She laid her revelations before them and they saw that it was good, and it was so.

If the angels or spirits ever flew in or out, they were invisible. Its owners occupied it and lived there, the Margraves came too; success gave them confidence, and they grew insolent as they grew great; the servants of yesterday dictated to their masters of to-day, and while the angels and spirits were at work above, devils incarnate were darkly plotting below. They came to the surface in the troubled pool, and brethren no longer dwelt together lovingly in unity.

The Rev. Hummer took moonlight walks on the bluff with the spiritual Mary; but this caused no commotion. Rev. Hummer lost a colt and thought it had been stolen. He went to Mary for a revelation where to find it, and Mary told him, after consulting the spirits, just where it was, and described the place, the farm of a widow Smith over across the river, and a party was sent to the farm and captured what was supposed to be the colt. The widow protested it was her colt, that she had raised it; but Dr. Margrave and his crowd put it on a sled, there being snow on the ground and the river frozen over, and hauled it off triumphantly to Keokuk.

But the end was not yet; the Smith family did not submit tamely to this trespass or mistake, or by what ever name you would call it. They came to Keokuk and replevied the colt before a Justice of the Peace. A tremendous excitement was created by this movement in Illinois and Keokuk, the whole town was in an uproar. Witnesses were subpoenaed on both sides, and a cloud of witnesses appeared at the trial.

Lowe appeared for Hummer and the case was tried by a jury who decided the colt belonged to Hummer. Mrs. Smith took an appeal to the District Court, but was again defeated. On the trial it turned out that Mary Margrave, who lived at Hummer's house, where she worked, had given him the revelation where to find his colt. He did find a roan colt so much like his that the jury gave it to him. He took it and kept it and broke it, and as he said, while breaking it he was whipping the devil out of it. Betsy Margrave, another medium, a sister, but inferior as such to Mary, as she never became noted and was therefore not much mentioned, lived with and worked for Lowe, he and Hummer occupying the same house built by Mary Margraves revelations.

Dr. Margrave kept his horse in Hummer & Lowe's stable. The property purchased by the Parson Hummer, he kept in his own name, not making any of it over to Lowe, who had paid his money on the purchase expecting to come in as an equal partner according to their original agreement. Hummer went on selling but not dividing; he still walked with Mary, the medium, and trouble grew apace; his wife became dissatisfied. Mary had in the meantime made

THE OLD SETTLERS.

many revelations, had told them where Captain Kidd's piratical treasures were buried by the deep sea in the east, and first Hummer then Lowe went east and consulted a noted medium, Lucretia Le Moine. She gave new revelations and they became still better satisfied that the Kidd treasure would be found, that they would find it and it would make them rich and independent.

Parson Hummer and Mary were more intimate than ever; they were followed and watched, and from suspicious circumstances attending their long walks in the woods, Mary and Hummer were arrested for adultery.

The spell had been broken, Hummer and Lowe had quarrelled about the property, the Margraves taking sides with Hummer, and the people with Lowe, whom they believed was the victim of a conspiracy. He had been deceived by the Margraves and Hummer. The Grand Jury at Fort Madison indicted Hummer and Mary Margrave for adultery. They had separate trials; McFarland prosecuted and Cyrus Walker defended.

We do not think from hearing the evidence that a good case was made out against them, but they were both convicted. George H. Williams, Judge, afterwards Attorney-General of the United States, passed sentence upon them. Hummer went to jail for a few hours, when S. T. Marshall got him released and brought him home with him and kept him several days. At first he refused to come out of jail, and insisted on remaining there all night.

Mary was sent to jail for ten days.

Hummer had nailed up the stable door and Lowe opened it. Margrave came to the rescue and interfered by attacking one of Lowe's little boys. Lowe was too full of fight to stand this, and though genial and good natured generally, he would fight at the drop of a hat. He attacked them and drove them away, and everyone said he was right.

On the trial of Hummer, Cyrus Walker, his attorney, wanted to set up the plea of insanity in defence, but Hummer would not permit it. But at the same term of Court a jury found him insane, and Col. Wm. Patterson was appointed his guardian to take charge of his property. He quit his church, or rather the church quit him, and stopped him from preaching, and his voice in the pulpit was silenced. His wife left him and they were divorced; he recovered from his infatuation, and through Judge J. C. Hall and S. T. Marshall, attorneys, an amicable settlement and division of the property was made between Lowe and Hummer, except the treasures of Captain Kidd relinquished to Mary Margrave.

The Margraves left Keokuk, which became too hot for them, and moved back into the interior of Iowa, and the medium Mary, and the dog fennel doctor, Becky and all the tribe of Margraves have gone to the spirit land. Parson Hummer sold out and moved to Kansas City, Mo., married again, preaches yet occasionally, and still resides there and is in prosperous circumstances.

THE CANDIDATES.

Captain Curtis F. Conn was the author of "Hiawatha" on the candidates for Mayor in Keokuk, in the spring of 1858.

Christain Garber referred to, was for a long time one of our leading wholesale merchants, was a Virginian by birth, and has always had a spotless reputation for his commercial integrity. "Bill" Timberman, "Berkshire," and Rentgen, "Burns' Bill," were then Bachelors. Charlie Moore was a big blacksmith and a democrat then, and took an active part in politics, and was a leader in all mischief. Devil Creek Bill Clark was the first Mayor of Keokuk in 1848, and "Old Rouser," Capt. Bill Holliday, sometimes called Paunch-us-Pilot, on account of his large stomach, was a member of the first council. Silas was Captain Haight, and Old Bucket was Henry J. Campbell. The maker of city scrip was Hawkins Taylor. The "Great Wapsie" was Hugh W. Sample, who once whipped a big Irish bully named Napoleon B. Boyles, and the reference made to the "Major" arose from his having a difficulty with Major Floyd, at a yellow hand bill meeting. In explanation of these "yaller hand bill meetings;" they were free and easy citizens mettings, gotten up at the Athenum and were something like a third house or mock legislature. In these meetings any citizen could be attacked, and they generally took these criticisms good humordly.

Major Floyd, who was then the government agent, was a Virginian, and prided himself on his aristocracy. It is reported on him that he once whipped his blooded dog for playing with a common cur. The Major called the machinery by which the trip hammer was worked on his chissel boat the "masheen." Sample, who understood his weak points, took him off at one of these meetings. The Major got furious and sent a challenge for a duel to Sample by Dr. Page and another Kentuckian, his friend Huston. Sample said he would cowhide any man who presented him with a challenge, and he had the cowhide under his coat when they met him on Second street. Under the laws of Iowa, sending or carrying a challenge was a penitentiary offense. They asked Sample if he would accept a challenge?

He replied, have you got one?

They repeated their question, and he answered repeating, "have you got one?"

Page and Huston were afraid of arrest, kept their hands on their pistols, while Sample kept his hand on his cowhide.

The challenge was not presented and neither the cowhiding nor the duel came off. Sample was a tanner when a young man, and it used to be told on him he "tanned dog skins," but this did not trouble him in the least.

The "Native Chieftian" was David W. Kilbourne, he and Judge Clagett, when whigs, both wanted to be candidates for the nomination of Governor, had a little personal war of words at the Leclede Hotel, and growing excited attacked each other with arm-chairs when they were separated.

Kilbourne was elected Mayor on the Know-Nothing ticket in 1855.

"Young Pidgewiskee" is his son, George E. Kilbourne, and Edward Kilbourne, the candidate for Mayor, is his uncle. Just previous to this he was the father of twin boys, and the "Bold Emprize" refers to the Gas Works, of which he was then proprietor; a friend of his writing east, who visited him, called them the "Bold Emprize."

THE OLD SETTLERS.

The General of the Home brigade was General Van Antwerp, a Knickerbocker, from New York, well known in the state in which he held many offices, as he was an active democratic politician.

The "Colonel" referred to is Col. Patterson, who figured in the Missouri war about the boundary line betwixt Missouri and Iowa. He was then post master. On the Nebraska question he was understood to be non-committal, and was undecided which side of the Lecompton nigger question he stood on. The point was just this, the administration was Lecompton, he held office under it but was for Douglas, but it was not necessary for him to be expressing any opinion at all. It was reported he sent his son Joe to tell men in his employ at the pork house how to vote, from the fact that they voted the democratic ticket. The Colonel was a shrewd politician and laid his plans so well, his purposes were not found out till his work was accomplished.

General Arthur Bridgman is referred to as trading pork for dry goods, and was one of the old land officers at Fairfield, and for many years a prominent wholesale dry goods merchant. He was many years Alderman, and was Chairman of the Committee on City Scrip.

Silas Haight ran a steamer up the Des Moines and got on a sand bar. During the gold excitement in Hardin county, he got a specimen of gold quartz which he limped about and showed to the would be gold hunters, so as to get them as passengers on his boat.

The "Hickory Quaker" is Major John M. Hiatt, who came from Indiana, ran a mill, used to drive a fast horse, "black bob tail," when Bob Gray, Rufe Wilsey, Jim Paul and Bill Ivans all used to drive fast horses. Hiatt was afterwards Mayor.

The "Buck-eye Prophet and Reformer" was William Rees, from Cincinnatti, Ohio, who laid off Rees' addition to the city, was editor of the Post newspaper, and sometimes preached on the streets.

"Hiawatha" created much merriment at the time, and few of the candidates taken off in the poem took any offense at it.

THE CANDIDATES.

AFTER THE MANNER OF "HIAWATHA."

"Should you ask me" how I know it,
How I know the things I tell of,
How I learned these great new doings,
Where I got my information—
"I should answer, I should tell you"
I was here and I was "posted,"
When this river was a spring branch,
When Old Garber was a small man,
When Bill Timberman and Rentgen
Were both young men and not old ones;
When Charley Moore was not a Loco;
When we had no broken brokers;
When we had no trading preachers;

THE OLD SETTLERS.

When we had no "five per centers:"
When we had good times and jolly:
When old settlers here on this side
Of the river—and the Mormons
On the other—kept just such laws,
And broke such ones, as they chose to:
Time when Bill Clark was the Mayor,
And "Old Rouser" in the Council,
Time when Silas bought the "Sardines:"
Time when "Rat Row" shone in glory:
When "Old Bucket" ruled the settlers:
"Long before they hung the Indian"—
Since then I have watched their motions;
Listen to me while I name them.
Listen to the first in order.

Of the "City Scrips" the maker—
Of the market ground the buyer—
Of the "Pendulum" the builder—
Of the water works the champion:
His history is in the Journal,
Written by a clever fellow,
Who forgot some little items
Hinted at in the foregoing,
He did beat the mighty "Wapsie"—
Does his best to beat him once more.

Next "Great Wapsie"—he aforesaid,
For your votes is very anxious,
He will suffer for your glory,
He is valiant, he is mighty,
Though he didn't fight the Major,
Though he doesn't wear mustaches,
Though he never goes to battles:
Yet he'd fight—but not with bullets—
But with tongue he's "numerous pumpkins,"
And with fist he's quite persuasive—
General Boyles this fact will swear to.
He's the man that whipped Napoleon,
He's the man that "tanned the dog skins,"
He's the "yaller hand-bill" champion,
And his tracks he cannot cover,
Though for Mayor his chance is better,
Since there's nothing left to plunder.

Now another I will mention—
Won't say all the things I know of:
(Brother to the "Native Chieftain,"

THE OLD SETTLERS.

Who was once himself a Mayor,
But will never more be called so;
Named for him who slew Goliah
With a "dornick," not an arm chair,
As he used in fight with Clagett,
In the "Governor war," so famous,)
Uncle of "Young Pidgewiskee,"
Daddy of the brace of babies;
Of the "Bold Emprize" the owner;
He will serve you if you pay him
Gold and silver—nothing Shorter;
"Nary Red" of scrips or paper
Will he for his pay put up with.
Candidate of the cod-fishers—
Candidate of the Railroad cliquers.
Candidate called out by signers
In these matters rather verdant,
'Less they want to kill their man off.

Now, again, I know another;
Always ready, always willing;
On hand always for an office,
Of the "Home Brigade" the General,
Hailing from the Hudson country.
From the land of Knickerbockers,
From the State of "Spirit rappers,"
From the State they call the "Empire,"
From the State the Mormons came from.
He has claims above all others,
He has labored for his country;
Once he edited a paper—
Held an office since his boyhood—
"Only that, and nothing more, sir!"

Yet another still I tell of
In the war with "Pukes" the Colonel,
'Cross the Des Moines in Missouri,
Touching bound'ry lines or something,
All gone by, and all forgotten.
He for office has such longing
Two at once—and three, it may be
You will find are wanted for him;
Tells the locos who to vote for,
When he sees them, or sends Joe to;
The greatest trouble now about him—
Hardest thing for him to settle
Is which side of the Lecompton
Nigger question he shall stand on.

You may think our list exhausted,
But another claims our notice:
High in rank—no less as a General
Than the heroes we have mentioned;
Originator of the notion
That the hogs would come for calling;
Buying pork without the money,
Trading it away for dry goods;
Hogs to represent the dollars,
Little pigs the dimes and quarters;
Chairman of the "Scrip Committee,"
Sent to snub the tricky bankers,
Found them tough and very dogged—
Left, and said no more about it.

Done with Generals—done with Colonels;
Now the Captains we must come to,
One at least is out and running,
Of a river steamer, Captain.
Navigator of the Des Moines;
Stuck his steamboat on a sand bar;
Stuck her fast and there he left her;
Quit the river much disgusted;
Never more trod deck of steamer,
On the "ocean wave" don't like it,
But prefers to be on dry land,
And is willing to be Mayor.

Yet another, still another,—
Hickory Quaker, and saw-miller,
From the land of "yaller breeches,"
From the country of the "hoosier,"
From the "chill and fever" country;
He who the "black-bob-tail" driveth,
Driveth fast as lightning goeth,
Faster than Bob Gray or Wilsey,
Faster than Jim Paul or Ivins;
Fast enough to catch the devil!

Latest comes the "Buckeye Prophet,"
The Reformer—the street preacher,
With his crooked stick and gray beard,
Of the ancient race of humbugs,
Once his slipshod lamentations
Filled the streets of Cincinnati—
Now he's lord of Rees' Addition—
Now he says he must be Mayor,
Or the City's gone to ruin:
Writes Inaugural Addresses,
And upon a "Post" he nails them.

Now I've told you who they all are;
Now you see the willing martyrs:
For your glory they will suffer,
If you pay a thousand Dollars.
—[SHORTFELLOW.

BRUDDER DULL'S COLORED SERMON. THE KUKLUX SCARE. SUGAR LIPS AND SKIN JOHNSON.

The Colored Methodist Church in Keokuk had been organized for some time, and was vigorously beating up for recruits in 1860, as they then had no church and held their services in a Main street hall, up stairs. They had a loud spoken preacher, brudder Dull, who was a lion in the jungles with the colored sisters, who adored him; and the brothers were compelled to come to time and pay the preacher. With broad cloth of shiny black, and well polished boots, plug hat and black hickory cane, the inevitable badge of office of the colored preacher, he strutted about the city with his head thrown back, and his stomach swelling out very much after the puffed up fashion of a toad in a thunder storm. He bowed and smiled, and shook hands and talked to the colored sisters on the streets, and all the young bucks looked at him admiringly as he passed, counseled among themselves and talked about him, and what an easy time he must have, and what good pay he got, a thousand dollars a year, and every one concluded by his wishing he was a preacher. They all went to the church. The American citizen of African descent is noted for his inclination to be pious, particularly when under excitement, and at a religious revival, no matter if he should rob a hen roost afterwards on his way home from church. They love their church, dote on their ministers, and winter and summer they love parades, festivals, and pic-nic excursions. In the summer their time when not occupied as bootblacks, barbers, waiting on tables at hotels, or washing clothes, is spent at pic-nics, or ice cream saloons at nights, and Sundays in riding about town in buggies, eating water melons, or fishing for cat fish and red horse in the river.

It was not in summer now, but winter weather, and snow on the ground, when brudder Dull was having a revival, and had got up a tremendous excitement. The brothers and sisters were wild, and outside sinners were repenting of their wicked ways, and uniting by scores with brother Dull's church. On the night in question a party of us had been out in town, and coming along Main street, heard a tremendous racket up in the colored church, of shouting and singing, clapping hands, loud amens, and occasionally the words "glory to God!" We went in, the singing and shouting had ceased, and a young boy about fourteen years old was lying full length on a long bench near a red hot wood stove. We heard it said in a low tone, "he is in a trance!" We had the

curiosity to watch the proceedings to see what was done in a case of trance.—
So all who could gathered around him, one prayed aloud, and when he finished
they all kept kneeling down and singing:
We'll bow 'round the altar!
We'll bow 'round the altar!
till all of a sudden the boy in a trance, who had only been asleep, waked up
and rubbed his eyes, when they all left him and went back to their places, and
brother Dull then delivered an exortation. He had got no converts that night
and was apparently very much disgusted.

He threatened the brethren with the terrors of everlasting damnation unless they repented, and was much excited. Throwing up his arms he cried out at the top of his voice, (which was a very fine one, the peculiar voice, just imagine it, of the colored minister,) *"you sinners!* On the day of judgment you'll cry aloud, like Richard the Third: A hoss! a hoss!! my kingdom for a hoss! And dar'll be no hoss dar on which to flee from de wrath to come!— Come brudders and sistern, and seize de horns of de altar of de Lord!" That was a clincher, and made six new converts.

THE KU-KLUX SCARE

took place in the fall of 1874, and was at the time the subject of much merriment, creating a great sensation. There was at that time two very worthless colored citizens of African descent, one called "Sugar Lip" for short, and the other Skin Johnson. There was just previous to this, much talk in the newspapers of the Ku-Klux-Klan, mobbing and killing their colored brethren in the south; more were killed on paper and in telegrams than died, but the sensation and reign of terror created was no less startling. "Sugar Lip" and his companion were all eyes and ears, and listened intently to everything that they heard. Eaves-droppers never hear anything good of themselves. It was soon perceived that they were listening and making frequent inquiries. Stories of the Ku-Klux seemed to attract their particular attention. A lot of young gentlemen, some of them limbs of the law, others in different kinds of business, resolved to perpetrate an innocent sell, and make them the victims. For this purpose they laid their plans, and laid them well. They kept talking of Ku-Klux and Ku-Klux raids so they could hear them. They described in glowing colors, most horrible to relate, the description of these fiends in human shape in all their hideous deformity, and how they could travel by water as well as by land. They were amphibious and had great glaring eyes, forded rivers with ease, burnt cities and towns, and their march was like the march of a pestilence, a prairie fire, or the devastating flight of millions of grasshoppers. They had springs in their heels and springs in their toes, one of the party said, and could make sixty steps or a spring of sixty steps, at a single stride. The plot was thickening, and had become noised about town that a Ku-klux raid was soon to be made. At last the time arrived to execute it, and it was well done.

Every one knows the wonder and credulity of the colored race; it is constitutional with them, and they are not to blame for it, even if it does subject them to ridicule: Just after dark one Sunday night, when the first church bells had tolled for religious services, a party of young men were gathered together talking mysteriously in a drug store much frequented by Sugar Lip and Skin Johnson, who just then opportunely made their appearance. They were at once told that the Ku-kluk had burnt Alexandria and Warsaw; were crossing the Des Moines river four miles below, armed to the teeth, in great force, and that another party were coming on board the packet steamer Andy Johnson, that they had robbed and murdered every one as they went, and were coming direct to Keokuk, covered with blood, and breathing the direst vengeance on the colored population. No time was to be lost, the Ku-klux were coming sure enough. Sugar Lip and Johnson, with their eyes bugging out, rushed forth, filled with alarm. They went to the colored Methodist church first, it was the farthest off. A large, portly, saddle colored minister, brother Brown, was holding forth in a sermon, and was in the midst of one of his loftiest flights of oratory, about the children of Israel marching through the Red Sea dry shod, when they appeared breathless and excited, and called out: "The Ku-klux are coming! The Ku-klux are coming!!"

All was hubbub and excitement, and the children of Israel in their march through the Red Sea came to a sudden halt not in the book. Brown stopped suddenly, his face and forehead covered with perspiration, and called for an explanation. They both talked at once, and told how the bloody Ku-klux were coming, and called upon them to save themselves, while there was yet time.— Preacher Brown put on his hat and cried out to the brothers: "Go home! go home, bruddern and sistern! Save your wives and your children! I'se your Minister, and for my part, I'se gwine! *I'se gwine!*" By this time the aisles and door ways were crowded with refugees rushing and jamming, and hustling, and crowding madly, in their terror, against each other; men, women and children, mixed up pell mell, some of them without their hats, shawls or bonnets. They rushed ahead of the preacher, who saw an open window, and as he said again, "I'se your Minister! I'se gwine!" he struck with lengthy and hasty strides with his long legs over the benches, and made for the window, got out of it, and was off on a run to hide himself, some say, in a sewer.

The work of the missionaries here was over, and they hastened to the colored Baptist church, where a great tall, and very black old Kentucky brother was holding forth to his hearers. His subject was baptism, and he had just put Paul and the Eunich down in the water, when Sugar Lip, Johnson, and a dozen others, appeared and cried out: "The Ku-klux are coming! The Ku-klux are coming!" The congregation were all on their feet at once. Their hair was too kinky to stand on end, but some of them were badly frightened. Not so with the preacher. He was full of grit, and wanted to know further about it. They explained, and brother Shelton, at the request of the Deacons, stopped the services, but he told the brethren to get ready for fight—he was just as ready to die then as any time. This put a new face on affairs, and those who did not hide in cellars, went home and got muskets or clubs.— When the Andy Johnson came in, and was about to land, some three hundred with muskets and clubs, of the colored Baptist and Methodist churches were there to stop her landing. Another party guarded the railroad and wagon bridge crossing the river.

It was some time before the officers of the Andy Johnson understood what the trouble was. It was finally explained to them, and a mutual understanding took place.

The steamer landed and a few bolder than the rest, who were armed with muskets, boarded the boat and made an unsuccessful search for Ku-klux! Not a Ku-klux was to be found! They made inquiries. Warsaw and Alexandria had not been burned, and no Ku-klux had been seen. There was subdued tittering, and some loud laughing and hurrahing upon the part of the spectators as the American citizens of African descent left the landing.

Some were in a violent rage. They wanted to lynch Sugar Lip and Skin Johnson, but they had taken the alarm and hid themselves away, and were no where to be found. Next day several of the young men were arrested and taken before the City Recorder, charged with inciting a riot. They appeared and defended, and, as a matter of course were discharged.

So ended the Ku-klux scare. Those who had retired to the safe security of dingy cellars, and the damp recesses of the city sewers the night before, were out next day telling what they would have done had the Ku-klux-klan come upon them and reminded one of the hero at an election. Some one in the crowd struck his brother! He jumped up and down, rolled up his sleeves and smacked his fists crying out: "*Who struck my brother Bill! Ten dollars for any one who will tell me who struck my brother Bill!*" A little short freckled faced, sandy haired man, stepped up to him and said: "I struck your brother Bill! What have you got to say about it?" "Why," said our beligerent friend, slinking away, "all I've got to say about it is you struck him a terrible blow!"

THE DEVIL WITH HIS POT-METAL BOOTS. DR. ISAAC GALLAND AND THE DREAM OF (COMPROMISE) ROBERT ROBERTS.

It was while the settlers were first engaged in a suit to set aside the decree of partition for fraud as alleged, and it is not necessary for our purpose to go into recital as it would be a tedious detail of court proceedings in chancery, in which no one now has any interest, as all questions growing out of the decree title are long ago settled, but it is only requisite to say that Johnson Meek and Robert Roberts, the latter of whom figures in this anecdote were then the managers selected by the settlers fighting the decree title, to manage their suit in the courts brought by Meek et. al. vs. Spalding and others, to consult with the attorneys employed by them.

Dr. Galland was also then at war with what was called the New York Company, but he was slippery as an eel, and though he claimed to be with the settlers, he was all the time for himself, and while they were friendly with him they looked upon him as doubtful, and considered him so uncertain that they did not always know where to find him. General Hugh T. Reid, David W. Kilbourne, L. R. Reeves, and many others, owned land under the decree title. Reid and Reeves being then attorneys, fought to sustain the decree title in the courts, the District Court of the county being now in session at Fort Madison. Roberts expected to go to court, and was then living on his farm near Sandusky. Dr. Galland came along very early in the morning and stopped at his house, and calling to him, bade him good morning and inquired how he felt.

"I feel very sad," replied Roberts.

"How is this," said Galland; "what is the matter?"

"Oh, I have had a terrible dream!"

Galland listened, looked at him with astonishment, and said:

"A dream! that is nothing; but tell me about it!"

"I had a terrible dream, and I feel sad over it yet. I have been thinking about it all morning."

Galland was interested, in spite of his seeming coolness.

"Don't keep me in suspense; out with it Mr. Roberts!"

"I dreamed that I was dead; that I went to hell, and when I got to the door, all bewildered as I was, the door opened, and I heard a loud voice calling my name and telling me to walk in!"

"Darkness was at my back, black pitchy darkness, and in front of me I saw furnaces of glowing red hot fire, and smelt a sulphurous smell, which filled the air with vapors, and nearly suffocated me. I stepped in and an Imp walked directly up to me and ordered me to take a seat, and I sat down on a red hot chair."

"The Imp asked me where I was from."

"From the half-breed tract," said I.

"The Imp started off; I did not see where he went."

"Presently he returned, and immediately afterwards the Devil himself came in with his fiery eyes, his great horns, his cloven foot, and long tail, and addressed me:"

"I hear you are from the half-breed tract. How are things getting along down there?"

"Well," said Roberts, "the settlers are about to win their suit."

He turned then to the Imp, and in a terrible voice, which echoed as from the depths of a great cave, cried out:

"Bring me my pot-metal boots!"

"He brought them; they were red hot; he pulled one of them on, and then stopped and commenced to question me."

"Who was attending to the business when you left?"

Reid, Kilbourne, Cyrus Walker, and Starr, for the decree."

"I want to know who was for the settlers?"

"I mentioned Johnson Meek, myself, O. H. Browning, and Rorer, attorneys, and others, and finally I mentioned you, Dr. Galland."

"He stopped me and called to the Imp: 'bring me my boot-jack.' He brought it, and he pulled off one boot, and as he did so looked at me and said: 'Then it is no use for *me* to go there; if Dr. Galland is there it is just as good as if I was there myself!'"

Roberts was a very quiet man, but full of wit, and made some masterly hits.

On one occasion he went to town and stopped at the house of old Mrs. Gaines, and dismounted to go in. At the door he met Dr. Hogan, (Terror,) who lived at her house, and saluted him:

How do you do Dr. Hogan?

I don't want you to speak to me!

"Very well," replied Roberts, "I always considered you beneath my notice, and I am very glad you have found it out yourself."

CHAPTER VI.

Old Clifton the He Possum. His Speeches in the Legislature—General Mc-Carty—Thomas W. Taylor—Judge Leffingwell Shoots a Fly from off a Soldier's Nose, etc.—Price of Property in 1857—Letters of Great Men—General Curtis, Governor Lowe and General Belknap—Fillibustering Period and the Sons of Malta—Midnight Procession—The Circus and the Side Shows—Huldah Jones Rides the Elephant and gets into Good Society.

JUDGE LEFFINGWELL, OLD CLIFTON, GENERAL McCARTY.

The old settler, Thomas W. Taylor, was lame in one leg, and came from New York, and claimed to belong to the Old Knickerbockers—probably he did —the vainest family we ever knew, and one which had the most fools in it, and boasted of their blue blood claimed to be descended from Oliver Cromwell, the protector, whom the John Bulls, long after he was dead, had drawn and quartered, and his bones hung in chains as a traitor, which was very much like the wrathful boy kicking a stump he had fallen over. We had no doubt of the validity of their claims, as John Cromwell the only son of the Protector, was an imbecile and so was Knickerbocker Taylor. He claimed to have been a Major in the Black Hawk War of 1832, and that he fought at the battle of the Bad Axe, and was, when we knew him, keeping a little country post office named Tuscarora; he was a near neighbor of Josiah Clifton, the old "He" Possum, as he was called, a Campbelite preacher, and a representative in the First Iowa Legislature at Iowa city, in 1847, elected on the Possum ticket. Taylor was an aspirant for the United States Senate; Clifton was his friend and supported him and Jonathan McCarty. Judge Leffingwell reported old Clifton's speech. The Judge was a brick, could make a speech, or tell a story with the most pathetic voice we ever heard, so as to bring tears to one's eyes, or make you laugh at his ridiculous figures, and could write as well as speak, so he reported all of Clifton's speeches in the legislature, *ver batum et literatum*, with his faults of grammar, his scriptural quotations, in which the Apostle Paul of Tarsus, who saw the great light brighter than the sun, the light from heaven before which he fell down blinded and trembling, was converted, and his great plea before the most noble Felix. Bringing down his horny hands, or great paws—corn field hands used to the plow, for he had always been a hard worker, and was as honest as he was ignorant and unsophisticated. Leffingwell's description of the speeches were a description of the man as we have seen him a hundred times piling up the school books, hats, hymn books, and bibles, before him on the table, dressed in his jeans, butternut or blue homespun, with his wife Sally sitting near him. Butternut was the prevailing color of his dress, as walnut bark was plenty, and indigo high priced. It was a feast, not a feast of reason, and a flow of soul, but an entertainment, such as a bear dance, a bull fight, or a Roman gladiator's fight in the arena, with its thousands of spectators, looking on, and cheering bruin in his love passes, Taurus rushing at red flags and sashes, or the armed fighting followers of Spartacus and Cataline. It differed in this, there was fuss and froth and blustering fury, but no blood. To see his great mouth fly open reminded us of the opening of the mouth of a cavern, as illustrated in the ancient geographies representing Fingal's Cave in Staffa.

Neither the Democracy nor the Whigs in this first session of the Legislature, or General Assembly as it is designated by the constitution, had a majority. Clifton was elected on the Settlers or Possum ticket, and while the politics of Major Jacob Hunor was understood to be democratic, and Col. James Sprott as whig, the old *he* Possum was neutral, or non committal. Dodge and Jones, the prominent men, and aspirants of the democracy for the Senate, who subsequently at the next election were made Senators, were anxious to get his support, but Hunor, McCarty and Taylor, were aspirants as the "friends of the settlers," and it was "nip and tuck" who would get him, as it depended on Clifton's vote from Lee county, and the vote of N. King of Keokuk county, a refugee from Lee, on the charge of meat stealing—grand larceny. On the preliminary examination, before a country Justice of the Peace, Mr. Marshall, his attorney, finding the evidence against him was sufficient to convict him beyond any doubt, in case he was committed, advised him, it is said, to escape, which he did, and from occupying a place as representative in the penitentiary from Lee county, got to represent Keokuk county in the Legislature.

Two other seats were contested, the members representing them having removed outside of their several districts. George Berry had been a member of the Constitutional Convention from Lee county. Clifton had talked with Berry about what was the construction put by him upon the intention—his own intention, and the construction put by him upon the intention of the convention, as to whether a member lost his right to sit by removing from his district.

Clifton contended they did lose their right by removal, that he knew it was so, "as sure as gun's iron," and he was certain of it, for one of the members of the convention, George Berry, had told him so!

He made another speech, we recollect, and as it was about old Keokuk men whom he supported for the Senate, we will give its substance as Judge Leffingwell reported it.

He was in favor of General McCarty, he lived at one eend of the rapids, and of Major Taylor, because he lived at the other eend, and had boated over the rapids for nine years, and knew every "iddy" in the river from one "eend" of the rapids to the other "eend." McCarty got a complimentary vote but lacked one vote of election on joint ballot, but stood no better show of being sent to the Senate than of being turned to a pillar of salt. Taylor had a large wheat crop that year, and as the Mormons were committing many robberies, he hired two men, old Luke Allphinn, and another to guard the post office, at two dollars each per night for sixty nights. There was never over five dollars in money in this office belonging to the government.

He sold his wheat and paid the bills, and in the canvass at Iowa City for the Senate, he spent what was left and came home limping on his lame leg, cursing the ingratitude of republics, denouncing every one bitterly. Jonathan McCarty had been a man of prominence in Indiana, was clerk of the court and Surveyor General, from which latter he got the title of General, and elector for the State at large for Harrison and Tyler on the whig ticket in Indiana, in 1840. Was a member of Congress once, and subsequently defeated from bolting the ticket, adopted at a whig convention, which nominated Caleb B. Smith, by Andy Kennedy, a blacksmith and lawyer, who defeated them in a short and Napoleonic canvass, and when asked how he got to Congress replied he had beaten two whigs, and could have beaten half a dozen more just as easily!

McCarty had never been a lawyer in Indiana, but having been a long time clerk, was admitted to the bar, and commenced practice, was engaged in some important criminal cases, made speeches at settlers meetings, but never succeeded as a politician in Iowa, as he lost his health after coming here, was despondent from losing prestage as a politician. In his younger days, as a public speaker from the stump, he had no peer before the public in Indiana. He died in 1855, leaving a son, Edward McCarty, now prominent as a young lawyer in St. Louis.

Judge William E. Leffingwell, of Lyons, was never a resident of Keokuk, but made a democraic speech here as elector in 1852; ten years after in 1861, distinguished himself as a Captain of the 1st Iowa Cavalry, for his accuracy as a marksman, by shooting a fly off of the end of a soldiers nose with his

THE OLD SETTLERS.

navy revolver, while the steamer on which his regiment was embarked, while it was lying at our levee. Hence for this he may be remembered as one of our "Big Injins."

He was the rival of General Jesse B. Browne, also when on the rampage, during the days he figured in politics. As a criminal lawyer he carried with him great force by his eloquence as an advocate and strategy in management. Having trouble in the regiment after his arrival at St. Louis, he was put under arrest, but not confined to closer quarters than his tent, but broke his arrest, got on a glorious bender, such as General Browne did in his palmy days, and was re-arrested and put in the guard house, but here he was equal to the emergency, though guards were at the door, and pacing up and down the street.— He got a big bowie knife and hewed his way through the door, and was once more free. It is said of him he has defended successfully more criminals charged with murder than any lawyer in the State of his age, the number being at least one hundred. We once heard him bid good bye to a lot of Mormons in their camp near Iowa City: he did it for mischief, and spoke to them so pathetically and earnestly, he brought tears to their eyes, and many of them wept aloud. One old lady held on to the skirt of his coat, and he shook hands with her a dozen times. At last, when she trembled with emotion and burst into tears, he said to her, "good bye, mother! if I never meet you again on earth, may I meet you in heaven!" With "God bless you" on her lips she fainted and fell back into the arms of an Elder of the church.

KEOKUK LOTS IN 1857.

We give the letters of three gentlemen, all then residents of Keokuk, as a matter of curiosity, their estimate of the value of two lots, five (5) and six (6), in block thirty-one (31), in the City of Keokuk, at the corner of fourth and Exchange streets, in the spring of 1857.

All of the parties, General Curtis, Hon. David W. Kilbourne, and General Belknap, are well known, the two former being dead. We take them in their order, as dated:

HON. DAVID W. KILBOURNE'S LETTER.

Keokuk, January 9, 1857.

Messrs. George P. Bissell & Co.,—Gents.:

Mr. D. Redington has requested me to give my opinion as to the value of lots five (5) and six (6), block thirty-one (31), in this city.

The lots are on the corner of fourth and Exchange streets, well situated for business purposes, in a part of the town where extensive improvements are being made, and property rapidly advancing.

I should consider the lots ample security for ten or twelve thousand dollars.

I suppose they would now sell on the usual time, one, two and three years, with ten per cent. interest per annum, on which property is sold here, for twenty one to twenty five thousand dollars.

It gives me pleasure to say that Mr. Redington is a good citizen and an energetic business man, and I may add, has been quite successful.

Respectfully Yours,
D. W. KILBOURNE.

P. S. I am well acquainted with Messrs. Stempel & Harper of Fort Madison, and have entire confidence in their abstracts of title.   D. W. K.

GENERAL CURTIS' LETTER.

Keokuk, January 18, 1857.

Mr. Geo. P. Bissel,—Sir:

I am required by Mr. Redington to state to you the cash value of his property on the corner of Exchange and fourth streets, lots five and six, block thirty-one, Keokuk, Iowa.

I am acquainted with the property, and can say it is among the best in the city in its locality, and will soon be in the centre of the business part of the city. It would sell now from twenty to thirty thousand dollars, and if they were mine I would not sell them for that.

Mr. Redington is one of our best business men, successful in all his undertakings, is doing a very large business, and is considered a reliable and responsible man.   Yours very truly,

SAMUEL R. CURTIS,
Mayors Office, Keokuk.

GENERAL BELKNAP'S LETTER.

In my opinion lots five (5) and six (6), in block thirty-one (31), in the city of Keokuk, are worth from twenty to twenty-five thousand dollars. I do not think if they were mine I would sell them for less than twenty-five thousand dollars, and I consider them ample security for the sum of thirteen thousand five hundred dollars.   WM. W. BELKNAP,

Agent Phoenix and Hartfort Fire Insurance Companies.

Refer to Messrs. S. L. Loomis, H. Kellogg, and C. B, Bowers. Keokuk, Iowa, Feb. 2d, 1857.

SONS OF MALTA.

No society from its first organization in our city, ever recruited members so rapidly as the Sons of Malta. It was in the winter of 1860, the river was frozen over, snow on the ground and sleighs could go to Warsaw without any trouble, when it was first organized so a party went down there and got initiated into the order, and were so much pleased with it that a lodge was at once organized in Keokuk.

It went on swimmingly, it was a society for fun, as that was a dull winter, and we had little else to do than to make fun.

Captain David White, known as old Enterprise, a gentleman of pleasing address, and most insinuating manners, was one of its leaders.

We had many candidates as the election was to be soon, who wanted to run for various city offices. They were consequently anxious to use every means to secure votes and win popularity. We can see the old Captain now as he got men in a corner and very confidentially talked to them on every occasion so very earnestly, he impressed it upon them whether they were willing to believe it or not, that to win the day they must join the Sons of Malta. They might be incredulous at first, but he persisted and kept on talking to them, and finally convinced them it was just the thing; they came in as many sometimes as half a dozen and sometimes more every meeting, till we numbered nearly three hundred members. D. B. Smith, Senior, and many others were equally as active. We remember among our members the leading citizens, lawyers and members of the medical faculty, youths in their teens, and venerable grey beards, who were carried away by the seductive spell of eloquence of its advocates of the great benefits this society was going to confer upon them, advancing their future prospects, socially and financially. Without belonging to it they would be ostracised, would lose business and be tabooed generally. To those inclined to be patriotic it was intimated some great event, which it was necessary to keep secret, was about to take place, in which if they would participate therefore they must join the Sons of Malta! Peter, the Hermit, in preaching his crusades never met with greater success than our Missionaries, in making converts. They were every where. J. K. Hornish was a candidate for Mayor. Dr. Haines was a candidate for Alderman. Henry Bartlett was a candidate for Marshall. Charley Hubenthal was a leading butcher, and J. B. Knight was an active politician, and quite a number of others we could name, had their axes to grind, but we mention these only as leading characters. The lodge rooms were in the third story where the elm tree stands on Fifth and Johnson streets, and were sumptuously furnished and lighted with gas, pictures and mottoes of the order hung about the walls of the lodge room which was patriotically festooned and decorated with our national colors. Our sentinels armed with muskets stood guard, parading up and down the hall to impress the candidates, who were escorted into the anti-room, examined, disarmed and blind-folded, and then singly, they enter our hall with a guard on each side. Amidst solemn singing and music they entered, while in their black and white robes the sons sat about the hall, the G. R. J. A. at one end, and the A. G. R. J. A. at the other. The candidate was questioned and on answering, the words he uttered were sometimes solemnly repeated by the members of the society, as they signified their approval by the words "satisfied!" And again he was put through the manual of arms, asked about his being for or against the invasion of Cuba so very seriously that he began to think we were really fillibusters. Nearly all were ready to join the glorious expedition against Cuba. The swimming exercise, part of our ceremonies, was decidedly rich. Water was being poured out and could be heard to splash by the candidate while he was being questioned as to his skill as a swimmer; and finally he was laid out flat on his belly, and stretched with his arms and legs extended on a large piece of canvass as big as a wall tent fly, around which a dozen or more tall men gathered. The candidate was waiting and wondering what would come next, for we put them on this great piece of canvass one at a time. The men about it now raised the canvass with their hands high up, and the candidate was told to strike out, which he generally did as if swimming, and in this position was thrown up towards the ceiling and would fall back on the canvass bouncing like an India rubber ball up and down, greeted with the cries on every side, "Strike out!" "Strike out!" "Strike out!" and in this way was bounced up and down till the men were tired out or relieved by others, and the candidate was nearly exhausted for want of breath. To a fat man it was a trying ordeal. Many were badly frightened, but there was no escape; we put them through to the end.

The swimming process over, the candidate was made to walk up an inclined plane, all the time blind-folded, on his hands and feet, his all fours, a smooth plank leading to the top of a long box about a foot in length, and when he arrived at the top of the box he was seized, turned about upon his back, and rapidly pulled along to the other end of the box where there was another descending inclined plane, like the first, upon the board of which it was made, it differed from the first in this, every few inches a half circular piece of wood was nailed so it was as if a plank had been nailed on one side of a ladder, and over this, his face upwards, he was pulled by the feet, but so held that his head did not strike, but in his descent bump! bump! bump! making a noise lik an old timer with his pestle and mortar pounding hominy. The measure of his glory was not yet full, he was destined to suffer martyrdom still further, and as the blood of the martyrs is the seed of the church, our candidates when once initiated into the order resolved themselves into a committee of one to make new converts.

The last trying ordeal was when, on his knees before a large looking glass the brother received the staff of life; the bandage was removed, from his eyes, and he saw himself, as others saw him, gazing in the glass, his head gear a pair of asses' ears, and on each side of the glass the picture of an ass, one fat and sleek and in good condition, the other, old and poor, with his teeth out, he could not hold his oats, and above the two the Shakspearean quotation: "When shall we three meet again?" He had seen the end and his patriotic fervor for invading Cuba was ended; to complete his happiness he was required to contribute a keg of lager beer.

Some of the candidates at first were indignant, but in time they got gloriously over it and enjoyed the fun and took in their dearest friends.

Charley Hubenthal who was going out on the plains was caught; he was one of our best swimmers, and the next day he went out and recruited every butcher in the city. The admission fee was five dollars, and we had as much as five hundred dollars in the treasury at one time. Part of the object of our society was "to clothe the naked" and to "feed the hungry," and to the poor we contributed liberally; to poor widows and the sick and afflicted we gave wood and food and clothing, liberally appointed visiting committees, giving to a single poor woman as much as twenty-five dollars at a time, till the city was full of the fame of the "Sons of Malta," for their deeds of charity.

One night we had a grand midnight torch-light procession. Arrayed in white and black robes, decorated with colored crosses, grinning death-heads and cross bones, in two ranks we marched through the principal streets, the G. R. J. A., with his head covered by a Roman helmet, in the lead, with banners on which were "We feed the Hungry," "We clothe the Naked," and many other inscriptions of a like character. It was like a procession of Monks in solemn array, and at every corner we halted and called out in chorus the mottoes decorating the banners of the order, attracting the awe struck wonder and special admiration of the large crowd of spectators who followed in our wake all along the entire line of march and till we again reached the hall of the society. At least three hundred members joined in the procession which was one of the most noted, and created more sensation than that of any society which ever paraded our streets.

Through that winter we enjoyed ourselves, and as Spring was coming on one Clark, who was treasurer, absconded with all the money in the treasury went South and when the war broke out joined the rebel army, and it is reported got killed. Dr. Hughes fell heir to the robes and paraphernalia of the order, which shortly afterwards became defunct, as we had recruited in our ranks that winter nearly all the element who are charmed with the novelty, or impressed with the benefits they expect to derive from belonging to some secret society. The blind-folded candidate being initiated, while the ceremony was being gone through, would hear the sentinel at the door give a knock and announce the names of prominent citizens seeking admission, such as Col. Potter or Major Floyd and others who were never members, and would feel proud that he was to be a member of such a society. The wives of married gentlemen who joined it, tried to find out their secrets, but such gentlemen were mysterious and so badly sold they never disclosed them. It did no one any harm, and by its deeds of charity that winter, did more good in a short time than any society ever established here, and we all got more than the worth of our money in fun.

HULDAH JONES RIDES THE ELEPHANT AND GETS INTO GOOD SOCIETY.

Huldah Jones was a pretty country girl, and lived just in the suburbs of the village; and as Huldah used to tell us her daddy owned one of the best farms in the county, we used to go to see Huldah, and as she was wonderful nice to us, and her mother said she liked for Huldah to have a beau, or feller, from town, as she called it, who wore store clothes. We lived in town then, not in the village near which Huldah's daddy owned the farm, but in another town, ten miles away, and we used to go out and spark Huldah, who said she would rather have us "hug" her, hug was the word, than anybody that ever sparked her.

We always went to see Huldah on Saturday nights, and stayed over till Sunday, took her to church, and then left for home Sunday afternoon, and what is the nicest thing with the country girls, we always took her "buggy riding," and she liked that.

When we drove up on a Saturday afternoon, Huldah's little red headed brother always came and opened the gate and took our horse, unharnessed him, and gave him water, and put him in the stable at the barn, and just filled the rick with hay and rubbed him down, so that our horse got so, involuntarily, when we passed that way down the lane by Huldah's house, we could not stop him, he got as stubborn as a mule, must turn in any way, he wanted to be watered and fed in that stable, and must have been governed by some kind of instinct which told him we wanted to see Huldah; of course we did!

Then when we came, Huldah was looking for us, and did not always wait for us to knock before the hall door flew open, and we kissed Huldah with a smack; that is the way she said she wanted to be kissed; she did not want any of this half way timid kissing, like the country boys kissed; she wanted a "feller" who was not afraid to kiss her right.

There was always a commotion in the barn yard, a squalling of chickens, "yaller" legged chickens, such as the Methodist circuit riders got when they stopped, but Huldah's daddy was not a Methodist, and there were no Methodist preachers who stopped there, and we were glad of it, as a Methodist preacher would have had the best room and the big feather bed, but we got that always. Huldah had picked the geese and made it herself, and her mother told us when Huldah got married she was to have two big feather beds, and no end of quilts, counterpains, linen sheets and towels, and showed them all to us.

Huldah would kill a chicken and churn—they always killed a chicken and churned when we came to Jones' house. You ought to have seen Huldah wring a chickens head off; she could do it to perfection. And then we had such nice cool butter milk or peaches and cream and doughnuts; if there was anything good we got it, and they always had something good, for Jones was a rich farmer, and we always took him the papers to read, and told him the latest news. Jones was none of your sardines, he was not a country greenhorn, if he did live on a farm, for he had been about the world, and was a member of the legislature. When he went out away from home he wore store clothes and blacked his boots, he had a plug hat, and he never came to the table in his shirt sleeves when he was at home. Nor did he blow his nose with his fingers —he knew better than that—and always carried a pocket-handkerchief which Huldah had hemmed for him herself, and what was more he used it.

Sometimes a country beau with long yellow hair and gloves on, and a new yellow saddle would ride up, he had a place, may be, near Jones, and he wanted to spark Huldah, who had many admirers, for she was gushing and had just the sweetest lips, the prettiest white teeth, and such melting sky-blue eyes, full of mischief too—to look at her when we think of it now, is enough to make one's mouth water. Those country fellows meant business, they wanted Huldah and they wanted that land Jones was going to give her, for he told us so, and showed us the land. He took us walking one Sunday morning out in the fields and he kept talking about the crops and prices and lands, and we must confess we got a little fidgity, we were afraid Jones was going to ask us about our intentions towards Huldah, but he didn't, but said in a very knowing kind of a way what he intended to do for his daughters, said the boys had their share, that he had another place he intended for Jane, her sister, but Huldah was his favorite, and her mother's favorite, and he intended to give her the home place. We told him that was nice, that Huldah was the oldest and she ought to have it. And then we walked back, and we felt relieved that Jones did not go any further. Huldah wrote to us and we wrote to Huldah; they were sweet letters, and it was no use for the "fellers" with the new "yaller" saddles to ride up to the gate and ask to see her father for an excuse just to get to see Huldah; we didn't do that, but went in as bold as a lion, and made no excuses that we wanted to see Jones, and if Huldah was not there we asked for her, and if she was away from home visiting at a neighbors, they sent for her, and she said she would just give all those fellers with the new saddles the sack. What did they know? and she did it, and they swore vengeance, and looked daggers at us, but that was all that came of it. Huldah just laughed at them, and we brought her candy, and blue ribbons for her hair, and a blue sash, and Huldah was delighted, and we thought that was small pay for all that butter milk, horse feed, doughnuts, yellow-legged chickens and sleeping in the big feather bed. So we told Huldah we would take her to the circus. She was more pleased than ever, and the next week when the circus came we went out to Jones' and took a beau for Jane with us too. The circus came off in the Public square, that afternoon, and so the Jones family put up our horses and invited us to stay to dinner, and we got a circus ticket for Huldah's red-headed brother to go to it, and to do all the side shows; he grinned all over his face, he was so tickled. But he had been feeding and currying and watering our horse all this time, and deserved a show ticket, and to go to the side shows too. Circuses only came once or twice a year, and he was Huldah's little brother. He said he would rather have us come and spark his sister Huldah than any of them fellers; Jane's beau never gave him anything, he said; he went right straight out into the orchard and got us a big basket full of red June apples. Huldah's brother was grateful; he looked all over the hay mow, and in all the hen's nests, and got all the fresh eggs for dinner. We had an extra good dinner that day, and the Jones family were all pleased for we were going to take Huldah and Jane to the show, and Jane's regular beau lived out in the country, it was so nice to take Jane, for Jane was engaged. Mrs. Jones said she always wanted Huldah to get into good society.

So after dinner Huldah and Jane got on their white dresses and new hats, and were looking all glorious with blue ribbons, they washed their faces with castile soap, and came out with new shoes and new gloves, and looked so sleek —yes, just as sleek as a peeled onion—with red roses in their hair. We went to the circus; we escorted Huldah and marched in advance; Huldah said that was the place for us. Jane was escorted by the beau we brought her, and walked behind us. Huldah talked about Jane getting married, and we talked to Huldah about marrying till we got to the circus tent door, and went in; we saw the circus, and the animals, the bird of Paradise, the monkeys, lions, tigers, and the elephant, and then we proposed to take them into the side shows; but Huldah, who held our arm, pulled us back—wouldn't that cost too much money? It was only thirty cents more, but Huldah was a sensible girl and didn't want us to spend any more money for her; but we went the whole figure and took them to the side shows, bought them candy, lemonade, gingerbread and root beer, and they were happy. The poeple all stared at us from the country, talked among themselves about how nice the Jones' girls looked, and wondered how they always managed to get town fellers, with store clothes, for beaux. Huldah introduced us to a lady friend of hers, and we beaued her too, swinging on our other arm. Her beau was out at the time, and came in while we were looking at the rope walker; he looked mad; he was a great tall, stout fellow, and had just been shaved that morning, and had put on a new boiled shirt, and his face turned as red as a spanked baby; but we called him up and gave him his girl, and he was all smiles and graces. He talked to his girl in a low, confidential tone of voice; caught her by the hand, and they swung hands and walked round the circus ring swinging hands as they went. She told him Huldah Jones' beau took her into the side shows and bought her gingerbread and spruce beer, and intimated that he had better take her. He said he did not care what them stuck up town fellers did, he wasn't going to spend the money to take her. But she told him if he was going to be her feller he had to take her; if the Jones' girls could go to the side shows, she could go too, and he must take her; she was just as good as the Jones' girls! He wilted and took her, and got the gingerbread and root beer, and they did the side shows, saw the snakes, and came up to us swinging hands, while in the other hand she held, in a brown paper, a quarter section of yellow gingerbread, the top smeared all over and glistening with New Orleans molasses, and they both looked triumphant. Huldah had been talking all the time to us about good society; she had been reading the latest novels, and said her mother always wanted her to get into good society, and there was no good society about there, no one good enough for her to associate with.

 The elephant by this time came into the ring, a monster elephant, with a big castle of a saddle on his back, and recruits were called for to ride the elephant. The elephant knelt down, but no one came. The ladies were called for, but no one was bold enough to ride the elephant. So we told Huldah if you want to get into good society now is your time—go and ride the elephant. She would go if Jane would go—they were not afraid—Huldah and Jane could ride the wildest colt ever bridled, with or without a saddle. So we took Huldah and Jane into the circus ring, and we had them ride the elephant, and their fortunes were made. From their lofty perch way up on the back of the elephant they looked down upon the admiring crowd, and more than one wished to be in the place of the Jones' girls. Their eyes sparkled with delight, and their rosy cheeks glowed with pleasure, their blue ribbons fluttering in the breeze, when the elephant, commanded by his keeper, halted and knelt down and we received Huldah, and Jane's beau escorted her, we handed them to their seats. Now, riding the elephant was the top of the mode and all the rage. Our girl with the gingerbread and her feller, and several others who rode nice horses and new yellow saddles, with their girls, rushed forward holding each other by the hand, to ride the elephant. The elephant man waved them back; there was to be no more elephant riding that day, and Huldah and her sister Jane were the queens of society, for they alone, of all the girls in that part of the country, had rode the elephant.

Didn't we tell you so, we said to Huldah; they are all jealous of you because you rode the elephant. That's true, replied Huldah, and ever after all important events with the Jones girls took their date from or before the time they rode the elephant till Jane got married. We went to the wedding and "stood up" with the bridegroom and Huldah with the bride, her sister Jane, and they all said that it would be our turn and Huldah's to get married next. "'Twixt the cup and the lip there is many a slip." It was perhaps Huldah's fault not ours, "it might have been." We kissed the bride, we kissed her at parting the next morning, and as tears stood in Jane's eyes she bid good bye to her father and mother and to Huldah, and went away to her new home with her new husband. Huldah and ourself continued sweet on each other; we wrote each other love letters; she gathered us boquets, and we quoted poetry to her and slept in the big feather bed till Huldah went on a visit to Jane. We got letters from her still, and she got a new beau with store clothes; she was in good society; we traced it all to riding that elephant.

Huldah wrote to us again, and that was for the last time. And what do you think she said, after all our devotion, taking her to the show, buying that gingerbread and root beer! It was cruel—the unkindest cut of all. Huldah said to us, and she wrote by moonlight and under inspiration, "I don't see any use of your writing me any more letters unless you are going to marry me; if you are going to marry me I think it is about time for you to say so. I have plenty of good chances to marry here, etc."

We wrote to her if you have got a good chance to marry, take it, and she took it, and kept our cheap jewelry, and that's what we got for having her ride the elephant to get into good society. We had always heard republics were ungrateful, and now we believe it. We never saw Huldah again till years after that; then she was a gay widow with two children, blooming as ever, her deep blue eyes filled with that pensive melancholy all sweet young widows have when they sigh as they always do—who could resist it—we kissed the bride once, a widow now. Huldah sure enough got the home place, her husband left her a fortune, and she named her boy for us, and she said, but we did not believe much of that, she had always carried our miniature next to her heart. She pulled out the locket, held by a little gold chain, from her gushing bosom, while we sat on the sofa, and the little boy, our name sake, climbed our knees, she touched the spring and it flew open, there sure enough was our picture, a picture of a green looking boy, with no beard; on the otherside was that of Huldah, just as they were taken at the village, dating from the great day of her life, from which she still persists in dating everything, the day she rode the elephant.

CHAPTER VII.

The Ramshorn Railroad—General McKeans Duel—Anecdotes of Judges and Attorneys—The Penalty for Arson—Elkanah Perdew—Judge Rorer—Scroggins' Speech—Gus Goodrich—Judge Boyles—Monkey Johnsons' Breach of Promise Case and his Love Letters—Gil Fulsom and Judge Joe Williams—Henry W. Starr—The Quack Doctor—Pacing Johnson—The Meeker Family and others.

In 1851 a political project the building of a railroad from Keokuk to Dubuque and also to Council Bluffs was agitated and advocated by very many leading newspapers in the State. The idea advanced was that it was to be mainly if not altogether built by a grant of lands from Congress to the State of Iowa for that purpose. Every town of any pretensions on and off the river expected to get this railroad. Surveys were made, not for the purpose of establishing any route, but to attract public attention and to keep up the excitement and it answered its purpose, it had its day till the election of U. S. Senator was over and died. Like the track of a snake in the dusty road, it ran everywhere or appeared to run everywhere and ran no where It was ridiculed as the Ramshorn Railroad, as it was crooked as a ramshorn; this was necessary to accommodate everybody.

The local politicians of the different counties advocated the Ramshorn and held it up before the people as the thing that was to enrich them; it was to run through every county and by every mans' door, The Dispatch and Sharp Stick, edited by T. B. Cuming, afterwards Governor of Nebraska, Keokuk Daily and weekly papers, of which he was the editor, was its loudest champion, and he was going to have a railroad, the Ramshorn Railroad, built from Keokuk to Debuque without fail, via Iowa City and no mistake. It was a big thing for Cuming, and just the thing on which to make a United States Senator out of whom he could get an office, which he did. It was a bold aud successful strategy, and Cuming was an able writer and played his hand so skillfully as to accomplish his purpose.

Major McKean, who was a graduate of West Point, and distinguished himself as an officer in the Mexican War, was the Chief Engineer of the Ramshorn Railroad. He then lived at Cedar Rapids, was a Brigadier-General in the late war, commanded our division and was a very gallant officer, and as honest as the day is long, for he was not a politician. His being Chief Engineer of the Ramshorn Railroad connects him with Keokuk, and as he and Cuming are now both dead, we must tell a story on him.

GENERAL McKEAN'S DUEL.

He had just returned to New Orleans, from the Mexican War, in the winter of 1847-8, where he was temporarily stationed with his blushing honors as a gallant officer thick upon him, and as he was then young and full of life and vigor, he mingled much in gay society and was a lion among the first bloods of the city of New Orleans, then a fast place in which the code duello was recognized. General McKean told the story to us himself at the Tishimingo House one day at Corinth, Mississippi, and we can see him now, venerable and grey, dressed in his uniform, with the stars of a Brigadier-General on his shoulders, and shall never forget his description of the duel, and how with his sword he illustrated it, and the fire of excitement which glowed in his fine blue grey eyes as he seemed to be acting over the tragedy again. But we will tell it as near in his own language as possible. His favorite expression when excited, was, Ye Hogan to the Rescue!

He had a difficulty of no serious nature with a noted New Orleans duelist. McKean thought he might be mistaken, and as a gentleman, under such circumstances, he apologized, but the duelist no doubt, thinking it came from fear, grossly insulted him—he had killed seven men in single combat—was a Frenchman and noted for his skill with the rapier or small sword. But he was mistaken in his man this time, for McKean at once sent a note to him demanding an apology. He treated his friend with marked contempt and returned a beligerent message, on the receipt of which, negotiations being at an end, McKean sent him a peremptory challenge, which he accepted. The friends of the General all the while protested; the seconds tried to effect a compromise, but it was all to no purpose. The Frenchman had the choice of weapons, he was the challenged party; he chose small swords, the rapier used in duels. McKean's friends still tried to dissuade him from engaging in a duel, the articles of war prohibited it, and he knew nothing more about using a small sword than a child. They insisted it was an unnecessary risk of his life; his character for courage was already established as an officer in the army, he needed no vindication, and he would certainly be killed. McKean replied that to back out then would be dishonor, he would rather die as a brave man than be dishonored and branded as a coward. The preparations for the duel went on, the seconds fixed the time and place, the fight to come off next morning at seven o'clock. The parties, their seconds, surgeons and friends took carriages and were promptly on the ground at the appointed time and place.

The Frenchman looked confident; McKean was cool and collected, but his friends trembled with apprehension—they expected him to be killed. They took their assigned positions three paces apart, and at the last word one, two, three, they were to commence the contest of life and death. The single-handed contest began; the Frenchman commenced with his scientific movements, the guard, the false thrust, the parry, supposing his antagonist as a United States officer, was a skillful swordsman. But McKean, putting himself in position, made but one movement, crying out, Ye Hogan to the rescue! he threw himself forward, and with one furious thrust, ran the Frenchman through the body with his sword.

ANECDOTES OF JUDGES AND ATTORNEYS.

In 1855 Samuel Boyles, (called Biles,) was a candidate for re-election as County Judge, on the Democratic County ticket. Much complaint was made against him on account, as alleged, of his large expenditures of money in building the County Poor House, six miles out on the plank road from Keokuk, in order to excite the local prejudice of the upper portion of the county, and turn the votes for his opponent. He was to make his grand speech just before the election in Keokuk, the citizens of Keokuk, considering this attack on him as a local attack on their interests, many Whigs supported him. The time came for his speech; the place appointed was the Atheneum; the house was crowded to overflowing, and General A. Bridgman, a Whig, presided. Boyles was fortified with a large bundle of vouchers and written documents, and went on to make his speech, the audience listening with breathless attention. He explained the poor house expenditures to their entire satisfaction, and had the crowd with him and they voted for him at the polls. He wound up his speech with a grand peroration in speaking of the documentary evidence in his favor, he threw himself back, raised his right hand high in the air, and bringing it down with a slap on the bundle of paper before him, said: "*I tell you, gentlemen, the testimony is perfectly volumptuous!*'

THE PENALTY FOR ARSON.

Two countrymen, farmers of Pleasant Ridge Township, came riding into the village of West Point, at a furious rate, early in the spring of 1850. Halting near the east side of the public square, they hastily dismounted and tied their horses to the rack, and entered the dry goods store of Billy Stewart, where Elkania Perdew sat with great dignity in a split bottomed rocking chair, the sir oracle of the crowd of loafers whittling pine sticks. The orator paused as the countrymen entered, and all eyes were turned towards the new comers.— The tallest one, the spokesman of the party, approached the village attorney, and halting before him said: Sir! there has been arson committed out in our neighborhood! What's the penalty?

Imagine Caesar upon the banks of the Rubicon, or the earnest gaze of Moses over into the promised land, or the frog swelling with dignity at the approach of a thunder storm!

"He shook his tail and jarred the river."

Drawing himself up while the eyes of the crowd and his questioner were bent eagerly upon him he replied:

"He must marry the woman!"

So the penalty for arson was fixed forever.

Thomas Welch, Esq., tells a good one on Elcania Perdew, a prairie practice lawyer of West Point, who had a case before Welch, who was a Justice of the Peace in Pleasant Ridge Township. The case was tried, and Welch had made up the judgment and entered it on his docket. After the case was heard Perdew went on and made a long winded, loud speech, bellowing at the top of his voice, and concluded with, "now Squire, I want your decision!"

(Welch,) "I entered up judgment half an hour ago!"
(Perdew) "What did you do that for?"
(Welch) "Oh, I wanted to hear you spout!"

Perdew had another case before an old country Justice, named Bob Savill, in which he was sued himself on a note.

He plead want of consideration, but could not make up a successful defense, and he resolved to bluff the court, which he did, and in his speech said:

"If you decide this against me here, I'll take it up on certiarari to the District Court, and if beaten then will take it to the Supreme Court, and from there to the Supreme Court of the United States, and from that to the Court in "Bank," and thence to the High Court of Exchequer!

The Justice wilted and Perdew won his suit.

Judge David Rorer, of Burlington, lived in Arkansas before he came to Iowa, and was administrator of an estate in place of a deceased administrator, administrator *de bonus non*, and signed his name to the notices as such, and the people there named him little *de bonus non!* He used always by his antics and facetious remarks to be getting up a laugh in court as well as outside of the court.

Jo Sawyer kept the only hotel at Fort Madison at which all the attorneys stopped, Rorer with the rest.

Term after term there appeared on the table a painted wooden cake. All of us got tired of seeing it. At last the Judge resolved to get rid of it. Pulling the cake towards him one day at dinner, when the table was crowded, as if he was going to cut it, Sawyer came along and said:

"Sir! don't cut that, its wood!"

"All right," said the Judge, "then bring me a saw!"

That cake never appeared again.

SCROGGINS' SPEECH.

Scroggins was a loud mouthed attorney at Fort Madison, and when Douglas was a candidate for President, made political speeches. He had been reading Sheahan's Life of Douglas, and it appears that the first canvass he had for Congress, in its midst he took the bilious fever and was defeated.

Scroggins had committed the book to memory, and gave it in his speech right along *ver batum et literatum*. He was speaking to a large crowd in the court house, in a loud tone of voice. He had proceeded without hesitation till he got to where Douglas was taken sick, when he fairly roared out the words:

"And here he took the bilious fever."

He forgot the rest, stopped suddenly, and sat down, covered with shame and confusion.

The crowd burst into convulsions of laughter, the ladies tittered and the boys yelled and Scroggin's got down and out.

For weeks after that the boys would yell out at him on the streets whenever he appeared:

"And here he took the bilious fever!"

THE INTELLIGENT WITNESS IN COURT.

John Slinglerland was indicted for a criminal offense, and escaped conviction for want of the witnesses upon the part of the prosecution who appeared before the grand jury to get him indicted. This did not end it, for he was again indicted, and this time was charged with hiring the witnesses against him to run away and leave the county. An ignorant old drayman named Dean, was the principal witness, and he could not read or write. The notorious McFarland was prosecutor for the State. He asked Dean if he saw the money ($100) paid the witness!

(Dean) "Yes sir, I did."

"How much was it?"

(Dean) "One hundred dollars! A hundred dollar bill!"

(McFarland) "How do you know it was a hundred dollar bill?"

(Dean) "I know it was a hundred dollar bill, for I seed it. *It was as big as a newspaper!*"

The case was *nolle prosequied*.

John S. David, one of the old merchants of Burlington, a clever gentleman and good business man, "kept store," and had a brother, Barton David, for clerk. Times were dull and a party collecting came to get the balance on a bill. Col. David is very precise in his manner of speech, and wanted to let the traveling drummer or commercial traveler, know he had plenty of funds, and calling to his brother, he said:

"Barton David! go up stairs and bring down specie bag number 4!"

On another occasion it is told he said to Barton, pointing to a box of herring:

"Barton David! there are three more of those dried herrings gone! and I believe, by G—d, sir, you ate them! Such extravagance as that is enough to break up Stephen Girard!

Richard Montgomery T. Patterson was elected representative, and lived below Keokuk. He traded at Warsaw with Tom Perkins, the principal merchant, from whom he bought a pair of new boots. Going to Iowa City, the capitol, he and other members went up on a steamer; his state room was number fourteen. Some one told him to put his boots out to be blacked, which he did. In the morning he found his boots sitting out in front of his stateroom door, and looking at the bottoms of the soles, saw marked in big chalk figures, "No. 14!" He flew in a rage at once, and swore. "I don't wear number fourteen boots! That porter can't have any sense! I only wear number twelves, and I bought my boots of Tom Perkins, of Warsaw!

When Alf Roberts was city Marshal, and Jack Hardin deputy, an educated Irishman was arrested and put in the calaboose for being drunk and disorderly. After getting sober next morning he called to Marshal Roberts, saying:

"Are ye the Marshal?"

"Yes sir."

"Well, I'm a civil man. I was put in here for being intoxicated; if you'll turn me out of here I'll leave your town, as I came to it, with civility and decorum!

(Marshal Roberts) "Did you come here with Dick Corum?"

(Answer) "I came here with civility and decorum!"

(Roberts) "That's just the son-of-a-gun I want."

(Turning to Jack Hardin) "Jack, Dick Corum is in town, and I want you to get him!"

(Irishman getting beligerent) "If its Dick Corum you want, I'm Dick Corum, so help yourselves, d—n you."

THE MEEKER FAMILY.

The Meeker Family are the subject of many good and funny stories.

The name of the father of the Meekers was Ephraim, and he was about sixty years old. One day he went aboard of a steamer, and it commenced to move out. His wife was on shore and called to him. He ran out on the guards, but the steamer by this time was out in deep water. She was the boss, and ruled him, and cried out, "jump overboard, Ephraim! Jump overboard, Ephraham!" He did not dare to disobey, and jumped, landing up to his neck in water. A skiff went out to rescue him, or he would have been drowned. His son Clark went to take a crazy woman away from town; he took her up the river to some town above, and turned her loose. The people caught him and the woman, and put them both in a queensware crate, and shipped them back to Keokuk by the first boat.

Wes. Meeker had a wife, but went south, and while away got married to a big red headed woman. When he got ready to come home he deserted her. When he married her he gave his name as Carr. She followed him to Keokuk. The first parties she met were Dan Hine and Tom Crooks. She inquired of them if they knew Mr. Carr. They did not know any such man. Just then Meeker came along, and she rushed up to him, throwing her arms about him said: "Here's Mr. Carr; my dear husband!"

Meeker took her to his wife, compromised the matter, and got her away. Ever after that he was called Mr. Carr.

EDWIN MANNING

of Keosauqua, one of the oldest living merchants of the Des Moines Valley, Commissioner of the Des Moines River Improvement, a large land owner and now a banker, is very quiet but has much dry fun in him, with a keen sense of the ridiculous. At one time he had several dry goods stores, one of which was at Keosauqua which he stayed at personally. One morning he had just stepped out but kept an eye on all corners into the store. A man about town well known, whom we shall call Mr. Doosenberry, came in, and having on a tall high crowned wool hat, seeing no one about, helped himself to a hatfull of eggs, putting the hat on his head again. Mr. Manning saw him and in a short time came in. Doosenberry saluted him, and Mr. Manning, all smiles returned his greeting very cordially with, good morning Mr. Doosenberry! I'm glad to see you! at the same time brought down his right hand on top of the crown of his hat. Broken eggs covered Doosenberry's confused countenance.

POLITENESS EXTRAORDINARY.

Rev. Wm. H. Williams who was at one time an owner of considerable amount of property, built a stone octagon house for a Young Ladies' High School, a private institution of his own, for which he was eminently fitted, for he was a man of fine education, and a classical scholar, was very short sighted, so much so that he wore glasses, and then could not distinguish any one he knew across the streets. He was very polite to every one, and always made it a point to bow and lift his hat to the ladies of his acquaintance.

One morning he was coming down town, and as he crossed the street from one side of third to the other, on High street near his residence, a cow passed immediately before him.

He saw something, and seeing the cow he thought it was a lady, and at once taking off his hat said to the cow, "good morning, madam!"

Henry W. Starr, a very able and learned lawyer, was arguing a case before the Supreme Court of Iowa, Joseph Williams Chief Justice, John F. Kenney and George Green, associates. Starr had been indulging in fire water, and withal had a great contempt for the legal learning of the Court. He laid down a proposition as law, and supported it by a learned argument, citing authorities. Some members of the Court interrogated him, questioning the infallibility of his propositions. Starr grew indignant, and pulling out a five dollar bill offered to bet the Court that they were wrong and he was right. He knew more law in a day than that Court knew in a lifetime. They did not fine him for contempt.

Chief Justice Joe Williams could fiddle and dance, play the flute, sing a song or tell a story which would convulse any crowd with laughter. He was always called upon at dinner parties and public meetings for a speech and he never failed to put any assembly in a good humor. As an actor in comedy he would have been a decided success. One warm day at Iowa City when he was presiding as Chief Justice, Gil Fulsom was arguing a case, became overcome with the heat and perspired freely, he said, "With the Court's permission I'll take off my coat."

"Yes!" replied Williams, "you can take off your breeches too, as you'll show yourself before you get through!"

Stephen W. Powers was arguing a case before George H. Williams, Attorney-General, then Judge, involving title to the half-breed tract, and had before him a table covered with authorities which he proceeded to read, and kept reading for several hours. Finally he came to a long quotation in the old Normon law latin, and stumbled along with it for some time, and finally stopped reading it, and looking up at the Court said, I'll stop reading this latin, *I don't understand it myself and I presume the Court don't either!*" There was more truth than poetry in this, but Williams considered it a reflection on the Court, and admonished him if that thing was again repeated he would fine him for contempt. He had a habit, too, of calling out to Williams, Hold on there! Hold on there! when he was delivering an opinion, till he had to threaten to fine him for this also.

Gus Goodrich, Prosecuting Attorney, who was naturally gifted with brilliant talents, and an eloquent advocate, never took the trouble to read much and always made the mistake of saying *sonans tonans* for *idem sonans*, *participas criminatibus* for *particeps criminus*, and *testicle* for *technical* phrases. Gus got demoralized, was caught stealing county warrants from the treasurer's safe, and "jumped the county. He was several months in jail at St. Louis for stealing a valise, but was not convicted on the charge, as the witness failed to appear.

Judge Trimble told a good story of a quack doctor at the old Settlers Meeting at Bloomfield, Davis county, which happened in the early history of the "Hairy Nation." We regret we have not the names of the parties. A countryman was sick with chronic diarrhea; he tried every one else and as a dernier resort called in a quack. An eminent physician was called into consultation and said to the quack, it is necessary for me to know what you have been giving this man. Oh! nothing, said the quack, except a teaspoonful of fine white sand three times a day.

Esculapius looked wise, and raising his glasses, said, Sir! upon what principle of philosophy do you give this man white sand as medicine?

Quack—I don't know anything about your philosophy, but one thing I do know, that his innards got so slick they would not hold anything, so I gave it to him to roughen up his stomach and bowels so they would hold it.

Esculapius gave a parting lecture to the wife for employing this empyric, and left in disgust.

Strange to say the sick man got well.

Pacing Johnson was J. Nealy Johnson, a lawyer, who went to California, and when the Know-Nothings triumphed in that state in 1855, was made Governor, being elected by that party; he had a lama like shambling gait, in consequence of which he was called Pacing Johnson, and died some years ago a Supreme Judge of Colorado. He was a great story teller and sir oracle barroom talker, and nothing delighted him more than that, to get the chance to entertain a crowd of interested loafers; he enjoyed it wonderfully, because he was then the central figure. His power laid in his smooth tongue; he was a good talker, a genial sociable spirightly kind of a surface man, and his talk was very much like that of some of our public speakers, very good if you hear it once, if more it becomes stale: that speech wants to be moved about to a new place every time it is made, for it was the same old speech, and so with pacing Johnson's good stories.

In a Know-Nothing Society he was no doubt much at home, as some men in all societies know the ritual rules and points of order, and have them always at their command on the end of their tongues, and can repeat them like parrots, and they know little of anything else. They are like Schuyler Colfax, who rose high as an Odd Fellow; he had a particular kind of talent, we mean that pacing Johnson was a first-rate bob-tailed quarter horse, but lacked wind and bottom for a long heat. His career was short, he soon played out and just then the Pacific coast and the Know-Nothings took up and embraced cheeky adventurers. J. Nealy could button-hole them, and still continued to go for office with the chronic appetite of a home guard, pacing along, always pacing like a servant girl. We once asked old Col. C., an old time settler of Keokuk, who was a great friend of Johnson, what became of his son Hiram. Oh, he killed a Chinaman out in Idaho and they came very near hanging him, but he got off with the penitentiary for life. He found it was not so popular as it once was to kill a Chinaman. But I got him out; I got Nealy Johnson, who had gone over there and was a great friend of the Governor's, to go and see the Governor, and get him pardoned out. The Chinaman killer belonged to fighting stock, he had a big sister who went out to California, but got married before she left; she and her husband had a difficulty, but Sally did not tear her hair and shed tears, but whipped him in a fair stand up and strike from the shoulder fight, then turned him off, got a divorce, and never lost her appetite, but married another man in less than a week, and they have lived happily, for this time she had got a big, sandy-haired, long armed, long legged, slab-sided, bull-whacker, as stout as a mule, and found she could not conquer him, for on the first attempt, her slow-motioned Moses quelled the insurrection by spanking her till he raised blisters, with a codfish, crying out at every lick he struck, as he brought it down slap, slap, with his long arm, "Come into Court or show cause!"

The Moudy Family at Fort Madison all had sore eyes and rarely changed their linen. Sam, one of the boys, went to California and engaged in the stock business, and made quite a fortune, having several thousand dollars in gold. The Mexican greasers, employed as his herders, killed and robbed him. The news of his death came and the Moudy family were in great distress. His father was crying and wringing his hands.

"What is the matter?" inquired a neighbor.

"Oh!" said the father, "matter enough! The infernal Mexicans have killed our Sam, and what is the worst of it they got all his money!"

MONKEY JOHNSON'S GOOD FORTUNE COURTSHIP AND BREACH OF PROMISE CASE.

Johnson wooed and won a fair damsel with auburn hair. He was engaged to her and she relied on his promises. They were both young and John resolved to go to California and make his fortune. Jane did not object, and he went, fortune smiled upon him and he came back by the isthmus where he bought a monkey and took a steamer home at Greytown. The monkey climbed up the long masts and Johnson was in distress, he finally fell overboard and was drowned. The passengers named him Monkey Johnson. He came home well dressed, flourishing his gold.

Jane met him with open arms and everything went smoothly for a while. But a fair damsel with black eyes and corkscrew curls crossed his path and won his heart. He proved false to Jane and married his new charmer. She sued him for breach of promise, and John wilted and compromised. Before this his letters to her from California were exhibited to us by Judge Hall, Jane's attorney.

One contained an old fashioned scolloped valentine with such delightful poetry as this,

"The ring is round which hath no end.
So is my love to you my friend."

In another he said, "My dear Jane, I've seen the fair sect of Illinois, and there is not one of them to be compared to you by one sixteenth part.

Very respectfully your obedient servant,

JOHN S. JOHNSON.

CHAPTER VIII.

Some of the old Politicians, General Dodge, General Jones, Delusion Smith, H. W. Sample, Captain William Sample, Anecdotes of him and Joshua Owens and John Box—Daniel F. Miller and the Poll Books, his Race for Congress—Old Settlers of Fort Madison, Lee and Des Moines Counties—Julian Dubuque—Louis Honore Tesson—Cyrus Walker as a lawyer—The Knapp Family—Murder of Nathaniel Knapp—John S. Hamilton—Amusing Account of General Kitchell of Egypt—Clark Meekers' Bear let Loose—Furguson N. Wright Lyched by the Settlers—Old Blue Face Palmer.

Till the 15th of June, 1836, when Michigan was admitted as a State, Iowa, made part of its territory. Its Sixth Legislative Council on the 6th of September, 1834, passed an act to lay off and organize the counties of Dubuque and Des Moines west of the Mississippi river. Dubuque county had but one township, Julian, the county and township being named in honor of Julian Dubuque, its oldest settler, dating back to 1788, who held his title to the lead mines from the Spanish Governor, Baron Carondolet, under the name of the "mines of Spain," and died in 1810, his name being perpetuated in that of the wealthy county and great city of Dubuque. In 1830, Lucius H. Langworthy with others from Galena, attempted to settle at Dubuque to work the mines, but Col. Zachary Taylor directed his lieutenant, Jefferson Davis, the late Confederate States President, to drive them off, which he did in double quick time.

Des Moines county at that time embraced all the territory south of Dubuque county, in the Black Hawk purchase, till the third act of the Wisconsin Legislature divided it into Lee, Van Buren and Henry. Davis county was afterwards made from Van Buren, and became known as the "Hairy Nation." Lee county had the oldest settlements in the south; that of the "Old Orchard" now Montrose, at the head of the Rapids, dating back to the time of the old Frenchman, Louis Honore Tesson, in 1795, when he got a permit to trade with the Indians, and settled there, made historic in the celebrated law suit for a mile square, between the New York Land Company and the heirs of Riddick, in which the latter triumphed; one of them, Dabney C. Riddick, still living in Montrose. The length of time since the first settlement was established, very much like that of the age of a rattlesnake, you tell his years by the number of rattles on his tail. The ages of the old apple trees, said to have been planted by the old Frenchman, was fixed beyond dispute by sawing one into two parts, by which the yearly growth was clearly indicated. For years Montrose was a fast place, with many fast people from steamboats who stopped there temporarily, was filled with gamblers and reckless characters, but always had, as it has now, many good citizens.

On the 4th of July, 1836, Wisconsin was organized as a territory including the counties of Des Moines and Dubuque west of the Mississippi river, and Iowa territory separated from Wisconsin by an act dated June 12, on the 4th of July, 1838, and Burlington was the capitol till January 7th, 1841, when it was removed to Iowa City, and the first session of the general assembly, under the new state constitution was held there in the winter of 1846-7.

Robert Lucas, of Ohio, was the first territorial governor, was succeeded by Col. Chambers, a distinguished officer under General Harrison, who hailed from Kentucky, and afterwards James Clark, editor of the Burlington Gazette, brother-in-law of Gen. A. C. Dodge, a gentleman of marked ability, deservedly popular who died of cholera about the year 1852, his loss being deeply regretted. Judge Irwin, of Dubuque, was the first territorial judge, succeeding Judge, Lynch who presided in a murder trial at that place before there was any law, tried his man by a jury, who found him guilty, and he was hanged. John Box, the first member of the legislature from Lee county in the Wisconsin legislature. An elder in the Christian or Campbellite church, he was a good christian, an honest man, and in politics a strong democrat; he died about three years ago at Florris, Davis county, in the Hairy Nation.

The whigs used to tell this story on Squire Box. When a member of the legislature, some one asked him,

"What is the population of Lee county?"

(Box.) "Oak, hickory, hackberry and some sycamore!"

"I mean the population!"

(Box.) "Corn, wheat and rye!"

THE OLD SETTLERS.   111

Joshua Owens belonged to the same church, was a Whig, and lived in Washington township near Fort Madison, was a Justice of the Peace and one of our first sheriffs. It is told of him by Enoch G. Wilson, of Fort Madison, that he was chairman of a Whig meeting which was not a success, as there was a very slim attendance, and some one moved to adjourn over. The chairman Owens, put the question which was carried and thereupon declared the meeting *adjourned till some previous day!*

Captain William Sample, the father of Hugh W. Sample, came from Washington county, Pennsylvania, was an officer in the war of 1812, commanded a company at the battle of Black Rock. He had been a democrat and afterwards a whig editor. Hugh W. Sample, the father of Capt. Sam S. and William Sample, worked in his printing office when a boy, and there adopted his peculiar bold back hand, in writing the addresses on newspapers. Mr. William Sample was a decided whig partisan, and was several years post master at Fort Madison; an elder in the old school Presbyterian Church, and always stood erect in prayer. He sometimes made speeches, and it is told of him that in 1840 he made a speech for General Harrison, and in it said, "Where was Martin Van Buren in the war of 1812? Speculating in corn and whisky and selling it to the British in Canada!" He was a large, well formed man, with large head and prominent forehead, was very decided in his opinions, and of very dark complexion.

Hugh W. Sample was a little taller than his father, and much fairer, otherwise in personal appearance, they were very much alike. In the winter of 1848 he made one of a party going overland in a four horse conveyance to attend the session of the legislature about to elect U. S. Senators.

We stopped for dinner at a house in a little village in Washington county, the occupants including an old lady, were from Washington county, Pennsylvania, where she knew Captain William Sample over twenty years before. When Hugh W. Sample, whom she had never seen, entered, she rushed up and shook him by the hand delighted to see him. Explanations followed; from the striking resemblance of father and son she had mistaken him for his father.

Ansel Briggs was the first Governor of the State of Iowa, nominated by accident; Phillip P. Bradley, his private secretary, a man of ability, was really the governor; Briggs being very much like one of what are called "side judges" in a court, where the judge sits in the centre and presides, is the only lawyer. The side judges generally having more stomach than brains, being consulted only as a matter of courtesy.

THE OLD POLITICIANS.

We have followed the Star of Empire, as the wise men of the East followed that of Bethlehem, they followed their's till it set, ours is nomadic and never sets, but keeps onward towards the west. Tradition, tells us that in times long ago, the Mississippi river was a spring branch, but this must have been at an early period, when the state of Buncombe was a rural district, and Posey on the wild frontier, and before the days of "infernal" improvements and "raging canals."

Augustus Caesar Dodge, who hailed from Missouri, was the big injin of the Democratic party, and George Washington Jones, with his ambrosial locks cut the pigeon's wing at parties, and danced his way to the Senate as his aid.

But other politicians came who wrestled for mastery in the field, and for the public offices, and as Jacob wrestled with the angel, they finally prevailed. They were from both political parties, whigs and democrats, and came from Washington county, Pennsylvania, and Knox county, Ohio. They were Black Bill Thompson, who worked his mouth and talked about the "great American heart" in every speech, and walked into Congress.

J. C. Hall, the great lawyer, as the Governor of South Carolina, telegraphed to the Governor of Georgia, thought it was "a long time between drinks," and finally threw his weight upon the judgeship of the Supreme Court, which his brother-in-law, "Black" John F. Kinney had won before him.

Hugh W. Sample "tanned their dog skins," and was made President of the Public Works, and won laurels as the mighty "Wapsi." Gus Hall, with his great speech, in which the old hen always spread herself over innumerable eggs, made his way to Congress and Chief Justiceship of Nebraska, and Gen. Samuel R. Curtis, with his "hydraulics" and "porosity" got into Congress and immortalized himself as the champion of the Pacific Railroad, and afterwards as the hero of Pea Ridge. William Henson Wallace, of Hoosier, had to stand out in the cold and weep about the "iron hand of despotism," till a land office banished him to Oregon. The lost "Delusion" Smith bellowed up and down the plains, as another bull of Bashan, till a "green and yellow melancholy" came over his political aspirations, and he joined the church, had his sins forgiven, and made his way to the Pacific coast to turn up as Senator from Oregon. Thus the great lights of both political parties, who won fame and fortune in Iowa, came from Washington county, Pennsylvania, and Knox county, Ohio.

Judge J. M. Love, of the U. S. District Court, also came from Knox, and won his present high position on the bench which he adorns by his great learning and intellectual ability.

Governor "Bill" Stone was a Knox county boy, and being carried off on a stretcher, won the governorship, and went into retirement, as he failed to go to Congress or any place else except Knoxville.

There was yet a host more from Washington and Knox, and for a time Washington furnished all the candidates, and Knox supplied all the office-holders.

Washington was not then on the winning side, and as old Peyton Wilson said of George G. Wright when he wanted to be a candidate for Congress in a whig convention, at which Daniel F. Miller was nominated, "I tell you gentlemen, George G. Wright's time has not *ariv!* I tell you, it has not *ariv!*" In the canvass for Congress, Miller beat Black Bill Thompson who had lost all his money playing poker, and had nothing to spend, by making a vigorous canvass and securing the Mormon vote at Kainsville. The returns of that election from Kainsvilie were not received, and counted as they should have been, and Black Bill was admitted to his seat, but Miller contested the election, and charged that the poll books brought in from Kainsville to Monroe county, which had mysteriously disappeared, had been stolen. It turned out that Israel Kister, of Bloomfield, had taken them and put them in J. C. Hall's saddle bags. Hall kept them and gave them to Judge Mason, attorney for Thompson. Miller contested Thompson's seat, and while taking depositions in the contested seat at Keokuk, Judge Mason made the same mistake Cardinal Woolsey did with King Henry VIII, handing Miller the wrong papers—the poll books. This was a lucky thing for Miller, and he made the most of it. Thompson's seat was declared vacant, and Miller telegraphed from Washington that they were sent back to run the race over again, so as to make Thompson, the opposition candidate, which was done. Miller went through the district like a whirlwind; he was everywhere. He appealed to the Mormons, to the abolitionists, to the luke-warm democrats, the Germans and the Irish, and it is told on him that at a meeting composed of Irish and Germans, when asked where he was born, he said to to the Irish on one side, "I was born in Dublin!" and turning about to the Germans, "On the Rhine!" The colored troops did not vote then, but his versatility of genius won the day.

John W. Rankin, who came from Washington county, used to shake hands with every one and take them aside confidentialy to tell them a secret; the consequence was, when a candidate for senator, he was elected over a large democratic majority, and afterwards appointed District Judge. When Curtis was elected over "Cow and Calf Cole" in 1858, the democratic party was not in the ascendency in the district, and Cole was put up like any other bob-tailed scrub in a race to be distanced. Though a glib talker and popular speaker, hailing from Kentucky, he stood no more show of being elected than he did of being struck by lightning.

THE OLD SETTLERS OF FORT MADISON.

The old settlers of Fort Madison, who still survive, and many who are dead, are now or have been, while living, citizens of Keokuk. It was the old county seat before the act passed giving Keokuk a court; it was the most important town in the county while Keokuk was yet a village, filled with roughs principally, the foot of the Rapids, from which steamboats with two lighters, one on each side, ascended the river and sometimes got stuck on a rock and laid there for days.

Before our time, one John G. Toncray and Lorenzo Bullard kept hotels then in the upper part of town. Bullard kept the Madison House where Morrison's extensive Plow Factory now stands, near the mill just south of it; the flour mill, which was built by McConn and Palmer, on the site of the old Fort

Madison. The nigger-head rocky pavements of the old fort can be seen still, and any old citizen can point them out to you. To the curious they are worth inspecting as a land mark and link connecting the past of this beautiful and thriving city with the history, over which the fleet footsteps of our half century have passed like a shadow. We have known nearly all the old settlers of Fort Madison, Toncray and Bullard and Joe Woods among the rest, who used to use the words, "cotillion" for criterion, and Mr. Enoch G. Wilson used to quote from him, taking him off with the words, "that's no cotillion to go by!"

Alfred Rich was one of the first lawyers who lived there, but Philip Viele is the oldest living lawyer of the county.

Judge Viele shows the blood of the Mohawk Valley Knickerbockers in his face, which when young, glowed with the rosy hue of health. He was full of fun and French vivacity, and could be sublime, pathetic or facetious. He could work up the sympathies of a jury and shed tears himself when appealing to them as an advocate with dramatic effect.

General Browne was a friend of Judge Viele, and alluding to his roseate complexion at a supper given to prominent lawyers, politicians, etc., gave this toast, which created much merriment at the time: "Here's to Philip Viele! the deepest *red* lawyer in Iowa!"

We never saw Rich or Fred Buckhalter, the brother of Mrs. J. C. Parrott, a young lawyer there also at an early day. They both died young. Rich was the victim of consumption. He was, we believe, the first whig candidate for delegate to Congress from Iowa, and was defeated by Chapman. He had an extensive practice for that day, and a thousand stories are told on him by his old friends, in which he figures as the lion of some funny story or practical joke. He had many friends, was a Kentuckian, and was universally conceded as an able lawyer, gifted and brilliant; at that day he had no peer.

W. C. Stripe afterwards kept the Mansion House, and Col. C. H. Perry kept the Eagle Hotel for a short time, as the house belonged to him and he could not get any one to keep it, and while he kept it all the lawyers at court stopped with him, and one of them, L. E. Johnson, of Keokuk, used then to call Fort Madison "Perry's Landing." While we write many memories of the lawyers and the courts, and stories at which they laughed and were merry come to us. Henry Eno was one of the old lawyers, but not practicing when we knew him; he was the first judge of Probate of Lee county after it was set off from Des Moines, and John Whitaker, still living, was previously the judge of Des Moines county; the latter was a soldier under General Jackson at the battle of the Horseshoe, and a Tennesseean by birth. Eno left and went to California. Archibald Williams, O. H. Browning, of Quincy, and the late George C. Dixon used to come to the courts, and Cyrus Walker, of Macomb— they were the representative Illinois lawyers. Williams and Browning as land lawyers. Old Cyrus Walker as a great criminal lawyer. Williams was one of the ugliest man, except the Attorney-General, George H. Williams, in his younger days, we have ever met. His head was large, and his thin hair straight and at times stood in every direction on his head; he was tall, erect, and had a broad chest; his complexion was corpse like, and his teeth were large and looked as if they were double in front, and protruded beyond his scant pattern of lips, the material of which appeared to have given out when he was made, for they were too short. He was no orator but was prosy and spoke with deliberation, was a man of large brain, great argumentative powers and struck at the strong points in a case which he saw intuitively. He had no personal popularity, but was a great lawyer. Browning in his personal make up was the reverse of Williams; he was an orator of no ordinary caliber, with no lack of words, with a silvery voice, good, handsome, pleasant face; always went well dressed, had a winning address, and as an advocate before a jury or addressing the court, he had much influence and great power.

Cyrus Walker could not manage Judge Douglas, therefore he considered him an upstart who knew nothing about law. Douglas ruled against him and he swore that he never would practice any more in Douglas district, and he never did. He was employed in nearly all the great criminal cases in Iowa for the defense, and in some of the land cases. His forte was as a criminal lawyer, and previous to coming west he had practiced and been pitted against such great lawyers as old Ben Hardin, Wickliffe and Clay of the Lexington bar. He was altogether a self-made man, and could quote the old Norman law latin to the courts by the yard, and had all legal authorities at his tongues end. With a wonderful memory, he had great industry, was up late at night and rose early, and took regular exercise and long walks in the morning; was a very great reader, he read law and literature of every kind down to the latest novel. Walker was a man of wonderful capacity, and had no end to resources, If foiled on one point he seized another instantly, his legal tactics in the trial of a case were Napoleonic. His eyes were bright grey, and twinkled, and had the cunning look of a fox. He wore spectacles, but raised them up when cross-examining a witness which he did so very pleasantly that he made the witness believe he was his best friend, and if there was anything he could say in favor of Walker's client, that gentleman wormed it out of him. With great judgment of men, he selected a jury without knowing the men, from the shape of their heads or facial outlines of physiognomy, and his judgment rarely failed.

We have seen and heard all the great criminal lawyers in our early courts, and have no hesitation in saying that as an advocate before a jury he had no equal, and as a strategist his capacity was unrivaled by any of them. He never hesitated, but with the rapidity of lightning he maneuvered and managed so as to put his adversary off his guard, mislead him, divided his forces into skirmishing parties, swooped down upon them in detail, where he had a bad case, and vanquished them before they were hardly aware of his object. He smoked a common clay and sometimes a corn-cob pipe, walked with a quick, springy tread, and was very interesting and entertaining in conversation. We have talked to him by the hour and never got tired of hearing him tell his strategy and his triumphs in the management of criminal trials. One thing we learned from him, which in criminal cases, where if tried at once, conviction is certain, that to secure an acquital you must resort to continuances and changes of venue. The excitement blows over, the people forget, and the sober second thought enables them to weigh all the facts and do justice, when under the impulse of the moment or some rash leader they might hang an innocent man. Cyrus Walker was at one time the attorney for Joe Smith, the Mormon Prophet and after this the whig candidate for Congress in 1843, in the Nauvoo district against Hoge. Joe Smith had been arrested on a requisition from the Governor of Missouri for the attempted assassination of Governor Lilburn W. Boggs. Smith was arrested away from Nauvoo at the hotel of Mr. Heberling, in Adams county, and the parties arresting him were immediately surrounded by the Danite Band and carried off to Nauvoo, where Joe was discharged from custody on a writ of hebeas corpus, tried before the mayor, Cyrus Walker giving an opinion that the mayor had a right to discharge him.

Fort Madison is the oldest and first settled city in Lee county, in fact one of the first in Iowa. The first settlement was made by a dog fennel doctor Peter Williams, in 1832.

William W. Coriell, the father of Julian D. Coriell, was one of the commissioners who laid it off as a town, March 3, 1837, under the act of Congress of July 2d, 1836. Mr. Coriell married the sister of Mrs. Captain Edwin Guthrie, who is the mother of Southwick W. Guthrie, Adjutant of the 17th Iowa Infantry in the war of 1861, and now the efficient and able cashier of the Treasury at Washington, D. C.

Old Gus Horton, J. Horton, Richard Chaney, Aaron White, John H. and Nathaniel Knapp, were the first settlers. Old Gus Horton lived in a little tumble down, one story log cabin, half a mile below town, on the stage road running to Keokuk, and used to come to town for his grog very often; he was a peaceable, inoffensive old man, and lived there till he died, several years ago. Nathaniel Knapp was killed by a man named Hendershott, who stabbed him with a knife one night at a hotel in Farmington, Van Buren county, and nothing was ever done with Hendershott. Nathaniel Knapp left a widow, who, in her younger days, in fact till she became an old lady, was very handsome. She was a large, tall, well formed, volumptuous looking woman, with black hair, and large, black piercing eyes, shrewd and cunning, possessed of much vivacity, had a large finely formed head and great loquacity, and being put on her own resources took to business. She was a kind-hearted and benevolent, but a devil when circumvented in any of her favorite plans. Amongst men she was what you would call a masculine or *he* woman. She reared a large family, four boys and two or three girls, and was married the second time to one O'Reiley, who was a worthless fellow and finally deserted her and went to Oregon, then a territory. Her oldest daughter was married to one Enoch Gilbert in 1838, the first wedding in the town; she got to be a large corpulent woman, was a great talker, and you never saw her but what she was complaining of a world of trouble. She was a termagant and a pest, and finished her interview by asking you for the loan of five dollare, and if she got it that was the end of it; she never returned it, and never expected to. The Gilbert family moved to near St. Joseph, Mo., near which place Mrs. O'Reiley was last living. Her son, Sam M. Knapp, died of consumption; he was well read, well educated, a peevish but witty fellow. Charley got married to a daughter of Mrs. Ferris, widow of Johnson I. Ferris, a surgeon in the Black Hawk war, an estimable lady, whom he deserted for a fast woman without any good reason. "Charley" was a good looking, short, thick set, fast young man, with black curly hair, and bright, twinkling, mischievous, dark eyes, full of fun and frolic, and devoted most of his time to wine, women and cards. He had more of the ways of his mother than any of the family, being full of animal spirits. Nat. a younger brother, died; and a son by O'Reiley, Tom, was last living at St. Joseph. Mary was the youngest daughter; she married a journeyman printer named Forbes, who worked in "Old Peelhead" Spaulding's office, the Plaindealer, and afterwards studied law. He was inoffensive and good for nothing as he well could be, and we have heard he died while hunting rabits and snakes after an attack of delirium tremens, a disease to which he was subject. Mary, when a girl, was beautiful but dowdy. She had her mother's roseate complexion, but was much fairer; was of the medium height, with a well rounded figure, and gushing bosom; with brown hair which hung in ringlets or corkscrew curls sometimes, about her fair and beautiful neck, while her eyes were of that deep azure melting blue we see in the pictures of the Madonna, one can imagine as in life, when they are upturned to ours with a melting languor and half sigh, but which words cannot describe. She had a pretty little mouth, with pouting lips and evenly set pearly teeth, and a voice, when she sang and played the guitar, of ravishing sweetness. She was, in short, a beautiful little duck of a girl when dressed; yes, she was pretty without ornamentation, with a bewitching smile and captivating manners, but had little education. What she knew was principally picked up about the dingy old hotel, the Washington House, kept a long time by her mother, a place where she saw, all kinds of people, and much of the good and more of the bad phases of human nature; the travelling dead beat, the masked hypocrite, the "lone woman," the fast man, the gambler, pickpocket and counterfeiters, and occasionally a lady or gentleman. Brought up in such an atmosphere, with such surroundings, it is to be wondered she was never carried away by the falsehood and deceit about her; but she never was inclined to be fast, had she been, her mother would have put her foot down and stopped it at once, no matter what were her own individual short-comings. It is said the old lady knew all doubtful traveling characters, that they confided in her and told her their secrets, and when closely pursued by an officer for a criminal offense she concealed them, gained time by deluding the officials with fair stories, and finally helped them to escape. O'Reiley, her last husband, was said to be in league with counterfeiters, but nothing ever came out upon him publicly which left this a matter of surmise only.

The heirs of Nathaniel Knapp had an interest in the half-breed tract and that of two who were minors, was sold to Rev. Michael Hummer and Ralph P. Lowe. John H. Knapp, Sr., and Nathaniel Knapp were cousins. They built the first large frame hotels, the "Washington" and "Madison" House. Their families were not at all alike. John H. Knapp, named for his father, is now a member and the head of the great and wealthy lumber firm of Knapp, Stout & Co., in the pineries of the north. He was born and brought up in Fort Madison. William Wilson, an old citizen of Fort Madison, and a son-in-law of the late Thomas Hale, Sr., and brother-in-law of James L. Estes, is a member of the firm. White immigrated to Oregon at an early day.

The oldest settlers who came in 1835 and 1836, now living, are Judge Phillip Viele, Peter Miller, the first President of the first Board of Trustees in Fort Madison in 1841, and from being a blacksmith was familiarly known as "Old Tilt Hammer."

John G. Kennedy, at one time deputy-sheriff, a gentleman of much humor and remarkable memory of all the early history and good stories about the old settlers, and John C. Atlee, a prominent lumberman and mill owner, for a long time an alderman of the city. For many years he lived in Cedar township.

Judge Jacob Cutler has been dead several years; he came to Fort Madison about the same time as the last named gentlemen and Joseph Webster also, still living in Texas.

Thomas Fitzpatrick, Jacob Hunor, Henry M. Salmon and Billy McIntyre, whose faces used to be so familiar, are all dead, and Judge Phillip Viele, with uncertain steps, eyes dimmed by age, and palsied limbs, is trembling now on the brink of the grave.

John S. Hamilton, a lawyer from Pittsburg, came later; he was genial, whole-souled and popular, was killed by the premature explosion of a cannon he was firing at a democratic jubilee. He had been a soldier in the Mexican war, and killed a Mexican greaser at Perote, who fired at him from a parapet of the fort. He was a member of the legislature, a man of ability.

KITCHELL AND HIS DONKEY.

Wickliffe Kitchell was not one of the old settlers, but came from Illinois, from the rural districts of Egypt and the town of Hillsboro, a town watered by the classic stream of Okaw, where the wolves used to howl in the prairies, while the owls hooted at night in the deep green shades of its forests, dimly lighted by the flashing torches of coon-hunters on the war path. General Jackson during his first administration heard of Kitchell and took to him, and the Jack oak lawyer of Egypt was appointed U. S. District-Attorney that he might vindicate the insulted dignity of Uncle Sam as the shining light in the prairie practice. Kitchell grew up with the country, but in time there came too many great men to the kingdom of Egypt. He had grown grey in the service and would not follow where others led, and Alexander like, sought abroad new fields to conquer. He resolved to immigrate, to go west, and sold out root and branch, and came bag and baggage, with wife and children and household goods to Fort Madison in 1850. He bought property, built the first part of the building, now used as the Academy on Front street, to which Dr. Eads afterwards, when he became the purchaser, made extensive additions. This was not all; he bought the Island, now known as Kitchell's Island. He started a Ferry Boat across the river where Commodore Doerr's Steam Ferry now runs; but Kitchell's ferry was a concern propelled by two horses, which walked up, always up, on a revolving tread mill; they were blind horses, destitute of poetical musings, and did not understand their rights as they lived before the days of their coming friend, Berg, who has made himself famous by suppressing rat terrier dog fights, and the prone tendency of the age cropping out in cruelty to animals. "General" Kitchell, as he was now called, was not yet satisfied; he resolved to stock his island, bought horses, hogs and cattle and put on it in charge of a tenant. But the island with its occupants was yet too quiet, and he made another investment in a large bluish-colored donkey who had all the solemn wisdom in his countenance for which his master was famous when studying up a constitutional question. Kitchell was now one of the first citizens, and was elected mayor. The new constitution and then the code of 1851 had gone into force. Kitchell read the constitution and read the code, and filled up his time at the Court House, between his duties as mayor and running the ferry, in cursing the code and the bible, for he was a confirmed infidel.

He held forth to his auditors in the Clerk's office at the Court House, where he was listened to patiently by the clerk, our jolly old friend Peleg H. Babcock, (who enjoyed playing the fiddle, listening to a good story from others or telling one himself, and he had a thousand of them, and good ones to,) and there was sometimes Philotus Cowles and his brother Asa, who listened quietly, and John G. Kennedy, over whose fun loving countenance often stole a smile. But oftener still he made some sarcastic remark, good naturedly, of course, and as the General, who wilted under ridicule, got in a towering passion at him, he would habitually burst into a loud ringing laugh, which was contagious. Making frantic motions with his head, which was of sugar loaf pattern, tapering backwards very much like one end of a fishing worm, cursing furiously, he would rush from the room, and was seen no more that day. Kennedy one day, just after such a daily scene, put a leading question to the crowd:

"Do you know why General Kitchell don't believe in the bible?"

They gave it up.

"Because he didn't have any hand in making it!"

He made war on the code, the bible, and on Bill Thurston. He cursed all hypocrites, and was bitter in his denunciations of all churches, and we believe to-day, that Kitchell thought when he died he would go back to hover as a departed spirit, watching over his old stamping grounds in Egypt or else go straight to General Jackson. Whether he ever turned from his evil ways and sat down under the willows and wept, we never learned. He was the same unregenerate sinner when he left for Egypt, where he died at a green old age. But while he was Mayor of Fort Madison, his poor human nature asserted itself in his assinine will, which no two bull dogs and and a policeman could successfully resist. He make war on everything and everybody who would not consult him and agree with him, and wrote lengthly and learned opinions on constitutional questions, which in many words said little. He made war relentlessly and bitterly on city scrip, because it was printed. The constitution, said Kitchell, prohibits the issuing of any paper to circulate as money. The printed city scrip was destroyed because Kitchell said it ought to be written out. Some of the aldermen rebelled against his rulings, and there was war and revolution. In one short year his administration had six city marshals, four clerks, three supervisors, and two city attorneys. On he went like the horse in Hudibras "with brandished tail and blast of wind," till the first of January, when his time expired, and there was general rejoicing. A new years address, abounding in prose and classic poetical quotations from the "Ghost of Buster," and other sweet American poets, referring to the "spider and the fly," "little children, let not your angry passions rise," printed in slips, was circulated as a new year's gift, portraying the glories of his administration, and made him swear that the author "thought he knew more than General Jackson," his great patron. Now the dogs barked at him; his ferry boat was dubbed by the poetical name of the "Horse Fly;" he grew restless and dissatisfied, and his heroic donkey, which was ferried back and forth from the green pastures of the island upon the "Horse Fly," whether from disgust at the misfortunes of his master or from "true inwardness" so facetiously referred to by our friend Sprague, as a part of the Republican platform, he grew melancholy and serious, his ears drooped and he ceased to awake the echoes of the island with his loud braying, which had become as familiar to the women, children and dogs as Mrs. Alley's long tin dinner horn which tooted at the old settlers re-union had been to the harvest hands of old in Green Bay bottom. He raved and spoke out at a democratic meeting in the Court House one night in opposition to everything. And now came the tug of war, the unkindest cut of all, the last straw that broke the camel's back. Jim Hardin moved to appoint a committee to decide the question whether General Kitchell was a democrat. He added insult to injury by saying he had a head shaped like a Mormons. That was the last of Kitchell in a political meeting; he left in disgust. Soon after he sold out his house, his island, the Horse Fly, and his venerable friend, the melancholy donkey, and shaking the dust from his feet, returned again to the scenes of his early triumphs in Egypt.

CLARK MEEKEKS' BEAR—KEOKUK.

Old Rouser, Devil Creek, and Alderman Mackley were out of amusement. They had a pack of hounds and there was snow on the ground. Clark Meeker had a bear, a great black, shaggy haired heathen, which he kept in a log pen near his house, at the corner of First and Johnson street, and was fattening it up for Christmas, as he kept boarders, and expected to make a nice speculation outside by selling bear steak. Meeker must be got out of the way, and he was over persuaded to go on a hunt in Missouri. He left in the morning, and our trio with other friends, resolved to turn his bear loose; next day they would go on a grand bear chase, tracking him through the forest with their pack of hounds, while they followed on horseback to be in at the death.

It was midnight; the moon was on the wane, and a dim, uncertain star light, showed the log cage where Meeker's bear, all unconscious of the conspiracy to release him, was confined. The family consisted of the wife and the hired girl cook, had retired, and everything still and quiet as the grave without and no one was stirring on the streets. Armed with an axe and a two inch auger our party approached the bear house, built near and immediately back of Meeker's dwelling, next to and inside a high picket fence, and commenced the operation of boring him out. For two hours they worked, boring with the auger a great circle, to make a door through the logs, whence bruin, impatient of confinement, could make his exit, and breathe the free air of heaven amidst his own native hills. Relieving each other at intervals, they worked away with a hearty good will, till the opening was made, and Mackley, with the axe, with one or two blows, knocked out the logs which had been bored through, and they saw the bear. He was not lying down in repose but up and waiting the issue of their labors. The logs had scarcely fallen inside of the big log pen, when bruin, from his position on his haunches, made a sudden movement to escape, which took him through the door quicker than you can say "Jack Robison." There was a grand scampering then, and all got out of the way as quick as their legs would carry them, except Old Rouser. They rolled and tumbled over each other with a hurry scurry, helter skelter rapidity. But Old Rouser weighed over two hundred, and his locomotion was not so rapid. He had, however, reached the picket fence, and felt the bears paws upon him, and his hot breath about his head and face. There was no time to be lost; he made one frantic effort to scale the fence with its sharp topped palings, and "made the riffle," for he was a skillful pilot, and left the fence betwixt himself and the bear. He did not stand on the order of his going, and as he went the seat of his new doe skin pantaloons were caught on the fence and hung there. He was safe from the bear which could not follow him, but his friends said he hung out a flag of truce as he retreated, and they thought they saw at the same time the full moon rising, though it might have been an optical delusion. Rouser did not get further than across the street, when he halted. Turning about with the other dare devils, they must see what had become of bruin. Entering the house he ranged about in the kitchen supplying himself liberally with sugar, meat and all the good things coming in his way. With his stomach stayed, his curiosity must now be satisfied, and mounting the stairway proceeded to the upper story, and bursting in the sash of the cook's window, he stood erect on his hind feet at the head of the stairway. Loud screaming and shrieking was now heard from the female voices, that of Mrs. Meeker and the cook, murder! murder! help! help! rang out upon the still night air. Old Ephraim Meeker, the father of Clark, living next door, heard it. Ready for any emergency, he rushed out with his loaded rifle; he heard the commotion up-stairs, and approaching nearer saw his bearship, and taking in the situation, fired upon him, and he fell down dead. There was no bear hunt next day with horse and hounds, but bear meat was for sale on the streets, and Old Rouser's scaling that fence was the general subject of comment.

FURGUSON N. WRIGHT WHIPPED BY THE SETTLERS.

Old John Wright was the father of Furguson N. Wright, and a large family of boys, he drew an interest in the decree, but claimed he had other interests not admitted, and commenced a law suit, in which other settlers joined, who claimed interests also, not admitted in the decree of partition. "Furg," as he was called, was one of the managers for the settlers, and collected money, in all five hundred dollars, to carry on the suit. The New York Company compromised with Wright, admitting just what he claimed. The settlers were exasperated, and charged him with bad faith. They insisted he should pay back the money, five hundred dollars, which he refused to do, but finally consented to an arbitration by two referees, to meet at Montrose. He selected William Lamb, a farmer, the settlers selected Dr. J. M. Anderson, a well known citizen of Montrose, a gentleman of high character and standing. Before the day fixed, Wright told Lamb not to go, but went himself. When the arbitration was talked of, his excuse was, that his referee was not there.

The settlers had found out from Lamb that he had been told to stay away. Major Benson and Andrew Keithler, a committee of the settlers, told him this. Wright insisted he would not pay a dollar, and said they were all a pack of fools Benson told him if he did not pay it they would take it out of his hide. He then lived on the middle road leading to Montrose, from Keokuk.— The settlers resolved to take him out of his house at night and lynch him.— They selected a captain, and a party to do the whipping, of a few men only. But about thirty men surrounded the house at a distance, while the select few, under the orders of the captain, were to approach. They knew he was always armed, and would shoot if he had any intimation of their intention to whip him. They, therefore, resolved on a ruse to induce him to come out of his house to the fence on the road. The night was warm, and they called to him, telling him his brother, Mitchell D. Wright, had been badly hurt. He came out to the fence in front of his house, in his night clothes, wearing nothing but a shirt, in great haste. They had exchanged but a few words with him when it struck him like a flash that something was wrong, he suspicioned their object, and turning about retreated rapidly to his house, shut the door after him, which was bursted open. He ran up stairs. A ladder was secured and put up on the porch, fronting to the upper story. None dared to go up till the captain took the lead, and entered the upper story. Wright, in his haste, had forgotten his fire arms below, concealed between the bed ticks. He got down stairs before he could be prevented, and here, before he could get his fire arms, was struck over the head with the but of a loaded whip. It did not fell him to the floor, but while stunned by the blow he was seized and taken out in the yard. Here a gunny sack, which had been brought along for the purpose, was put over his head, and as a lamb to the slaughter, helpless and unarmed, and nearly naked, he was hurried to a retired place, a short distance away. It was now again insisted that he must pay the money or be whipped.

Wright was obstinate, and with all their threats starring him in the face, insisted he would not pay a cent.

The whipping commmenced. Whack! Whack! Whack! sounded the lash upon his bare back. He bore it with the fortitude of a martyr, and scarcely a cry or a groan escaped him. He was importuned again to pay the money, but was still obstinate as ever. He would not agree to pay a dollar.

The whipping still went on, but he stood up under it till the captain thought he had enough, and ordered it stopped.

A big stout Englishman then stepped up with a big whip and belabored him most unmercifully, and he succumbed, falling to the ground. About this time a cowardly fellow struck him with the but of a loaded whip or a club, on the head, against orders.

He was left where he fell, senseless, and bleeding profusely. The settlers left for home. Wright moved to town and swore out a warrant for the arrest of several of them. He had a tenant in the house whence he was taken and whipped, who knew all the party, but on the examination he swore he did not know any of them. They were discharged. Wright kept the money, but with a sore back and a sore head held on to it, and did not die till several years afterwards. We give no names, as some of the parties engaged in the whipping are now dead, and we do not like to take the liberty of using the names of those still living.

The settlers no doubt had great provocation, the remedy they resorted to was severe, and Wright showed great pluck and power of endurance.

It was thought he knew them all, and no doubt did know them.

It was further expected he would take summary vengeance and kill some if not all of them in detail. But from some cause he bore all in silence, and never did any injury to any of them as far as can be ascertained.

The whipping took place in the summer of the year 1852.

"OLD BLUE FACED PALMER."

Old Blue Faced Palmer was at one time a partner as State printer of Geo. Paul, of the firm of Palmer & Paul, and was a prim, precise, dressy old bachelor, who made his home at some hotel always in Iowa City. He was a democrat, a local politician, and was always at conventions and sessions of legislatures, and was familiarly called, not to his face, but by his acquaintances, "Old Blue Face." This originated from the blueish tallow color of his skin, for his face always looked blue. He was very proud, wore a claw-hammer-spike-tailed-coat and plug hat, carried himself erect, and affected to consider himself a man of importance. Blue face had been crossed in love, and his sweetheart was a maiden lady in Iowa City, one of several daughters. He was proud, and aristocratic in his ideas, and the father of his sweatheart had a false pride too. He was a shoemaker, but did not want that known at home. He made shoes by the piece, and took them down to Muscatine, walking all the way, and went frequently. "Blue Face" found this out, and this broke off the match; he could not think for a moment of marrying the daughter of a poor shoemaker. But he was still in love with her, and she could not have a beau but "Blue Face," with his great white eyes followed her to church, or whereever she went. For years every night, almost, "Blue Face" would go past her house, he had a mania, a weakness which pursued him like a phantom dromedary for going past her house and looking in at the windows before he slept. It was a hallucination, and "Blue Face" used to tell us how he loved her, but he would never marry a shoemaker's daughter, and could not bear to think she should ever marry any one else.

"Blue Face" thought he had enemies who were mean enough to assassinate him, and we encouraged him in the belief.

One night in the winter of 1856-7, while the legislature was in session, he went on his nightly patrol past the house of his lady love; it was very dark, and two mischief-loving young clerks secreted themselves near the house, fired two pistol shots in the air, and footsteps were heard on the pavement. He commenced running, and they pursued him at a distance; he fell in the mud, ran into a lot of mortar, but, like Lazarus, rose again. He smashed his plug hat in the race, bursted the seat of his pantaloons, and when he came to our rooms, bloody, breathless, muddy and excited, and when we saw the rent in his pants we applauded, and asked him if that was the new moon rising! He swore like a trooper, and never forgave us. Next morning every one had heard of his race—the race of "Blue Face" and his attempted assassination.— If he appeared on the streets a troop of boys followed him, and for two weeks he stayed within doors, having his meals taken to his room, venturing out stealthily at night.

TRIGGER-LEG HILDRETH.

"Trigger-leg" Hildreth was so named for the reason that the knee cap of one leg was injured and made it stiff at the joint. He was a great hunter. His gun got out of order, and he went to blow in it to see if it was loaded, and touching the trigger with his toe, it went off and killed him, and this was the last of "Trigger-leg."

OLD SETTLERS.

The first Brewer of Fort Madison was August Trenchell, and Hon. Henry M. Salmon, who was a member of the constitutional convention, and Post Master Harmon Dingman, were among the first German settlers. George and Ferdinand Keil, the Schwarts family, and Joseph Ehart, came before the Hodges were hung. "Double Head" died early, and "Leather Breeches" is among the old time land marks. Lee Hull is the oldest nursery man in the county, and Fort Madison is indebted to him for the beauty of its public parks. Benedict Hugel was one of the noted settlers of a later day; was many years in the city council with George Robers, Bernard Durrenkamp, and Fred. Holtzberger, was once State Senator and Post Master, in the time of Andy Johnson.

The Albright family are the most numerous of the old settlers. R. W. Albright was editor of the Lee County *Democrat*, in which office J. W. Delaplain, the veteran typo of Lee county, who set the type of the first copy of the Keokuk Daily *Whig*, published March 2nd, 1854, learned his trade. Mr. Allbright was the first Clerk of the District Court of Lee county, under the State government. His brothers, Jacob W. and William Albright, have always been and still are merchants.

THE OLD SETTLERS.

Robert McFarland, a resident of Fort Madison since 1839; in 1849 was elected Clerk of the Board of Commissioners; in 1851 County Treasurer, which he held, and other offices of honor, till 1860. Was Mayor of the city, and is now in the drug business. "Mc" knows all the interesting reminiscences of the city and county, from the time when Harmon Dingman buried the Possum till Daniel F. Miller, Esq., got that anti-phlogistic plaster from Dr. Cowles, and used to come to Keokuk to church, when Rev. Leonard Whitney preached, and the Unitarian church since so popular was called the "insurance office."

The act of the General Assembly, establishing the District Court at Keokuk, was drawn up by General Hugh T. Reid, and Hon. William J. Cochran, then a member of the legislature, introduced it into the House; it passed and became a law.

Wood, Estes & Co. built the first stove factory in Iowa, and turned out the first cooking stove on the 4th of July, 1855. Before this date we only had machine foundries.

The Steamer "Old Dominion" sunk in 1846, on Dominion Rock, near Keokuk. Captain Tyler commanded the boat, and William Ralston, the California fast banker, was the clerk.

Ed. Riley killed Barney F. Barron at Keokuk in 1840, the first killing of a white man in the town. He was sent to the penitentiary for two years.

The first brass band established in Keokuk in 1848-9, was taught by an old Frenchman, who married the widow Van Fossen. Horace H. Ayers, Lee Springer, Morman W. Starkweather, were among its members. The band drenched the old teacher with cider.

The Rapids Convention was held at Burlington, Iowa, 23d of October, 1851. Governor Stephen Hempstead was President of the Convention.

HON. A. T. WALLING—THE FIRST GAS LAMPS—AN OLD NEWSPAPER ; ITS CONTENTS—GENERAL JESSE B.. BROWNE STOPS AN OX TEAM.

In looking over an issue of The Daily Evening Times, Vol. I, No. 10, dated Keokuk, Iowa, Wednesday evening, Sept. 26th, 1855, how many memories come to us as of yesterday of the persons and things named in it.

Walling & Hussey, proprietors.

Walling is now in Congress from Circleville district, Ohio, democrat.

Old Dr. G. St. Clair Hussey was afterwards an Episcopal minister, then a republican politician and was last at Natchez, Mississippi.

Let us see what they were doing and what they talked about.

THE ADVANTAGES OF KEOKUK

Is the leading article which we recognize as from the pen of Mr. Walling, who was an able writer.

"The advantages of our city are such as should draw to it the merchant, the mechanic, the capitalist from the east, in preference to any other point. That it has superior advantages, both in relation to the internal and external circumstances of the state, will not be doubted by any who have ever visited it, or who have any knowledge of the geography of the country. Situated at the foot of the Des Moines rapids on the Mississippi river, it is virtually at the head of navigation on that noble stream. No stage of water but permits a constant steamboat communication between this and all points below, while the greater portion of the year boats of even lighter draft cannot pass the rapids, but are forced to discharge their cargo here to be passed over by means of *Lighters*, hauled around, or what is more common, go into store here, to be distributed to the vast and fertile regions rapidly filling up to the north and west of us.

We are also at the mouth of the Des Moines river, a stream extending northwardly through the entire state, watering by itself and numerous branches a country greater in extent, than is watered by the exclusive stream of any other state, and of fertility not surpassed by the valley of the Wabash or Miami, while in beauty of scenery, salubrity of climate, and general facilities for a desirable agricultural location, the valley of no eastern river bears no comparison. Keokuk receives the drain of this great water shed. Its business finds its natural outlet here—and here its comes—doubling and trebbling from year to year in a manner that excites the undisguised astonishment and admiration of the traveler who visits it to-day after an absence of but a single year. The natural divide between the Des Moines river and the rivers north of it, furnishes a highway unsurpassed, to the very northern limits of the state—and along it may be found the teams and wagons of the thousands constantly engaged in the carrying trade from this point to the interior. But while Keokuk posesses these superior facilities as a point naturally, she is not unmindful of the advantages to be gained by artificial improvement, and in this respect equally to any other does it recommend itself to the eastern man seeking a business location in the west. We refer to railroad and river improvements. Two railroads are already commenced—the one to be extended from here along the Des Moines valley entirely through the heart of the state—the other from here to Muscatine, on the Mississippi above the rapids, giving us a connection with Chicago, and through it facilities for the northeastern markets as we already have with the southeastern. Besides this, most of the connecting links of a road from this to St. Mary's on the Northern Cross Road in Illinois, has been graded and but a small amount of expenditure, and a short time is necessary to complete a direct eastern railroad connection."

He then speaks of the great importance of the work of slack water navigation of the Des Moines river being prosecuted vigorously by a New York Company of ample means, to extend to the Raccoon Fork, now Des Moines; also the height and beauty of location of the city, situated on a high bluff, rising abruptly from the river, from 70 to 100 feet, to the level of a rolling prairie back; and its entire freedom from low or miasmatic lands any where in the vicinity." He concludes, "These advantages are appreciated by all who visit us, and the effect is seen in the number of new comers commencing business here, and the large number constantly arriving who are unable to get business houses, even with the amount in course of erection. A more general knowledge abroad of our position would produce corresponding results. To extend that knowledge is a duty, as it should the pleasure, of every citizen, in which we pledge ourselves to do our full share."

The next article is a notice of Professor James Hall, the recently appointed State Geologist, having just passed through Chicago on the way to Iowa to make a geological survey of the state. A great battle between General Harney's command with the Sioux Indians, some other general items of news, a quarter of a column of unimportant telegraphic news, and Governor Grimes' Thanksgiving Proclamation, setting apart Thursday, the 22d of November as a day of thanksgiving and praise. Under his administration, which was far-seeing and liberal; the State Hospital for the Insane was fully established, and it is therefore important in view of the important services of the distinguished Governor of Iowa, and the U. S. Senator from our state, we will give it. The Governor says:

"The last year has been crowned with blessings to our state. We have been exempt from pestilence. Abundant harvests have rewarded the toil of the husbandman. We have been preserved from intestine commotions and bloodshed. No distracting evils have occurred to impede our prosperity. Our population, wealth and productive resources of every character have been greatly multiplied. Steps have been taken to establish charitable institutions, corresponding to the progress and spirit of the age, and the demand of humanity. There are evidences all around that the state has made unexampled progress in everything that tends to promote her best physical and moral interest. As citizens, we have enjoyed liberty without licentiousness, civil and religious freedom, without distinction of party, sect or nationality, have been enjoyed by all. Our nation has been prosperous. Peace has been preserved. While other nations have been plunged into bloody and desolating wars, we have been preserved from that calamity. For these and for numerous other blessings, it has been deemed proper that a day should be set apart by the Executive of the State for praise and thanksgiving."

The same paper of the 26th of September, 1865, in its local column says: "We saw yesterday, at the Mayor's office, a specimen of the gas lamps to be used in lighting our streets. It is the intention to have seventy-five of them put up by the first of January, if sufficient pipe is laid by that time."

The city was not then lighted by gas, and we had no eastern communication by railroad, and in fact no railroads at all, as the Valley road leading towards Des Moines was only then built to Belfast, twenty miles, and what is now the C. B. & Q. R. R., was only running to Sandusky, six miles, half way to Montrose. We had the Keokuk and Rock Island mail line of steamers, the J. McKee and Ben Campbell, making daily trips, connecting at Rock Island with the cars from the east, and the St. Louis and Keokuk mail line of steamers, composed of the "Die Vernon," "Westerner," "Jennie Deans," "Keokuk," also the steamer "J. W. Sparhawk," running as a regular daily packet from Keokuk, in connection with the cars of the Northern Cross Railroad at Quincy, leaving Quincy at 8 o'clock and arriving at Keokuk at 12 m., and leaving Keokuk on return trip at 5 o'clock. To get east we could take the steamer and go to Rock Island, and there take the cars of the Chicago and Rock Island Railroad, or take the steamer from Keokuk to Quincy, and there take the cars of the Northern Cross Railroad, or going north you could leave the steamer at Burlington, Iowa, and take the stage to Galesbnrg, striking the railroad east. To go directly east from Keokuk you had to cross the river on a ferry boat, as we had no bridge then, and take an old lumbering stage coach and strike the Northern cross Railroad at Plymouth, from twenty-eight to thirty miles distant. In case the river was not navigable on account of the thick ice running, which made navigation dangerous, ten chances to one you would be delayed for days at a time.

Dry Goods and groceries, sent into the country, were sent overland up the "Divide" road, following the route over the prairies, west over the plank road, of which Thomas W. Clagett was then president, which was built over what was once Muddy Lane, and ran in the direction of Charleston, about fourteen miles, and had two toll gates, one near the present residence of Captain Israel Anderson beyond the city limits, and one six miles further out, near what is now the County Poor House. The notice of Judge Clagett will show that the means of transportation to Montrose was then by hacks and stages, when not by the river.

PLANK ROAD.

TRAVELERS TAKE NOTICE.

All persons traveling on this road will be required to pay their toll at the gates. Persons living within the townships of Jackson, Montrose, Charleston and Des Moines, going and returning to or from Keokuk the same day, upon paying full toll at the first gate can return free. All hacks for the carriage of passengers between Keokuk and Montrose, and which habitually travel the plank road, can go and return the same day by paying one full toll. Those who only use the plank road when other roads are bad, will be required to pay full toll each way.

No person will be allowed to stop their teams to water on the bed of the road, or to remain with their teams at the gates any longer than may be necessary to pay their toll.

The law will be rigidly enforced against all persons who disregard this notice.

THOMAS W. CLAGETT, President.
By order of the Board of Directors.

General Jesse B. Browne was in 1855–6 a toll gate keeper at the first toll gate, as he was old, poor, and without an office, and his friends wanted to give him something to do, so he got the toll gate to keep.

Long lines of covered wagons, drawn principally by horses, prairie schooners, as they were generally called, such as were formerly used in traveling the

THE OLD SETTLERS.

plains, generally four horses to a wagon, could be seen at any day scattered along the road, sometimes four or five together. All the goods sent into the country were transported that way, supplying the Des Moines Valley and the tributaries of the Des Moines River. Sometimes ox teams were used to draw these wagons, but not often.

All who recollect General Browne, know how tall, erect and military he looked, so grim when he chose, may not remember the story how he frightened the countryman driving an ox team coming to Keokuk· As a terrible swearer he could discount the army in Flanders and not half try himself.

An ox team came along one day when the old General had been indulging freely, and was on one of his terrible benders, and drove up towards the toll gate, when the General rushed out with his long bowie knife, towards the innocent countryman wielding the ox whip, and in a voice of thunder, swearing, as only he could swear, that he did not allow any ox teams to travel on that road, and as he made tracks for the countryman, flourishing his knife as if to cut him down, he made off as fast as his legs could carry him, frightened out of a year's growth. Browne, in the meantime, was charging about, up and down the road, threatening vengence on the drivers of all ox teams, and ox teams in particular. The road became blocked up with teams, in front and behind the ox team, and continued thus for two hours or more, the countryman not daring to go near his team, and other drivers, who did not know Browne, looking on and wondering, till some one from town happened to come along in the nick of time who knew him and could manage him, got him in the house, and the ox team then passed through safely. About all the people in the immediate vicinity, at that time, brought to town in these wagons was cord wood or hoop-poles, and on top of nearly every wagon could be seen two jugs, one for molasses and the other for whisky. There were no gardens on the route between Keokuk and Montrose, and the coldest day in winter, as you passed the log houses on the road side, you would invariably see the doors open.

General T. I. McKenny, Agent of Lee County, at No. 80, sign of the Golden Mortar, advertised

"For the sale of spirituous liquors for medicinal, mechanical and sacrimental purposes only."

The contents of one of the jugs on the wood wagons it is but charitable to suppose was for sacramental purposes to be used in Sugar Creek bottom or Hog Thief hollow.

BLACK HAWK.

CHAPTER IX.

The Black Hawk War—The Battle of the Bad Axe—The Old Steamboat Captain Throckmorten, of the Warrior — Otis Reynolds—General Gaines—General Atkinson—Black Hawk's Surrender—General Street Indian Agent—Col. Zachary Taylor—Lieutenant Jefferson Davis has Black Hawk and others in charge as Prisoners—Black Hawk's tour through the Country; Anecdotes of Him; his Wife and Daughters; His correct likeness taken at the close of the War in 1833, etc.—Bill Thurston—Lou Green the one armed Lawyer—Turner, the Schoolmaster, breaks a Girl's rib—Abner Clark Bull-dozed, etc.—John Hiner's Hog Claim.

Captain Carson, who was an old pilot on the Mississippi river, says, that the Rosalie, commanded by Captain M. Littleton, well known to the author, was the first steamer which made two regular trips to Keokuk from below in 1838. Its commander left here for California in 1849, and engaged in running a steamer on the Sacramento river. His son Henry was long afterwards a pilot or clerk, was a fine singer, and a gay lark, and spent much of his time brushing his ambrosial curls, playing his guitar, and serenading the ladies of moonlight nights, singing

"Come to the lattice lady love."

This however was at a later day in 1847-8; his father, at that time, being still on the river.

One of the old time steamers, before refered to, in 1832, was the "Warrior," Captain Throckmorten, and if for nothing else is worthy of mention, from the fact that its captain was present with his boat at the last battle of the Black Hawk War, the battle of the Bad Axe, fought at the mouth of the Bad Axe River, on the 2nd of August, 1832. Here Black Hawk and his warriors were most signally defeated, many of them were killed or captured, and the great chief made his escape by flight. Black Hawk was a Fox and a chief of the Sacs and Foxes, and as his defeat in this battle had important historical results, and as "Keokuk" and vicinity was at one time his favorite resort, a short sketch of him and the Black Hawk War, in which there are many yet living who took an active part, may be of more than passing interest. Previous to the ceeding of lands east of the Mississippi river by the Indians to our government, Black Hawk, with a band of about four hundred Sacs and Foxes, was living on Rock River, Illinois, about three miles from its mouth. In 1821 this land was sold by the Indians to the United States, with the understanding however that the Indians were to continue in possession until the land was put in the market for sale to actual settlers. In 1829-30 the land was put in market and sold to individuals, including their village, who settled upon it, the Indians moved west of the Mississippi. Not a single chief signed the treaty ceding these lands, it is said. In 1831, however, they recrossed the river and took possession of the site of their old village and corn fields, as Black Hawk alleged on invitation of the Winnebago Prophet for peaceable purposes only, to raise a corn crop. The whites state that they were insolent, and committed many acts of violence, which were most probably provoked. The government sent Gen. Gaines to Fort Armstrong, Rock Island, in 1831, with a military force to remove them west of the Mississippi river. While the troops under command of General Gaines were at the Fort, Nathan Smith, heretofore referred to, who was an interpreter and spy for General Gaines, was sent to see and talk with Black Hawk at the Indian village, and induce Black Hawk to go and see the General, which he did. This interview with the General was short and conclusive. General Gaines told him that he was not a peace officer but had his orders from the government to drive them across the river. He had no discretion, but that he did not want any trouble, and that he had understood he had agreed to leave peaceably. If he did not leave in ten days, he would fire on his village. Black Hawk agreed to leave and never recross the river, and made a treaty to that effect. At the expiration of the time fixed for Black Hawk to leave, General Gaines marshaled his forces and with his artillery took up his line of march for the Indian village, and found it deserted; the Indians had re-crossed the river.

In violation of this agreement the British band of the Sacs and Foxes attacked the Menominies in the fall of 1831, at Prairie du Chien, killed twenty-eight of them, and though remonstrated with, refused to surrender the agressors. They vainly tried to induce every other Indian nation to join them for the extermination of the Americans, and asserting that the English had promised to join the Indians, they resolved to commence war themselves. They therefore invaded the east side of the Mississippi river in April, 1832, and this invasion was called the Black Hawk War. About eight hundred warriors, headed by Black Hawk, Nah-pope, We-sheet, the Ioway and other chiefs, were joined by the Winnebago Prophet, with his band, after crossing. The Prophet, as he was called, was the principal fomenter of the disturbance, working upon the credulity of the Indians by his incantations and pretended gifts of prophecy. The volunteers were called out by the governor of Illinois and commanded by Generals Henry, Posey, and Henry Dodge. General Atkinson commanded the regular troops, and mildly expostulated with the Indians trying to persuade them to return. He understood little of the Indian character and was taunted by insolent messages from the hostile savages. He was no doubt a respectable grand-mother, not a general.

He advanced on the Indians from Fort Armstrong, and chartered the steamer "Java" with Otis Reynolds as captain, to go up Rock River. It got to the rapids but was unable to ascend any further. Some kiel boats were gotten over with supplies, and Atkinson's troops marched along the banks of the river through the high grass, reaching above their heads, and having accomplished nothing, returned to Fort Armstrong. The battle of Sycamore Creek or Stillman's defeat, brought on the Black Hawk War, through the hasty action of the militia who fired first on Black Hawk's flag of truce. The Indians were well mounted and armed, and scattered their war parties over the country, producing a universal panic, and succeeded in destroying much property, breaking up settlements, killing whole families, and scalping women and children. They way-laid the roads, cutting off travelers, and created sad havoc, till the volunteer troops reached their neighborhood. General Henry pursued them in the country north of Rock River, and across the Wisconsin river, through woods and swamps, almost impassable, till the rear guard of the Indians was overhauled, attacked and defeated on the banks of the Wisconsin river.

Previous to this, General Atkinson took five hundred men, embarked on a steamer for Galena, near which place Black Hawk, with three hundred warriors, was encamped at Dixon's Ferry. The General desired interpreter Nathan Smith, to take one company, and with it to go to see Black Hawk to induce him to make peace and return, but he refused to go with this small force, knowing it would be construed into a hostile movement and result in death to the entire party, but offered to go alone. He went out accordingly; near Black Hawk's camp, and sent for him; the meeting was friendly but reresulted in nothing, and though Black Hawk tried to induce him to go to his camp, he refused and returned to Galena. General Atkinson then sent out Savery, an Indian Agent, attended by one company to see and negotiate with Black Hawk. The agent and all the company but eight men were killed and scalped, and the general returned to Rock Island. Black Hawk, after his defeat and escape from the battle of the Bad Axe, was induced to come in and surrender to General Street, Indian Agent at Prairie du Chien. The Winnebagoes who went to him carried messages from the government authorities, promising him if he surrendered he would be released. Black Hawk is reported to have told them that he knew they lied, but for the sake of his wife and children who were starving, he would go, and went accordingly. The Indians at the time of the battle of Bad Axe were in a starving condition, and camped under the bluff where the troops, taking them by surprise, surrounded and attacked them. A squaw, who was killed in the attack, was found lying dead with her little girl pappoose wrapped in the folds of her blanket, with her arm broken from being shot. Amputation was found necessary, and while the surgeon was operating upon her, amputating her arm, she was given a hard cracker which she ate ravenously as a hungry dog, so near was she to starvation, paying not the slightest attention to the knife of the surgeon, and not making the least outcry.

The defeat of Black Hawk resulted in the treaty of Rock Island in September, 1832, which was made by Keokuk and other chiefs, and the ceding by the Indians of the "Black Hawk purchase," as it was for a long time called, lands west of the Mississippi river, now part of Iowa, by the terms of which the Indians were to give possession on the 18th of June, 1833. Black Hawk and his two sons were held as prisoners of war. By the terms of the treaty made by General Scott with the Indians, it was agreed that the captive chiefs should be kept in confinement during the pleasure of the President of the United States, who referred the matter to Congress. They were taken first to Jefferson Barracks and afterwards held at Fortress Monroe, and on their liberation were placed by the President in charge of Major Garland, to be taken on a grand tour through the country to exhibit to them the folly of ever renewing hostilities against the United States. They were told the people of the United States were as numerous as the leaves of the forest, and everywhere they went attracted much attention. At this time, in 1833, Black Hawk was, according to his own statement, a man of about sixty-six years of age, though looking much younger. He was about five feet eight inches in height, sinewy, with a broad chest, the high cheek bones of the Indian, high forehead and great penetrating black eyes, with the glance of an eagle, with dignified and majestic manner, though manifestly much depressed in spirits since his great misfortunes.

The accompanying likeness, which was sketched by an officer of the army who served in the Black Hawk war, and was at the battle of the Bad Axe, and at the military post where the captured chiefs were for a long time imprisoned, is the most correct likeness, it is said, ever published. He habitually carried his long pipe and a fan, which he holds in his hand, and for a long time was never without them, as it was thought to impress the officers having him in charge, that he considered himself and his nation no longer at war with us. His dress is that which he wore during his confinement. Catlin when engaged in painting the likenesses of the principal chiefs who were confined at Jefferson Barracks, proposed to Black Hawk that he should be represented with a spear as emblematic of his recent pursuits.

"No !" said Black Hawk, indignantly, "No spear for me ! I am forever done with spears !"

Col. Patterson saw him once at West Point, in this county, when he was dressed as an American gentleman, with a black frock cloth coat with metal buttons, pants, and a silk hat, says he walked erect as a soldier. Some ladies sent for him to come to the parlor of a hotel on the public square where they were stopping. This was after the war when he was lionized wherever he went. Black Hawk went to see them as requested, and an ignorant, rough old countryman, old John Stout, who was in the room, and by the way did not understand a word of Indian,' said to him, meaning to be complimentary, no doubt, puck-a-chee ! which means clear out ! leave here ! He arose, indignantly, his eyes flashing fire, and without a word, walked out majestically, mounted his horse and left the town at once.

The reporter of Chevalier Webb's paper, the Courier and Enquirer of July, 1833, tells some good stories on him while swinging round the circle. Among the ladies presented to him was one with very fine hair, who gave him a tomahawk. Black Hawk patted her on the head, and said to his son, "What a beautiful head for scalping!"

When at Old Point Comfort, Fortress Monroe, he was very dull, and many people supposed he might want amusement. A beautiful young lady played for an hour and a half the most admired Italian airs as she sat at the piano, and was delighted at the attention exhibited by the illustrious red man, who neither moved nor uttered a syllable, and on finishing, looked around for his applause, but found him fast asleep.

Another lady presented him with a bottle of ottar of roses, he tried to drink it, and threw it away in disgust, exclaiming "give me some fire water!"

At Washington he was much annoyed by the ladies who seemed to have nothing to do but attend the debates of Congress, trials for murder, and run after great men. On one occasion he got out of all patience, and turning to the Prophet, said, "What in the d——l's name do these squaws want with me?"

At Philadelphia he was taken to the theatre, and slept through the play 'till the applause of the audience, at the song of "Jim Crow," awoke him. He pricked up his ears, till it was encored for the fourth time louder than ever, when he remarked in disgust, "When these people come to visit me I will treat them to a concert of wild cats!"

On another occasion, in the same city, he attended a ball and was invited to dance; he sent for his ball dress which consisted, among other things, of a buffalo hide with the horns on. In this costume he gave them the war dance, capering and yelling, and creating a great alarm. The house was in an uproar; the ladies screamed, a celebrated little dandy, with eye glasses, fainted, the fiddlers got out of tune, but Black Hawk was delighted.

A host of good things, which are true, could be told of this remarkable chief who was always the friend of General Street, the Indian Agent for several administrations, to whom he surrendered. Street subsequently removed to Agency City, in Wappello county, where he died on the Black Hawk purchase. Black Hawk lived till the fall of 1839 when he died on the Reservation of one mile square, where Iowaville now stands, and was buried by a big spring near the residence of Mr. James Jordan, an old Indian trader, still living, who is full of reminicences of Black Hawk and the Black Hawk War.

Years ago his bones were stolen by a doctor of Quincy, Ill., and nothing now remains of what was once the proud war chief of the Sacs and Foxes, but the history and traditions of the past.

Governor Lucas made a requisition on the Governor of Illinois for his bones, and they were surrendered as a skeleton and placed for safe keeping in the territorial museum at the capitol in Burlington. A fire destroyed the building and its contents, and with them his skeleton was consumed in the flames. Zachary Taylor, then a Colonel, was in command at Prairie du Chien when Black Hawk surrendered, August 27, 1832, and Jeff Davis, then a lieutenant, took charge of the prisoners, and took them on the steamer Winnebago, to Jefferson Barracks, Mo. Black Hawk was in irons and complained that the shackles chaffed his wrists, but at the request of General Street, who became personally responsible for him, the irons were ordered to be removed by Lieutenant Davis, since so noted as President of the Southern Confederacy, who was at that time about twenty-eight years of age. Black Hawk had but one wife.

BLACK HAWK'S WIFE AND CHILDREN.

Black Hawk's wife was not a full-blooded Indian, but had French blood in her veins. Her daughters were much lighter colored than the other Indians, showing unmistakably their white blood. They were very handsome; one it is said was very beautiful. She spoke French fluently, and was much admired by a young officer of the army, who, but for his accidental death, it is authoritively reported, expected to marry her.

There are many still living who have seen Black Hawk and knew him well, and say he was a small man in stature, heavy set, and for one of his size possessed of great physical strength. It was, as we have said, on account of his wife and children that Black Hawk was induced to surrender, and to keep them from death by starvation. After his surrender, she came south with her little son, stopping near St. Francisville, Mo , and was frequently at the house of the genial, kind hearted and hospitable, Jere Wayland, the old settler, and one of nature's noblemen who sympathized with her in her misfortunes. Her heart was filled with despondency, and she thought Black Hawk would never return, but he assured her he would come back in good time. When he did return she was filled with joy, and his arrival was duly celebrated with big demonstrations and a great feast, at which both Black Hawk, Keokuk and their families were present.

It is related of Black Hawk, by Jere Wayland of St. Francisville, Mo., that the old chief was much astonished at seeing Durant go up in a balloon, from Castle Garden, in New York, and in viewing this, to him strange and supernatural sight, he said he had made up his mind to fight no more. Turning to one of his trusty braves, he said, "I have taken thirty-five white scalps with my own hands; for one year I have neither ate nor drank while the sun shined, trying to commune with the Great Spirit; but the white man could go up !" Black Hawk related to "Uncle Jere" Wayland an incident of the war of 1812, with which he was personally connected, which happened at Fort Edwards, now Warsaw. Returning in a canoe, with a young chief from down the river, where they had been on a war-like expedition, they saw a solitary sentinel measuredly pacing his beat at mid-day.

The young chief could not resist the temptation and declared he would kill this man, to which Black Hawk readily consented, and took his position at a high point on the bluff above, commanding a full view of the fort. The young chief, with the stealthiness of a panther, crept through the brush and up the steep bank, slowly approaching the fort. He was still beyond reach of his rifle; but the Indian warrior, to make his aproach unobserved, broke off a branch of a tree, covered with leaves, and holding it before him, approaching nearer and nearer till within range, then, when the sentinel's back was turned from him, fired at him, and he fell dead at his post. Before the alarm could be given, he had made good his retreat, rejoined Black Hawk, and they again proceeded on their journey.

It is a historical fact that when Black Hawk left the west side of the Mississippi, to engage in the Black Hawk war, his starting point for Rock Island was from Fort Madison, Iowa. Some of his party went by land, the braves on horseback, the women and children in canoes, carrying their cooking utensils.

Black Hawk and his chiefs at Jefferson Barracks were kept prisoners with a ball and chain attached to them like felons by General Atkinson. When prisoners at Fortress Monroe, from the 26th of April, till the 4th of June, 1833,

THE OLD SETTLERS. 137

when released; they were kindly treated by Colonel Eustis, and had many visitors, and received a great many presents from the ladies who came to see them.

The old chief Keokuk at one time had as many as six wives. When he got tired of an old one, he discarded her, and took a new one. The name Keokuk signifies the "Watchful Fox." He was born at Rock river in 1780, and was a native Sac Indian. Black Hawk was a Fox Indian. Keokuk was not a hereditary chief but won his way to that rank by the force of his talent, enterprise and courage. When but fifteen years of age, in the first battle in which he was engaged, he killed a Sioux with his spear on horseback, and this was considered a great achievement; a public feast, commemorated this event, and he was admitted to the privilege of a brave at this tender age; ever after he was allowed to appear on all public occasions on horseback, a rare privilege. He was a splendid horseman and always went mounted on a high mettled horse. He traveled in more state, and appeared on public occasions of ceremony in a style of grandeur and savage magnificence which exceeded that of any Indian chief in his day on the continent. Hence he attracted much attention, and was everywhere the centre of attraction. He succeeded Black Hawk as chief entirely, the latter being deposed after the treaty of Rock Island in 1833.

The causes which led to the Black Hawk war were deep seated, going back to the treaty ceding lands made with General Harrison at St. Louis, Nov. 3d, 1804, which the Indians alleged was not made with chiefs authorized to represent them, but with a lot of Indians who went there on a visit to get one of their nation released, and were made drunk, and then got to sign this treaty. There is good reason to believe there was some foundation of truth, as on the 14th of September, 1815, another treaty was made with the Indians at Portage des Sioux, to heal the bad feeling growing out of the war of 1812, in which Black Hawk took part with the British who incited the Indians to hostility to the United States. An Indian must fight when there is war; he will not be an idle spectator, but must fight on one side or the other, instead of being a home guard in the rear. They first offered their services to the United States which were refused. The reason for this refusal no doubt grew out of the fact that in battle the Indians could not be restrained from using the tomahawk and scalping knife, and the government did not want to countenance this mode of warfare. This treaty goes on to confirm the treaty of 1804, which was again confirmed by another treaty made on the 13th of May, 1816, and still again by the treaty of Fort Armstrong, made with the Sacs and Foxes by Maj. Thomas Forsythe, Indian Agent, on the 3d of Sept. 1822. We are irresistibly led to the conclusion that the first treaty of 1804 was known to be bad, and hence it was necessary, to keep down disputes, to have it frequently confirmed. Black Hawk and his party were always dissatisfied, and after they engaged with the British in the war of 1812, were called the "British Band." He was born, as he stated, on Rock River in 1767, (his father was Py-e-sa,) which would make him sixty-five years old at the time of the Black Hawk war. But an Indian is like a mule or an unmaried ancient maiden, of uncertain age; but one thing is certain, Black Hawk was an old man at the beginning of the Black Hawk war.

LOU GREEN, THE ONE ARMED LAWYER.

Lou Green, the one armed lawyer, lived at West Point, was young, handsome, talented and brilliant, full of fun, but very dissipated and played cards, and petti-fogged before country justices. He was once prosecuting a man for whipping his wife; the principal witness was one Beadle, who saw him whip her. He put this question to Beadle:

"Did you see this man lay violent hands on this lady?"

"Violent hands, hell ! he gave her one of the d——dst battle whangings I ever saw !"

The justice ordered the witness to sit down for using such language.

Green insisted that the witness go on with his story, and detail the circumstances of the whipping.

The justice ordered Green to sit down and refused to hear him.

Green seized him about the neck with his one arm, and with the stump of the other beat him about the face and eyes till they were black and blue. The justice fined him one dollar for contempt of court, and Green paid it, saying, that court was always a subject of contempt.

This is a sample of the early *prairie practice.*

BILL THURSTON.

Bill Thurston, of Fort Madison, was a noisy politician, a successful pettifogger and periodically got religion, and when the excitement was over, would fall from grace. He was once elected to the legislature, but defeated when a candidate for the Senate. He had at an early day been accused of hog stealing, and this was generally believed whether true or not. In any exciting contest the hog thief charge always came up. Once in the Baptist church he was asked by the minister to lead in prayer. A merchant, named Warren Hyde, said, "now the hog thief is going to pray, I'll leave!" He kept a harness shop and bought old copper and iron and put it in his back room. Some mischievous boys used to steal from his back room and sell it to him at the front door. He was hunting with one Jed Lewis on an island above town, when they found a dead man who had a good silver watch in his pocket. Thurston took it, and it got noised about, and to stop the pressure of public opinion he advertised an old watch, but not the one found, but it had no claimants.

A TIGHT SQUEEZE; TURNER, THE SCHOOLMASTER.

There was once a party at one Carmick's at West Point, a school teacher named Turner, was present, and having one of the girls cornered with his arms about her "squeezed" her so violently that he broke one of her ribs, and Dr. Sala had to be sent for.

The girl had him arrested and his fine and cost for this little courtship amounted to sixty-five dollars.

ABNER CLARK BULL-DOZED.

Just after the murder of McCardle by John J. Jones near West Point, Jones having escaped, there was a look out in every quarter for him and a supposed confederate, the latter being reported yet in the neighborhood. Abner Clark, a respectable farmer, came to town with two dressed hogs in a sleigh, for sale. Some parties who did not know Clark met him in Salmon's saloon, in the forenoon, and supposing him to be the murderer's confederate, seized him, tied his hands and feet, put him in one corner, and poured whisky over him, and he laid in this condition, scarcely able to move, when some one came in near night, who knew him, and he was released, to find his dead dressed hogs had been taken out of the sleigh and eaten up by live hogs which were still surrounding it.

TOM WHITE.

Tom White was a character, and was on his muscle. Having trouble with Old Sammy Hearn, who lived on the place where Noah Bailey now lives, and owns, opposite St. Francisville, he gave Hearn, who was a cranky, obstinate, disagreeable old fellow, a terrible whipping which cost him three hundred dollars. Hearn had a fine yoke of steers, and White, by way of a set off, stole the steers to get even with him, but had great trouble again in getting rid of a criminal prosecution.

JOHN HINER'S HOG CLAIM.

When hogs ran loose and wild in the brush, Hiner bought a hog claim, as it was called, from old "Jums." Hogs then were marked and turned out to run at large, without fear of being impounded by Simcoe, the hog-bouncer. Hiner was a butcher, commenced killing the hogs belonging to his claim, and killed them on the streets, in the alleys and in the brush, till he killed all the fat hogs in town. At last he killed one, and Colonel Patterson came along, and seeing it, asked if that hog was lame in the right hip.

"Yes!" said Hiner, "but it had my mark!"

"What is your mark?" asked the Colonel.

"A bit and a slit and an under clip!"

"But it's my hog," said the Colonel. "Can you split him?"

"Yes!"

"Then split him and divide, and stop killing!"

That hog was divided.

CHAPTER X.

The First Newspaper, the Register—The Gate City—Some of the old Newspapers, and their Editors—Lawyer Greasy—George C. Dixon in the Circus Ring—Wolf Hunt—Holding a Panther—Dr. Isaac Galland the Mormon Apostle and Counterfeiter—Miscellaneous Items.

THE KEOKUK REGISTER—J. W. & R. B. OGDEN, PUBLISHERS.

In 1846, the brothers, J. W. & R.B. Ogden, read the terse sentence of Horace Greely—"Go west, young man!"—and having faith in the old philosopher, they looked to Iowa as their best success. The younger brother, R. B. Ogden, laid down his composing stick in the "Republican Office," Springfield, Ohio, in September of 1846, and spent his first winter at the capital, Iowa City, at the time of the first state legislature. After looking over the entire field, and by the advice of Henry W. Starr, James Grimes, Judge Lowe and others, Keokuk presented the only opening for a *Whig* newspaper. At that time Mahaska county was the extreme western county. A dozen newspapers comprised the entire list of the state. The river counties, with Van Buren, Henry, Wapello, Mahaska and Johnson county, were about all that could boast of a weekly paper. The two young whigs soon discovered that Iowa politics was a one-sided thing. Whiggery was decidedly at a discount, and unpopular, and outside of "Proud Mahaska" and "High Henry," (both Quaker counties,) there was not the ghost of a chance for an office from street supervisor or constable up through the grade to that of Governor, but was laid siege to by the unterrified. Lee county was solid 1000, and the leaders of the party were old stagers, having, many of them, the stamp mark of Sam Medary all over them. Men of force and brains, and as a general thing didn't want Whigs fooling around in their established democratic vineyard.

Keokuk presented anything but an inviting home for our political adventurers. With a population of only 600, and the "vexed question of titles," which culminated in a political imbroglio; the exodus of the Mormons, and the worse enemies of good society, the "Jack Mormons" were all elements of discord, that deterred the better class from making it a home, and intimidated many who waited long for a solution of the question of "titles," and folded their tents silently and left.

The prospectus of the Keokuk Register was issued in April, 1848, and the first number of the paper appeared the following month, with a list of *three subscribers*, viz., Samuel Van Fossen, L. B. Fleak, and Ross B. Hughes. This was particularly discouraging, especially as their subscriptions were not prepaid. These same gentlemen had given their personal guarantee that the paper should have a paid up subscription of 1000. The new editors were young; the green was predominant. They simply had entire confidence in the promises of these zealous "settlers." Not discouraged they went to work and the result was a subscription list of 1800 at the time of the sale of their office to Messrs. Howell & Cowles, in 1849.

THE OLD SETTLERS.

The Register was ably edited by J. W. Ogden, and soon took rank as one of the leading journals of the state. His introductory was copied by the St. Louis Republican, Cincinnati Gazette, New York Tribune, and The National Intelligencer at Washington; a flattering compliment to the young editor. Some good things are told by the pioneer of the Register, in his experience with the early settlers, which will close this history of the first paper of Keokuk.

Col. Wallace, of Fairfield, told R. B. Ogden, at Iowa City, that he would give him a letter to a friend in Keokuk, who was a prominent and successful lawyer, Norton Munger, which he thought would be of value to him. Ogden called at Munger's law office on 2d street, on the morning after his arrival in Keokuk. Finding the door locked, he sauntered along towards Main street. On the corner of Main he met the only well dressed man he had seen, with polished boots, kid gloves, and generally exquisite in his make up. He accosted Ogden:

"Stranger, you appear to be looking for somebody."
"Yes sir, I called at Mr. Munger's office, and his door is locked."
"Professional business?"
"No sir."
"Have you just arrived?"
"Yes sir; I simply have a letter of introduction to Mr. Munger. Do you know whether the gentleman is in town?"

Without answering, he looked up and down the street, and espied Munger, at the distance of a square, and yelled at the top of his voice, Munger! Munger! come here!

On his approach he was introduced:
"Col. Munger, here is a gentleman who has a letter of introduction."

The Col. read the letter; read over hurriedly "that the bearer visited Keokuk with the intention of establishing a Whig paper, and as that was the kind of timber wanted in this benighted country, he hoped," &c., &c. The letter finished, Munger paying no attention to the introducer, ran his arm through Ogden's, and led him down Main street, to the foot of Water street, went into a doggery, and for the first time after receiving the letter spoke:

"What'l you take?"
"Thank you, Mr. Munger. I never drink."

Munger swallowed his whisky, took a look all over his new acquaintance, and said:

"Well, by G—d you'd better leave this country!"

Munger, after assiduously and fearlessly nursing many cholera cases, died of cholera himself in 1852, in the arms of S. T. Marshall, Esq.

I. G. Wickersham was the well dressed gentleman.

THE PROSPECTUS

of the *Register* was printed in a "Jack Mormon" printing office, at Nauvoo, in March, 1847. There was no press in Keokuk, the nearest office being at Warsaw. "*The Warsaw Signal*." Ogden procured a horse at Cave's livery stable, telling them that he was going to Warsaw, and would return the same day.—

No questions were asked. He found the Des Moines river full of running ice. The spring freshet had come, and there was no hope of crossing the river for several days. Nauvoo was his only chance, and making a bee line he struck for the Mormon temple. At Montrose he left his horse and crossed the Mississippi in a canoe, through running ice. He found the printing office deserted, and was compelled to spend the night at the Mansion House, kept by the dead prophet's widow. There was a dance at the house, which continued till the break of day. Drunkenness, cursing, bowie knives, and pistols, was the order of as devilish a looking crowd as ever congregated this side of the infernal regions. Next day the printers, either from being too drunk, or it being publication day, refused to do his work, but gave him the use of the type and press. At 4 o'clock in the afternoon he wended his way to the ferry house— the old stone house that still stands on the bank of the river—kept by a "Jack Mormon," named Hendricks.

"Can you ferry me over the river?"

"Yes, when somebody else comes along."

"How soon do you think that will be?"

"How in the h—ll do I know?"

Ogden looked at the ferryman, and concluded not to ask any more questions, but wait. Eight o'clock came, and no one darkened the door. It was a cold, cheerless, dark night. The wind moaned drearily. The stars shed no light, and they seemed further from earth than he had ever seen them.

He went out from the dismal house into the night, could see a few glimmering lights away over the great river; could hear the great fields of ice grinding and crashing in its mighty sweep, and as he waited, and waited, and listened for the coming of some one that would insure his crossing, a great gloom settled upon him. What a place and what a night for murder! this was his thought.

Nine o'clock. Going into the room he ventured:

"Don't you think the prospects are that there will be no other person to ferry over the river besides myself?"

With an ugly oath the reply came: "I will take you over when I have another passenger."

"What do you charge a passenger?"

"One dollar!" gruffly said.

"Well, I'll give you two dollars. It is now 9 o'clock and I have to be in Keokuk to-night by 12 o'clock."

All the reply vouchsafed was, "Do you take me for a d——d fool."

Ten o'clock. Ogden mustered courage and said, "I will give you five dollars to put me on the other side." There was no reply. The old renegade Mormon had a face of iron; he neither talked nor laughed nor smiled; he sat in his chair the whole evening, grim, silent, hard and devilish looking.

Eleven o'clock. Precisely as the clock struck, the ferryman arose from his chair, saying, "Now, young man, *your time has come!* Wait a moment! He went out, whistled sharp and clear, and our friend thought it singular and peculiar. Presently two men came in with the ferryman, with oars on their shoulders. They pulled their caps down close, buttoned their coats tight, and said, "Come."

THE OLD SETTLERS. 143

As he approached the boat, and was ordered to get in the stern, he thought that a good old fashioned prayer, if he ever made one, was the appropriate time to make it then. He was to be murdered and thrown into the river.

Twelve o'clock he was on his horse, riding as fast as the darkness would permit, for Keokuk. And he got there none too soon. The livery stable man had been told that he had seen a young fellow riding his sorrel horse like the devil north; the same horse that had been hired to go to Warsaw, two days before; *the sheriff had orders to go in pursuit.*

The prospectus of the *Register* was written in Squire Van Fossen's office. General McCarty had an office in the same room, an attorney and all politician. Ogden handed the manuscript to Van Fossen, he in turn, after reading it, handed it to McCarty, with, "General, what do you think of it?" The Gen'l read it aloud, and said:

"Not worth a G—d d—n! Not one word in regard to our interests, the great settler question."

Ogden fired up and said, "General McCarty, I hav'nt any thing to do with your question of settlers rights. I came here to start a Whig paper."

Van Fossen saw trouble, and the oily old rat said, "I think I can settle this, let me try."

He wrote: "In regard to the vexed question of titles, we shall pursue a course which shall be satisfactory to all parties!" and handed it to the General. His reading that sentence excelled any thing that the writer of the instrument had ever heard; and his earnest swearing was terribly eloquent. The new clause went in notwithstanding. After it was printed Ogden distributed them around town, and of course called on the leading merchants, Chittenden & McGavic. They were both gentlemen, having no sympathies with the "settlers rights."

McGavic read the paper, came to the last clause, read it over twice, and said, "well, by G—d. I don't want any thing to do with you!"

Ogden was getting discouraged.

The day after the arrival of the two brothers at the Mansion House, kept by Madam Guyger, on front street, a large crowd had assembled in the bar room, the most prominent and conspicuous of which was Devil Creek Bill Clark. The Ogdens passed through, noticing J. P. Reed and some others.—After they had passed out Reed said:

"Bill, how do you like the looks of the new fellows?"

"Well, J. P., if you want my opinion, it is that the little light complexioned feller looks like a pretty respectable cus, but the tall, black one, like a d——d hoss thief, and I am going to freeze to him."

This very complimentary opinion was conveyed to the publishers by an apprentice boy, who was present. A very positive feeling of anger by the injured one was felt, and it was thought best that this Bill Clark, whoever he was, had to be made an example of. In course of time Bill was met. Somebody said, "Bill, let me make you acquainted with Ogden.

"You old hoss thief," said Bill, "give me a shake of your corn stealer.—I've been hunting for you!"

And ever after Bill Clark was his truest friend.

ANOTHER.—Van Fossen wrote a communication for the *Register* over his own signature—a most vindictive personal tirade against the decree, and in which he charged D. W. Kilbourne with being a perjurer, &c., &c. The compositor made it read "forger." The next week Van Fossen wrote: "Your compositor unwittingly made me say that the party was a forger. I wrote perjurer, but I now say the compositor was right, and I am ready to stand up to the word.

Mr. Kilbourne was living then in Port Madison, and was justly indignant at the publishers. Mr. Kilbourne immediately came to Keokuk, bought a cow hide, and it was soon known that the cow hiding was to come off. Bill Clark saved his friend.

THE FIRST PAID SUBSCRIPTIONS AND WHAT COME OF IT.

Squire Chenowith and Bill Dunn were the first names on the subscription list. The old squire is still living on the half-breed tract; Dunn removed to Montgomery county some years ago. Chenowith and Dunn rode up to the Register office, on the corner of 3d and Johnson streets, where the Patterson House now stands, and called out to the publishers, "Come down here." The call was responded to by R. B. Ogden. The men gave their names, and two dollars each, one years subscription. Returning to the office with a radiant face, he cried, hurrah, John! first two subscribers! let's put their names in capitals, with a gold mark around 'em.

John (seriously)—"Robert do you remember the injunction that father gave us when we left?"

Robert—"Yes, oh yes! I remember it. It was 'that we give our first earnings to the Lord!' I remember it very distinctly!"

John—"What are we going to do about it?"

Robert—Well, John, I'm willing to give the first earnings, Chenowith's subscription, if you will only show me the Lord. I've been around more than you have, and I hav'nt seen him yet. I don't think the Lord ever set his foot on this tract of land, and as for giving it to him, I can't see how it can be done here!"

John found the Lord in the only church in Keokuk, the old Beehive, on the following Sunday, and Chenowith's two dollars went into the black bag, and from thence, no doubt, into Cardinal Woolsey's pocket, the first Keokuk Methodist preacher, and a good one; he was the father of our pious young friend Fletcher Woolsey, so well and favorably known for his talent as a bookkeeper, and his gallantry as Adjutant of the 17th Iowa.

THE GATE CITY.

What is called the Gate City now was edited by Hon. J. B. Howell and James H. Cowles, who previously edited a weekly newspaper in Keosauqua called the Valley Whig, and practiced law. Howell was a candidate for District Judge in that district, and was defeated by Olney by about three votes, and quit the law entirely, bought out the Whig and Register and moved to Keokuk in 1849, and uniting the subscription lists adopted the names of The Des Moines Valley Whig and Keokuk register. Cowles went south and soon afterwards died at Mobile of consumption. Mr. Howell continued the publication alone, fighting his way against great odds politically, and when out of a subject put in his time abusing Judge Joseph C. Knapp of Keosauqua, a democrat, telling the story on him that he once said, "the people are like a drove of sheep." In the last times of 1856-7, and till 1861, he had for partners J. R. Briggs, now deceased, and William Richards of Washington, D. C. On the 2d of March, 1854, he started alone the first daily newspaper in Keokuk, the "Keokuk Daily Whig,' the type for which was set by J. W. Deleplain, then a compositor in his office, afterwards his partner for about five years. The name of his paper being changed to the Gate City, he is still connected with it, being the veteran editor of the state. He rarely writes for it now. Once he sold out, at the close of the war, to a red-headed nephew who was in the hundred days service, and got the title of Colonel, (A. W. Sheldon,) fighting in the bloody commissary department. He made some money speculating in tobacco in Virginia, invested part of it in faro, gold watches and chains in New York, fast horses in Kentucky, came to see his uncle and bought out the Gate City, failed to pay for it, and Mr. Howell was compelled to take it back, and then announced his intention never to quit the editorial profession. He was once postmaster, and in 1870 was elected U. S. Senator for a short term, filling a vacancy, and is now a judge of the Court of Southern claims.

Hon. J. B. Howell in his time has been a man of pluck, and is entitled to much credit for his persistency of purpose, bold independent course as a public journalist, and his political opponents give him credit for consistency.

Sam M. Clark, son of one of the oldest pioneer Methodist preachers in Iowa, connected with the Gate City since 1854, is a forcible and elegant writer of much merit, and we consider him one of the ablest republican editors of the state.

The democratic editors of Keokuk have been, William Patee, afterwards Auditor of State; Russell, who died of cholera; T. B. Cuming, Governor of Nebraska; H. W. Beers, who became an Episcopal minister; A. T. Walling; John C. Turk; Dr. B. P. Rankin, the "Squatter Governor" of Nebraska, and U. S. Marshal now of San Jose, California; D. Redington; Oliver I. Taylor; Charles Smith; and our able and learned friend Judge Thomas W. Clagett of the Constitution, who had more friends among the people than any editor of either political party in the state. Hon. John Gibbons, his successor in that paper, as a democratic editor and as a writer occupies the front rank in his profession, and is considered by far the most efficient editor, and wields the most facile pen of any of his political compeers in Iowa.

SKETCHES OF A NOTED CHARACTER.

Dr. Isaac Galland, who gave the lands on which Nauvoo was laid out to Joe Smith, the Mormon Prophet, was blest with the fatal gift of genius. His busy brain was always forming new schemes, and his ready pen could describe anything in which he was interested in glowing colors. He was an able writer, but vindictive and revengful, an Ishmaelite whose hand was against every man's, and every man's hand was against him, for his temperament was aggressive, and he was always in a law suit or having a personal altercation with some man or set of men. Beadle in his book on the Mormons in Utah, says he was originally a horse thief and belonged to the Massie gang of counterfeiters. This information was given by R. H. McKinney, of Nauvoo, and since reading it and talking to him about it, we have further inquired of Tollifer Dedman, of Clark county, Mo., an old settler and reliable man who came to what is now Nashville, in 1830, and knew Galland from that time; Nashville not then being known by that name, and, as Mr. Dedman says, he himself was then a mere boy, and had no one to play with but Indian boys, who could beat him shooting at a mark with a bow and arrow, but when it came to wrestling he could always throw them down.

DR. ISAAC GALLAND AS A COUNTERFEITER.

Mr. Dedham lives on Fox river, below Alexandria, and first came on to the Mississippi river in 1828, with his father's family and to Nashville in 1830, and on account of the Black Hawk War in 1832, moved to Warsaw, then Fort Edwards, Ill., and afterwards to Missouri where he is well known. We started to tell you what he said about Galland:

When his father and family, on their way west, crossed the Wabash river, at Terre Haute, into Edgar county, Illinois, they found that there was great excitement there about a notorious counterfeiter named Galland, who had absconded, leaving his wife and two daughters in a log house, under the rafters of which was found concealed a large roll of counterfeit money. When they got to Nashville they found old Dr. Galland, the same Galland, who was the escaped counterfeiter at that place, and he sent back by Dedman's brother and brother-in-law, and they got his wife and daughters for him. He used frequently to talk to Dedman, and give his personal history and experience as a counterfeiter, which business he had then abandoned, as he said, it was no longer profitable on account of too much competition. He was a very fine engraver, and made the first county seal for Hancock county, Ill. He had been in jail frequently for counterfeiting and on other charges, and used to laugh and say, he had been guilty of everything laid to his charge except hog stealing, and he never owned a hog. He had studied medicine, and as old John A. Murrell, the noted land pirate did, studied law in jail. One of his exploits as a counterfeiter was making the plate on which was printed the hundred dollar bills representing the State Bank of Virginia. Striking off some of the bills he took one into a bank and said he had taken it in a trade and wanted to test its genuineness, representing it had been given to him by a party he knew, but had not seen since. He wanted the bill examined. The bank officers and clerks all examined it and could find nothing wrong about it. But to decide the matter as to whether it was a genuine or a counterfeit one hundred dollar bill, the bank officers sent out for an expert, who, after examining it particularly and comparing it carefully with the genuine bill pronounced it a good counterfeit. The examination completed, and this opinion expressed by the expert, became a leading question as to what was the difference between this new counterfeit and the genuine bill. The bank before this examination would have taken it without question, and they were thoroughly alarmed when the expert pronounced it bad. It was a dangerous counterfeit to be afloat. Dr. Galland, in the meantime, was perfectly cool, and had been watching the changing features of the bank officials, and had listened to them and the expert in silence till the expert expressed his opinion of the bill. Then he demanded what was the difference between this bill and the genuine?

"Nothing," replied the expert, "but this, the hair of Franklin on the counterfeit is too coarse!"

"That," said Galland, coolly, "is easily remedied."

"Then," said he, as he related this adventure to Dedman, "I went out and mounted my horse and went home, and changed the plate, so I could make just as good money as the bank could."

He was a bold operator, unscrupulous and dangerous, and there is no telling now what he did which is now hidden by the lapse of time, and the death of his confederates, from the eyes of the world. One thing is well known, that he was intimate with Joe Smith, the Mormon Prophet, and was one of the twelve apostles of that church, after their arrival at Nauvoo in 1839, and otherwise made himself useful as his emanuensis and private secretary. As much counterfeit money was in circulation from Nauvoo, and many titles to lands on the military tract in Illinois, including the patents from the government, and subsequently conveyances by old Judge Chandler and others, it is more than probable that he had much to do with all these operations. His capacity as an engraver would render him very useful to the prophet, who no doubt availed himself of his usefulness. He never stuck long to any one thing notwithstanding his versatility of genius, and soon got disgusted with and left the Mormons. It is claimed that at first he believed in the authenticity of their doctrine and revelations. This might do to tell to the marines but not to persons who knew Dr. Galland's intellectual capacity and ability. A man of massive brain, he had a large head, high forehead, broad and prominent as that of Napoleon I, or the great Pope Pius IX. The head of a Mormon convert in the days of Joe Smith, and in fact the heads of those who fly off on a tangent on every new issue, are conical, subdued sugar loafs, and lacking intellectual force, but one idea can enter the brain at a time, and to this they stick with great pertinacity.

Dr. Galland had too much sense to believe in Joe Smith's divine mission, though he might have believed that instead of divine inspiration he had peculiar magnetic power such as is ascribed to trance mediums and the juglers of India to-day, but living at that day when spiritualism was unknown, though now extensively believed by some very intelligent people, he was in advance of it. A Mormon, and being one of the twelve apostles, and commanded to go and preach, answered his purpose for a time, long enough to sell to his Mormon converts in New Jersey and other places in the east, large tracts of lands on the half-breed tract, to which it turned out he had no title, and he kept on selling the same lands till he sold them several times over. He quit the Mormons in disgust, when he could not make anything more out of them. When we used to see him he devoted nearly all his time attacking the courts, always found fault with them and cursed all the judges roundly. He used to be at war with David W. Kilbourne who was attorney in fact for Marsh Lee and Delevan, trustees of the New York Land Company, and wrote a pamphlet denouncing Kilbourne in the bitterest terms. Kilbourne replied in another pamphlet, in which he quoted Galland's history from the records of the courts, and of conveyances, and also quoted a revelation of Joe Smith relative to the "Lord's servant, Isaac Galland," and the command to "go and preach!" Galland felt this; he published another pamphlet, in which he was voluble, virulent and personally abusive, but Kilbourne took it coolly, only laughed, shaking his fat sides, while the old doctor ranted on, but the facts from the records effectually squelched him. He came to the surface once after this as a candidate for the legislature on the Possum ticket in 1851, when C. J. McFarland, General Reid, Judge Beck and John M. Walker, were candidates for District Attorney. At a meeting for joint discussion at Franklin Centre, all the candidates, or nearly all of them, were present, and spoke. Dr. Galland was personally very abusive towards General Reid, who replied in a very short, sarcastic and amusing speech, in which he read from the appendix to the Book of Mormons, the revelation of Joe Smith from the Lord, commanding "his servant, Isaac Galland, to go and preach." This was a clincher, the crowd roared and applauded, and Galland gnashed his teeth with rage, and left the place in disgust. He never made another speech during the campaign. He was a man of personal courage, but had generally a wise discretion, in this, he attacked a man he could easily whip, or whom he could frighten with that most terrible of weapons, before which sometimes the most courageous will fly, a sword cane which he habitually carried.

Devil Creek Bill Clark's favorite weapon was a bowie knife or double-barreled shot gun, and the old Doctor knew him too well to provoke a contest with him. Once Clark got out his double-barreled shot gun and ordered him to take the opposite side of Main street, and the Doctor, knowing his fate if he failed to do it, kept at long range of the shot gun and obeyed orders.

On another occasion on the way up to Fort Madison on a steamer, he attacked ex-Mayor William Leighton, making a thrust at him with this sword cane. But the wiley Scotchman, accustomed to boxing and athletic sports, and at that day full of vim and active as a trained wrestler in the ring, quiet and facetious in a company of gentlemen, but a dare devil in courage when insulted, quick as thought he seized the Doctor, wrested his sword cane from him, and snapped it in twain, threw it into the river. This was the beginning but not the end of it. Galland always wore a pair of gold spectacles, these he jerked off and threw down on the cabin floor, and seizing his adversary, punished him severely, fracturing three of his ribs before they were separated. A few days afterwards, Galland came to him and apologized.

On another occasion Lyman E. Johnson, raised a mob to attack him at his house in Keokuk; they were prowling about, threatening to hang him. .Galland knew who was at the head of the mob, and more, he knew that Johnson, its leader, had no personal courage. Lyman was in the background hissing them on. But knowing Galland's desperate character, they did not dare to attack him by entering his house, as they knew it would be certain death to some of them. While they parleyed, Galland appeared at his door, and addressing the crowd said Johnson was at the bottom of this mob, and pointing him out lurking on the outskirts of the crowd with his virulent tongue denounced him as a coward, and offered to settle the matter then and there, challenging Johnson for a fair fight, but he did not come to time and the mob lacking a courageous leader, left him and went away, his bravado and Johnson's cowardice saved him.

Dr. Galland was the author of some very interesting sketches of the North American Indians, long ago out of print. From his personal acquaintance with these savage sons of the forest, and his acute judgment of the character and motives of men, however much his mind may have been afterwards perverted by prejudice and poisoned by malice, owing to his heart being embitred by disappointments in after years, he, no doubt, gave a more correct statement of their characters than has ever yet been published. Bitter and vindictive, Dr. Galland had many redeeming qualities, he could be a rowdy and lead a mob, could swear like a pirate, and in latter years of his eventful life, filled with so many boisterous scenes, drank to excess, yet when he chose to be so amongst gentlemen in society, he was courtly and elegant, learned in his discourses, entertaining his hearers, and when in this vein was full of humor.

Whatever the faults and sins of his younger years and latter days of his life, over which let us draw the mantle of charity; he was a very remarkable man, one of those characters who come to the surface and figure conspicuously in the rough and varied scenes of a frontier life.

One verse of "Garret Davis'" old war song was:

"I met a possum in the road,
Just by a 'simmon tree,
He curled his tail above his back,
And swore the road was free."

JOHN H. LINES,

now of Salem, Oregon, was clerk of Judge Mason's court when the decree of partition of the half-breed tract was made in 1841.

Another clerk of his court was Orlando Savando Xenophen Peck. He was a cousin of "Cousin William," who taking offense at the Peck family, changed his name from Peck to Telford. They were from New York, and O. S. X. Peck, was last a lawyer on Wall street. Telford has been dead many years. He was the city attorney of Keokuk Feb. 19th, 1848.

Aragoni once kept an eating house and had pies for sale. A purchaser came and examined his pies, found they were spoiled, turned sour. "Never mind!" said Aragoni, "you no like him, no take him; steamboat come along and take him all!"
On his sign was two glasses of beer for 5 cents a piece.

Hon. William J. Cochran introduced the first white clover into Iowa.

Burns & Rentgen were the first agents of the American Express Company in Keokuk, and were succeeded by James Lloyd. Henry W. Linebaugh was the first jeweler.

Paul McClosky was partially insane; he was a shoe maker, and one day took a pair of shoes from Miller's store, and putting them under his arm walked off down the street. A clerk followed him and tried to wrest the shoes from him, but he held on to them as long as he could, saying, "Sir, I've got a mechanic's lien on these shoes!" His left arm offended him, and he took a hatchet and cut it off.

Father J. M. Villiars was the first Catholic priest, and belonged to the Jesuit order of La Trappe. He was very popular outside of his church, and delivered a very able lecture before a literary society by invitation, which was very highly spoken of at the time. He committed suicide at Indianapolis while temporarily insane. He gave the motto for the fine silk flag presented by the ladies to the Keokuk Guards, at the request of Captain T. B. Cuming,
"Sans Peur et sans Reproche"
without fear and without reproach; this motto was applied to Chevalier Bayard, who lived in the time of the French King, Louis XII, in the 15th century and was a most gallant knight.

THE FIRST DAYS OF KEOKUK AS A CITY—THE MAYOR AND FIRST ALDERMEN, WHO THEY WERE AND WHAT HAS BECOME OF THEM—TRAGIC DEATH OF MACKLEY AND READ.

Keokuk was incorporated as a city Dec. 13th, 1847. The first election for city officers was held Monday, Jan. 3d, 1848, and the city officers sworn into office, January 10th, 1848. Our printed City Charter and ordinances, published by authority of the City Council in 1872, contain the act of Incorporation, which is dated December 13th, 1848, which is evidently a mistake and should be 1847.

THE OLD SETTLERS. 151

The candidates for Mayor were William A. Clark, "Whig," and Calohill E. Stone, "Possum Whig;" 175 votes were cast, and Clark was elected by 86 majority. Stone was the veritable "Dornicks," and was a jack-leg lawyer, who first lived at West Point, moved to Keokuk and married a Miss McFadden, whose father kept the Mansion House; she had a sister, two stories high, called "Beck," a brother named "Shep," and another great wall eyed brother "Wall." Stone was once a candidate for the legislature, and when canvassing in the county, Al Donnell says, it was said he lived on hazle nuts. He had great white eyes, and General Browne said, his eyes reminded him of dog wood blossoms.

"Devil Creek" Bill Clark a Kentuckian, and his brother, Joe, (Jurisprudence) commenced business first at Fort Madison in 1840, and at Keokuk were the partners of J. C. Ainsworth & Co.

Clark and Mackley went overland to California in 1853, the party consisted of sixteen men and three families, among whom were Jonas W. Brown, second city clerk. William Van Horn, a singer, John Richardson and family, John and William S. Gray, and Henderson Mackley. James Mackley was killed by the Indians at Honey Lake Valley, on the east side of the Sierra Nevada Mountains, on the old Lawson Cut-off, on the 17th of Sept. 1853. The Indians stole a steer the night before, he took five men and went in pursuit and found its carcass hung up with a butcher knife still sticking in it, in a clump of wild flag trees. The Indians attacked them and Mackley was shot by an arrow in his left breast which emerged under the right shoulder-blade; at 4 p. m., that day, a carriage, which was sent for, came for him and he was taken to camp and died at about 7 p. m., and his remains were taken to Shasta City, California, and interred. He had been to California in 1849 and built the first house in Shasta, returned to Keokuk in 1851, and was going back to settle permanently. He was born in Jackson county, Ohio, came to Keokuk in 1840; he was the first president of the city council in the absence of the Mayor, a man of much enterprise and very popular.

William C. Read was a lawyer, came from Missouri; his wife was a relative of Senator Louis F. Lynn, who once cowhided old Dr. Galland. Read's wife died in Keokuk; he was a democrat and member of the legislature, and was killed by the blowing up of a steamboat at New Orleans, while on his way to California in 1853. Mackley and Read were aldermen of the First Ward.

Captain William Holliday, (Old Rouser) and Heman Bassett were aldermen of the Second ward. Holliday died Aug. 8, 1868, in Keokuk; he was one of the best pilots on the river, was captain of several steamers, and was a very large man, weighing 300; was full of humor, was large hearted, put no value on money, was liberal to a fault. On account of his large stomach, W. C Rentgen named him "Paunch-us-Pilot."

Heman Bassett was first a blacksmith at West Point, then a merchant in Keokuk, and owned a lot of hacks; he went to California, was engaged in mining, and died at the Centennial Exhibition, at Philadelphia, in June, 1876; his identity was established by his certificate of membership of the oldest Masonic Lodge in Keokuk, which was held first in the upper story of the old frame building still standing on Johnson between Second and Third streets occupied as a furniture shop.

J. M. Huston was deputy sheriff under Alexander R. Wheat, was a defaulter for $800, and started to abscond in 1852 but was arrested by Dr. Eads and brought back to Fort Madison. There was snow on the ground at the time and he had started over the plains with wagons. His father became security and paid the money, and he went on to California and is still alive. He lost the money gambling. The writer was once fined five dollars by J. C. Parrott, Justice of the Peace, for contempt of court, which consisted in striking this fellow, Huston, over the head with a little jack oak club, on the trial of a case in which he made himself a little too officious.

John W. Ogden is still living in Ohio; on January 31st, 1848, he moved the appointment of a committee of three to procure rooms for the District Court, and the Methodist Episcopal Church or old "Bee Hive," then in the hazle brush, was hired at $2.50 per day, and rooms for the Grand Jury and Petit Jury were hired from George C. Anderson at $8.00 per month. January 25th, 1848, the office for Mayor and Council was rented from L. E. H. Houghton at $4.00 per month. February 8, 1848, one Dagger was City Engineer; the last meeting of Clark's Administration was held April 15th, 1848. Clark died about a year ago at a little farm he owned near Portland, Oregon; he enlisted as a soldier in the late war in the Washington Guards, which was a mounted military organization, was thrown from his horse and ruptured, and was discharged on surgeon's certificate of disability.

Dr. Justin Millard succeeded Clark as Mayor, April 17th, 1848. Thomas F. Anderson was clerk and wrote out the proceedings in full, and on the 18th of Aug. 1848, says the "Mayor stated there were several bills before the Council and was anxious to progress with and settle them. Alderman Watkins said he considered that action upon the previous minutes would properly be the first business in order; he addressed the council at some length, stating that the accumulation of matters important to the credit of the city, induced the several adjournments in order that a quorum might be found for the transaction of business daily accumulating. Soon as Alderman Watkins took his seat, Mayor Millard rose, and in an abrupt and uncourteous manner said, "*I adjourn the Council!*" and left.

Not signed by the Mayor."

"THOMAS F. ANDERSON, Clerk Council."

Mayor Millard resigned Oct. 17th, 1848, to take effect Nov. 1st, 1848, which on motion of Alderman Silas Haight was unanimously approved, and an election ordered for the 28th inst., to fill the vacancy, and Uriah Raplee was elected to fill the unexpired term, and was again re-elected in April, 1849, and resigned September, 1849. October 19th, 1848, Alderman Creel moved to dispense with the services of Clerk Anderson, and Oct. 19th Jonas W. Brown was elected clerk-protem, and Col. S. R. Curtis appointed to ascertain the grade of Main and Blondeau streets. Alderman Watkins moved that the Marshal be directed to make a demand on Anderson, former clerk, for the "Book of Ordinances with all other books and papers now in his possession, and upon refusing to deliver the City Attorney commence suit." Dixon & Wickersham and L. E. H. Houghton were employed to assist the Marshal; November 4th, by request of attorneys, the charges against the clerk were made known, viz,: "that Mr. Anderson made unnecessary charges in advertising ordinances, by writing more words than the ordinances contained. 2nd. That he altered the records of said Council. 3d. That he was incompetent for the business from time to time when the Council was in session." Anderson still held on to the books against the Marshal and three attorneys, and Clark Johnson, a big alderman, replevied them by taking the books away from him by force and shoving him out of the office. "Tom" Anderson was the clerk of the "Bully Osprey';' he and Dr. Millard are both dead; he died in Central America, and Millard in Oregon.

CHARLES HUBENTHAL, ALDERMAN,

was born in Hesse Kassel, Germany, on the 25th of June 1833, and imigrated to the United States, landing in the City of New York early in the year 1851, and moved thence to the city of Keokuk in 1853, where he has since resided except when temporarily absent in the territories, on the plains, and in California. Engaged in business as a butcher, full of life and enterprise, he has crossed the plains three times since he has lived in Keokuk, the first time in 1863. He returned in the fall of the same year, and in the year 1864 took back a lot of wagons and a drove of mules and remained absent till the winter of 1867, returning in 1869 he was absent till August, 1870, in Idaho, Montana, New Mexico, Utah, and Los Agelos, Southern California. He lived an adventurous life, dealing in stock which he purchased in California and took to the northern mines in the mountains. He has been twice elected alderman of his ward, once in 1873 for two years, and again in 1875, and has served during that time as chairman of the Committee on Cemeteries, as a member of the special Committee on Taxes and many other committees. As an alderman he has exhibited marked executive ability, and has performed his duties in a very able and efficient manner. In politics he is a democrat, and for his genial manners and liberality he is highly regarded by his fellow citizens and is deservedly very popular.

All the members of the legislature and delegates to both the Republican and Democratic conventions, just held at Des Moines in the spring of 1856, were coming down together to Keokuk on a little Des Moines river steamer. The delegates got into a discussion, and M. P. Sharts, a Keokuk alderman said, "I tell you, gentlemen, the democratic party is badly split up! but the republican party is a eunuch! its a eunuch, sir! I tell you its a eunuch!" It has been singing bass ever since.

CAPTAIN H. M. PATTEN AND CAPTAIN BOB FERRIS JUMPING THE CROTON DAM WITH A STEAMBOAT.

The Iowa legislature declared Skunk and Des Moines rivers navigable streams, and might just as well declared the man in the moon a legal voter, or made him conductor on an under-ground railroad. Steamers ran to Des

Moines up that river in 1858, but it was obstructed by dams, and Capt. Patten, one of our old time steamboat captains from 1845, commanded the Clara Hine which was caught above Croton, where the dam was broken, and the water ran around the lock so the boat could not get through it. Capt. Bob Ferris was at the wheel, and on consultation they resolved to jump the dam, which had fourteen feet fall, and turning about went up half a mile, put on a full head of steam, jumped the dam with the boat without any accident.

WILLIAM BLOM, ALDERMAN,

one of our prominent citizens and most active and successful business men was born near Amsterdam, Holland, in November, 1835, came to Keokuk in 1857, commenced work as a clerk at $12 per month, with Kellogg & Birge, saved $80 from his wages, and then he began business on his own account as a Soap and Tallow Chandler Manufacturer, in, which he has been successfully engaged ever since, and in connection with the same runs the Produce, Flour and Meat business; his sales amounting to $150,000 annually; he ships 1000 boxes of soap per month to all parts of the country, and is the largest soap and tallow manufacturer in the state. As alderman of the Sixth ward he is active, efficient and popular; is chairman of the special tax committee, and is on the important committee on fire, streets and alleys. In politics he is a republican, in religion, a member of Chatham Square Methodist Chnrch. A man of tireless energy, he has acquired his fortune by the dint of industry and business capacity. Five different parties had failed in the business of manufacturing soap, etc., on the same ground where he started, which did not deter him, and for fifteen years he has carried it forward with energy and made it a marked success.

HARMON DINGMAN BURYING THE POSSUM.

Harmon Dingman is the oldest living German settler in Fort Madison, and last year celebrated his golden wedding. He is an odity in his way, a good natured old man. He has held many offices such as sexton or "section" as he called it, and City Supervisor. Nothing suited him better than being about the courts, where he sat as a juror or listened to the proceedings, and made comments upon them, while he kept on knitting, (what the ladies call crocheting now,) at a pair of woolen yarn mittens, with a bone hook. In politics Harmon was a democrat, except once, when he bolted and voted for Dan'l F. Miller for Congress, Mrs M. making a five dollar bet with him that D. F. would be defeated, and he wanted that $5. When the Possum party was defeated, on one occasion a big procession of democrats was formed at the Court House, and marched by moonlight, with music through the streets, Harmon at its head, carrying a possum. As he was the "section," he claimed the right to bury it. A grave was dug at the foot of a hickory pole on the levee. Harmon held up the possum, and repeating the baptismal ceremony in German, baptized and buried it, while the procession halted and laughed at and cheered him.

While Dingman was supervisor it was part of his business to bury the carcasses of dead animals. He got his pay in city "Shrip," which would not pass for "Shool" tax, and was only worth fifty cents on the dollar. Fifty cents each was the fee for burying dead hogs. This did not include pigs. An old swine with a litter of thirteen pigs, just a baker's dozen in the family, died in an alley. Harmon was intent on financeering so as to bring city "Shrips" up to par, and buried the drove, and brought in his bill for intering fourteen hogs which was allowed. When teased about it, he insisted that a pig was a hog!

AN OLD LAND MARK.

The oldest house now standing in Montrose, was built for a store house in 1839–40 by D. W., and Edward Kilbourne, who occupied it as a store house Chittenden & McGavic, then Geo. L. Colman and many others have since occupied and used it and it is now used as a meat market stand by Fred Hahn who lives in the rear part. The weather boarding, made of old clap boards shaved smooth with a draw knife, are still in a good state of preservation, though the house is thirty-six years old at least.

Cyrus Peck of Montrose, who died several years ago was a Connecticut yankee, a merchant, and one of the oldest settlers of that place. A man of business, of much energy and pluck, he hated the Mormons and all their rascally coadjuters, and frequently gave the officers information through which they were arrested. They threatened his life but he did not fear them. He often rowed a skiff back and forth to Nauvoo and was remarkable for being able to light his pipe which he always carried on the river, while the wind blew a perfect hurricane.

THE OLD COUNTERFEITER SPURLOCK.

We never heard any other name for him but "Old Spurlock," and by this name he was known over thirty years ago, and as the old counterfeiter,

We never saw him and he never was arrested or tried for passing counterfeit money.

Yet he had the reputation of making counterfeit silver coin. He was an oddity, and a first class swindler, and confidence man. Old sheriffs bailiffs and policemen, who knew him, have frequently told us how he managed to make money on his bad reputation. Taking trips through the country, he exhibited good coin half dollars &c., promising to sell the bogus at fifty cents on the dollar. He made engagements for considerable quantities of spurious coin, and got money advanced on his contracts for delivery at a certain time. The time rolled around, but no Spurlock and no bogus coin was forthcoming. The victims who had been sold did not dare to tell it, and old Spurlock sought out new ones, and thus had the reputation of being a noted countefeiter.

ANECDOTES OF WEST POINTERS.

West Point had many Germans who drank much beer: Jim D. Peebler an old American settler at that place, started a beer saloon, and being much of a wag, put up as his sign "*Beer is what the peoples wants.*"

We asked him who lived in a certain little frame house where Dr. Kuechens father once lived. I know that man said Jim, and have tried to count his children several times, but could'nt do it. Once I counted fourteen, but think there must be more. They kept running in and out of the house so I could'nt see them all together, some were in the house and some were in the yard. He's got fourteen children certain, and I can't tell how many more!

WEST POINT CELEBRETIES.

The early celebreties of West Point were old Dogfennel Wilson, who lived in the suburbs, a gambler named Barton, a noisy constable and bailiff, D. M. Sherman, Adolph Salmon who was post master, and sold whiskey and castor oil; the sir oricle was the old tailor McDanel, and those who came from the country to have a good time in town, were Tom Points, a fist fighter and horse racer, the Stout family, John Duke who burnt lime, and ever looked limy, Solomon Fine who always talked loud enough to be heard across the public square, and last but not least, but the greatest oddity, was Luke Allphin, who lived about three miles out on Sugar Creek, west of town in a bottom full of black haw bushes.

ODDITIES OF LUKE ALLPHIN.

He had a daughter Peggy, a grass widow, and used always to be bragging on "my Peggy."

Luke had two sons, the oldest "Zeb," the youngest a stripling familiarly called "Bud." A young man named "Brad" Wilson lived in the neighborhood, and "Jo" Stotts who "sheriffed" around that neighborhood (stopping in frequently to see "Peggy,") tells us of a surgical operation performed by "Zeb" on "Brad" Wilson, with a "*peggin' awl,*" when he was overdosed with black haws.

Luke pegged at shoes and sitting on his bench cried out.

Bud! Oh, Bud! Where's the "peggin" awl?

I don't know dad!

It's a d—d lie, by g—d you do know!

The last I seed of it dad, Zeb had it picking the black haws from Brad Wilson!

That "peggin" awl was lost. Salmon who watered his whiskey well, could afford to treat, and did treat the country people quite often, and Luke always took what he termed a big "snort" or "mules ear full" at a drink. The price was then a picayune, and Luke knew this well.

Mr. Salmon, said Luke, what's the price of a drink of whiskey?

(Salmon.) A picayune!

What's the price of a drink of castor oil?

(Salmon,) It's all the same sir!"

Then give me a drink of castor oil!

Salmon handed him down a pint bottle of castor oil.

Drawing the cork, he drank the full pint without "batting his eyes."

Putting down a silver picayune on the counter, Salmon took it, smiled quietly, while Luke walked out to entertain a crowd, who were waiting for him on the public square.

Speaking to them of his early life, he said he was just as good a man as he ever had been.

To which! to which! said Luke, I did'nt know a buscuit from a stone, till I was nine year old by g—d (with a loud voice.)
"I was born in Kentucky cradled in a trough,"
"Swam the Ohio and caught the whooping cough."
When the Mexican war broke out, Luke wanted to go. He was over forty-five years of age, and his hair sprinkled with grey. He went to Ft. Madison to volunteer, but was too old. He went to a barber and got his hair dyed and kept trying, but could never get in. He was a reckless, brave, good hearted man, and rendered efficient aid in capturing the Hodges.

OLD JIM BOX AND THE ALCOHOL.

Jim was a good story teller, and lived near West Point in Pleasant Ridge Township, "Cat eyed" Box a relative of his tells a good story on him.

Jim liked brandy, not that he indulged in it to excess, unless it was at some one else's expense.

Knowing his weakness, "cat eyed" Box who was visiting at his house, took the label off of a pint bottle of Perry Davis' Pain Killer, which in color very much resembled brandy, and put it up on his mantle piece.

He put it there especially for old Jim's benefit, and watched him till he came in. Old Jim came at last, and casting a stealthy glance about him to make sure no one saw him, spied the bottle. With cat like tread, he approached it took it up, looked about again, and seeing no one, gulped down half its contents at a single draught.

The Pain Killer swallowed, old Jim sat down the bottle crying out as he sprang or rather bounded madly up in the air, *A-k-e-h-o-l, be gad!* "Cat eye' just then came from his concealment saying: Uncle Jim, that's Pain Killer! while he roared at old Jim's antics.

ORRIN WEBB'S CUB BEARS, AND THE TWO FANCY NEW YORK DRUMMERS. BUCKET, WHARF RAT, AND DEVIL CREEK BILL CLARK.

Bucket Campbell, Wharf Rat, and Devil Creek, went into the billiard room under the Old Rapids Hotel. There was but one billiard table then, the first ever brought to the place, and it was much in demand. They had come to play, but two well dressed, fancy looking, New York drummers, occupied it exclusively. Our party stepped up to the bar and waited till they got tired out from waiting, but the drummers played on, and it seemed as if they would never stop. They gave themselves airs, and ordered hot drinks, while our spectators, looking on, grew more impatient. Putting their heads together they consulted, and made up their minds that our eastern gentlemen were proud, and must be taught a lesson. In a whispered conversation their plan of action was agreed upon. In the rear of his store, up on the hill, Orrin Webb had two half grown cub bears, in a kind of a half cellar, or deep scuttle hole, covered by a trap door. Off they posted, trudging through the mud, up the hill having made up their minds to get those bear cubs and have some fun. Arrived at the spot where they were kept, as they did not consider it necessary to consult Webb, they burst open the trap door. Old Bucket was let down in the dark to get the cubs, and secured them, and with one under each arm commenced to ascend, holding on to the rope by which he was let down. It was a new thing for the cubs, and they were restless, and commenced to scratch, and Bucket dropped them and came up. Devil Creek swore he would get them, and this time he descended into the den and brought up the bears.— Bucket took one and Wharf Rat the other, and very unconcernedly the three entered the billiard room where the fancy drummers were still playing, each standing with a billiard cue in his hand by the table, opposite each other.— Bucket advanced quietly, while Wharf Rat did likewise, and at the same moment put down a cub bear before each of the drummers, on the billiard table. This was done so suddenly that it seemed to the astonished drummers as if they had fallen from the clouds, and they were startled from their propriety.— Wharf Rat gave one of his unearthly war whoops in his loud, clear, inimitable voice, and Devil Creek and Bucket, as if by concert, joined in the terrific chorus. One of the drummers fainted on the spot, the other gave a wild stare, his eyes standing out with the insane glare of a maniac. He stood as if transfixed, for a moment, gave one bound, cleared the door, and fell down in the muddy street. Had he been kicked by a mule, he could not have received a more violent shock. With the clay mud sticking to his store clothes, he gathered himself up and ran till he was met and stopped in his mad career by constable Harriot, who, having heard the racket, supposed he was an escaped felon. A bucket of water was thrown over his partner, who recovered consciousness.— A crowd had gathered in by this time of all the "Rats" in the vicinity, who now had a big time at the expense of the drummers, who joined in the revelry, laughed heartily at their own discomfiture, and now, instead of being considered "stuck up," were the most popular gentlemen in town. They told the story to their friends in the east, and remembered Keokuk and their romantic adventure to the end of their days.

THE MISSOURI PUTNAM—A WOLF HUNT.

George Heywood was one of the oldest settlers of Clark county, and died only about a year ago at the age of eighty-five years.

His son, William H. Heywood, Esq., now residing at or near St. Francisville, who came there with his father when a boy, and is now over sixty years old, and a fine looking specimen of a man, tall, erect, well proportioned, and is possessed of a winning address, fluent conversational powers, and has a remarkable memory. He has told us many amusing stories of the old settlers. His father kept the post office where he now lives, and the old army officers from Fort Des Moines used to come there for their mail matter on horse back. He knew them all, and on one occasion saw Robert E. Lee, then a Lieutenant.

He told us a good story of a wolf hunt, in which Col. Montgomery and Senator George K. Biggs figured as the heroes. For daring and courage on the part of Biggs, it rivals the adventures of Putnam, so familiar to every school boy.

One winter night, in 1833, they had been to church to hear Rev. Mr. Allen preach, down on Fox river; before the days when our old friend Frank Hagerman hunted deer and wild turkeys on the Wyaconda, (Wakendah). Going home on horseback, the ground being covered with snow a foot deep, they heard on the prairie the loud howling of wolves rivaling in its sounding fury the echoes from a Methodist camp-meeting revival. They bantered each other to go on a wolf chase, and starting from the sand ridge on a gallop, soon swooped down upon the noisy pack, disturbing their amusement of picking the bones of a dead horse and snarling and snapping at each other. Soon they were in their midst, and the cowardly wolves took to their heels. Montgomery was armed with a huge horse pistol, Biggs was unarmed. Each selected his wolf, thinking it would be no big job to run him down. The wolves took different directions, and the John Gilpin race commenced. Montgomery's wolf took to the high grass on the prairie, and he pursued him for two miles when he took the back track and was killed near the starting point. Biggs' wolf, a huge timber monster, took the direction of Churchville, thither he pursued him, his festive venture, as the sequel will prove, well nigh ended in a tragedy. At first the wolf distanced him, but his powerful and fleet horse soon gained upon him and the wolf, panting, with his tongue lolling out, and foaming at the mouth, finding he was about to be overtaken, turned with glaring eyes in an attitude of defense upon his pursuer. His great open red mouth, full of long, sharp, glittering, white teeth, could be distinctly seen by Biggs in the moonlight. His horse halted suddenly, not from fear, but from being taken by surprise at the sudden halt made by the wolf. His rider, strong, powerful, full of activity and courage, spurred him onward, charging on the wolf, with one hand he reached down and seized him by the neck. The quick shock of the meeting dismounted him, and he fell to the ground, but did not lose his hold of the wolf. His horse, with almost human intelligence, stood still while they struggled in the deep snow. The wolf snapped and bit at him, but his heavy, full-cloth overcoat, with its three heavy capes, buttoned up to the chin, was too much for the wolf, and saved him from death. With a grip of iron, he held the wolf by the neck with one hand, and with the other he managed to get out his big pocket knife which he managed to open with his teeth, and then, with one thrust, he stabbed the monster to the heart. The snow was covered with blood, and those who saw the wolf say he was one of enormous size, one of the largest timber wolves. The snow bore evidences of a most terrible struggle, and the feat of capturing and killing that wolf was a rare specimen af the heroic courage of the times, which Biggs took to be a matter of ordinary occurrence; but Rev. Mr. Allen wrote him up in the Salt River Gazette, and the story of his terrible adventure has become familiar to the old settlers and their children as household words, and Hon. George K. Biggs has been honored by many places in the gift of the voters of his county, and is now a representative in the Missouri Senate.

HOLDING A PANTHER BY THE TAIL.

Jonathan Clark, of Clark County, Mo., John and Bill Hurst, of Hancock County Illinois, went on a hunt in 1834 near St. Francisville, Mo., and sending out their dogs soon "ruffled something," which took to the first tree a hundred yards distant. John Hurst fired with uncertain aim and wounded the animal which proved to be a very large panther. Infuriated by his wound it sprang to the ground and attacked the dog, and was about to prove too much for him. Here Bill appeared upon the scene, and seeing his dog in danger seized the panther by the tail with both hands. The panther now attempted to turn upon him, and the dog let go his hold on the "varmint." The panther made desperate efforts to bite him, but when he turned Bill would give him a sudden jerk when he would spring forward jerking Bill with great violence after him. Thus they had it, Bill jerked the panther and the panther jerked Bill. His "faithful dog" looking on as a disinterested spectator, while John was attempting to load his gun, but the ball got fast mid way the gun barrel. Clark ran towards the nearest timber for a club. Bill by this time was nearly exhausted, but his dog had recovered his wind and his courage and again seized the panther, which now changed the base of its operations from him, to attack the dog in front.

John cried out, now is your time Bill, go for blood! Letting go the panthers tail with his right hand, he drew his huge bowie knife made from a mill saw file, and with one desperate thrust plunged it up to the hilt in the panthers bowels. As the animal fell to the ground dead, he sank down where he stood exhausted by his terrible struggle. In a moment however he recovered and sprang up to view the dead panther; which was found on measurement to be eleven feet long from the end of his nose to the tip of his tail.

The people all over the country for miles about, came to take a view of the battle ground and see the " Painter," and the victor at the fight and when at the funeral declared that he was " a hoss of a feller."

THE TWO LAWYERS IN THE CIRCUS RING MAKE A NIGHT OF IT. DIXON & BLENNERHASSET.

R. S. Blannerhasset a noted criminal lawyer of St. Louis, and said to be a relative of the crazy Englishman Herman Blannerhasset, mixed up with Aaron Burr's projected conquest of Mexico, and his alleged treasony used to come to Fort Madison to court as attorney for the settlers on the Half Breed Tract. George C. Dixon, Esq., and himself, were employed by them to defend in a large number of ejectment suits brought by owners of lands under the decree title against the squatters called settlers. Dixon & Blannerhasset made a written contract with them for fees, fifty or more of the settlers signed it, and it was what is called a joint and several contract. The lawyers could sue one alone or all the settlers jointly, in case they failed to perform their part of the stipulations. Our lawyers were at Court, and stopped with W. C. Stripe at the Madison House,

Jo Schmelzle kept a pigeon hole table in his restaurant, half a square from the hotel, and between the hotel and Joe's place, was an open space used by all shows and circuses. There was a regular circus ring or pathway for the elephant and horses, trampled into the earth, where Ulysus and the pony, as old Jesse Grant had it, " went round and round!"

Mr. Dixon was lame in one leg, which was shorter than the other.

One dark night Dixon, Blannerhasset and Charley Hyde, a well known citizen, went down to Joe's to play a few games of pigeon hole, as amusements then they were few, in a little town, time hung heavily on their hands. It rained, they got interested and kept playing until it was past midnight, when they all concluded to go to the hotel. They started, Dixon in the lead Blannerhasset next, and Hyde last, and reached the pathway in the circus ring and following it Mr. Dixon went on limping as he went, Blannerhasset covering his file leader, and Hyde covering his file leader, and thus they went on supposing they were on the direct route to the hotel.

Mr. Dixon was a good walker, and tramped along rapidly, his companions following without question where he led.

It seemed a long way to the hotel, but they marched on, and thus tramp, tramp they went, and still the hotel was no nearer. They marched several hours thus, and the weather being warm they grew tired and perspired freely.

It was too dark to see their way, but at length the grey dawn came, then streaks of sunlight in the east, and it was day light—they could see their way! Mr. Stripe was an early riser, "early birds catch the worm;" and he was up early that morning looking for the worm!

He looked down the river toward Schmelzles, and there he saw the three beleagured wanderers marching about the circus ring, Dixon still in advance, his shortest leg in the inner side of the ring, bobbing up and down as he led them!

Stripe called to them, they answered and the thing was explained; they had been marching about that circus ring all night, to get half a square to the Madison house, Stripe's hotel, and were not there yet, though all the time they thought they were on the way.

This was just as good a thing as Stripe wanted—he told it on them, and they enjoyed hearing it themselves, for no one liked a joke better than George C. Dixon, even if it was at his own expense, and few could tell a story better. Blannerhasset was jovial and loved to mix in a crowd and talk, for with his rich Irish brogue, and his inimitable way of telling a story, he was always the center of attraction in the social circle. All recollect the late George C. Dixon, Esq., as a very learned lawyer. But few here knew Blannerhasset, who in his day at St. Louis, was at the head of the bar as a great criminal lawyer. He was at no lack for words, and was an eloquent and effective speaker, but he was not a land lawyer. But this did not matter, the settlers employed him on his great reputation as a criminal lawyer, and he came; they had no case, but he made an effort for them. Dixon furnished the legal authorities and read from them, he had a cart load of them in court, and Blannerhasset did the speaking, commenting on the authorities, but they were defeated and the settlers refused to pay their fees, and they sued them on the joint and several contract, sueing every settler separately. The settlers defended and claimed the attorneys had not attended to their business, and set up that as a defense, and one case was selected as a test case, from all the suits brought, and tried before a jury, the attorneys themselves Dixon & Blannerhasset, agreeing with the settlers to abide the result of this suit, which was to decide all, if the settlers got beaten in this one case they agreed to pay the fees in all. The trial commenced, the contract was read and submitted, its execution was not denied and plaintiffs closed their case.

11

It was now time to hear the defense who had Charley Hyde and W. C. Stripe for their witnesses.

They went on to prove by Hyde about the games of pigeon hole they played at Schmeltzles, and he closed his testimony by telling in his quizzical way, how they marched all night around that circus ring, and as he told his story, and told it well, the court and lawyers listened and smiled, and some of them disturbed the gravity of the occasion by laughing aloud.

Stripe confirmed Hydes story, and the country jury thought this was awful and gave a verdict for the defendants.

Dixon & Blannerhasset got no fees except their retainer, but had no end of fun about that nights adventure in marching around the circus ring, following in the tracks of the elephant.

Frank Jolly, was an old timer who lived in Green Bay bottom, and was the only son of Lewis Jolly, an old settler, who was always a delegate to democratic conventions. Frank used to chop wood on Green Bay island, a great resort for wood choppers. It was near Lost Creek, a creek which at high water overflowed the low grounds of the whole country, and at low water was used by the Christian Church for baptizing its numerous converts. Frank and some of the wood choppers had a row, and he tore down their log cabin.

He was arrested for it and brought before Squire James D. Gedney. On the day of the trial Frank was there, and so were the wood choppers and several spectators. Here in their presence the quarrel was renewed, and Frank, shaking his fist in the face of one of the wood choppers said d——n you, I tore down your cabin *but you can't prove it!*

LIBERTY ELISHA HOLMES HOUGHTON. KEOKUK'S FIRST ASSESSOR.

Was a noted character in the early days of our city, going back to 1840 in the days of "Rat Row," and to the time of all the notorious characters who cavorted about as scallawags, played poker and gave the war whoop, and pranks on their neighbors by letting their bears loose, and were first at a fight and in at the death. His front name was not short and sweet, nor a name at which the world grew pale, he signed it as a Notary Public to deeds, it appears on the records L. E. H. Houghton, very many times, from the days of the oldest inhabitant till he left here for Texas in 1857, but it cannot be said he left his country for his country's good for he was harmless and innocent as a child.

We have given his initials as he wrote them, and many have forgotten that such a man ever lived. But his life may still point a moral or adorn a tale. As our caption indicates, his full name was Liberty Elisha Holmes Houghton! That his mother was a woman of brilliant imagination is indicated by his name, that she transmitted many of her qualities to her gifted son there can be no doubt, but whether Elisha was ever fed by the ravens, we have no record to tell us, but there were times when a contribution from them would have been as gratefully accepted as the donation of a congregation of the Methodist Church to the starving family of one of their pious and self sacrificing circuit riders.

He was a little short man with iron grey hair, and when he walked about with his long waisted blanket coat which he wore winter and summer, with red and blue and brown rings around the tail, he was always looking up—looking as if gazing at the stars—he was said to be moon-eyed.

He was better off in the way of children than "Old Shady," of the song who

"Had a wife and one little baby,"
"Way up north in old *Canady*,"

for he had a wife and nine children, and in him the old adage was verified, a fool for luck and a poor man for children. He kept a dog and a gun, and took the children to all the circuses including the side shows. During Court he walked about looking wise above what is written carrying some law books under one arm, and in one hand, a long green baize bag filled with legal papers—the papers filed in chancery cases to set aside the decree—and at his heels, walked in solemn procession, old Benjamin F. Messenger, with the map of the Half Breed Tract, Dr Green and Frederick Parks with his red face, and ponderous stomach, puffing and blowing and talking loud, they were all *settlers*, looking for an earthquake to shatter the Decree into fragments so they could "get their rights."

Notarial business was good in Houghtons time, and he had most of it and got well paid for it. He understood this if he understood anything. He was very poor but took in considerable money, but his large family were scantily clothed and badly fed, and at times went hungry to bed. When Houghton got a five dollar bill, instead of buying bread, meat, sugar and coffee, he posted off to the first fruit stand and bought banannas, marched to a grocery store and got cans of oysters, a big dressed turkey, then marched home to his family who were looking for his coming, for they had nothing for dinner. It took little time to cook, they were too hungry to wait, the dinner once on the table, they sat down and feasted as contrabands in the army used to do when they had three days rations issued to them at once, their masters had been in the habit, of issuing a single meal to them at one time when slaves, so they kept on eating and eating as the victim of a tape worm eats, till everything before them was gone. They continued living on from one day to another, for weeks months and years, always hopeful, for Houghton was not a hypochondriac, he was happy, Macawber like, waiting for something to turn up.

He was resolved to make a spoon or spoil a horn sometime, he was looking through the long lane which must sometime have a turning, at the landscape in the distance peopled with golden prospects, with its halo of brightness glittering in the sunshine, where the old grey horse was browsing amid the red May roses. The ravens fed Elijah, manna rained down from the heavens, and quails came in flocks to the children of Israel in the wilderness as they followed the cloud by day and pillar of fire by night, and why then should not a rosy future come to our hero, the chancery lawyer with his moon-eyes and ringtailed coat!

He consoled himself with his fishing rod, and put out trout lines from his skiff, buoyed by stone jugs—the origin of the noted "stone jug fishing club," and sometimes killed a wild turkey or captured a deer while in the water swimming the river.

He was the first assessor, acted for a time as city attorney, started a book bindery and ran it until 1852.

Shortly after, property commenced rising, fortune must come to him now, and come it did.

He got a partner.

He was a singing master and elocutionist.

He could make a loud ringing speech, a speech with many words and little in it.

All political aspirants and young half fledged orators made speeches then to the settlers.

One night there was a settlers meeting and his opportunity came to make a speech, his first speech.

They strode about in the dog fennel and listened to him with open mouths and upturned faces toward the speaker; the balmy air of flower crowned June carried his eloquent words through and beyond the listeners who applauded and cheered him. The pale moon and bright stars looked down approvingly from the cloudless blue skies above them upon the orator and patriot, the new recruit who has come to live and die with them—he is "friendly to the settlers!" They take him by the hand when he has concluded and congratulate him, he has made a ten strike, and visions of Congress come to him in his dreams, he is proud of his effort! Houghton is proud too, the settlers come to their office and consult them, and they look wise and talk learnedly, get down the authorities and show them how they can win, and the settlers go away impressed with the idea that this man the new lawyer, with so many books must be the man to break the decree, he must know it all, and talking about him among themselves say he has more books than any lawyer in town—wonder if he has read them all!

HARLOW H. BELDING.

He came from across the waters of the great Mississippi from the city of Nauvoo and the Mormon prophet, to seek his fortune, a young lawyer, a widower, comely in person with a winning address and pleasing manners, and with the well modulated musical voice of a singing master. He had some money, something rare in that day, a large library, and a large capital of brass, for cheek in a new country and to a stranger in a strange land is at the beginning a winning card.

He wants a partner, a partner for life—a partner too in the law, and having looked over the happy surroundings, he falls in with the great chancery lawyer who tells him of the brilliant prospects and he is enraptured, and they form a law partnership, and open an office.

There was no money in catering to the settlers, and Belding soon found it out. He must make his fortune, so he rushed into land speculation, and took Houghton in with him. They bought a tract of land for sixty dollars an acre, and sold it for one hundred and fifty; and now Houghton was rich, he owned several houses, and his family fared sumptuously every day, on the fat of the land.

He was now resolved to be a public benefactor.

THE FIRST THEATRE OF KEOKUK.

He started the first theatre in the city of Keokuk, located on Main street between 3d and 4th, up stairs, over the dry goods store rooms, the building having been erected by the Hon. Robert P. Creel, an alderman of the city, also member of the Legislature in 1856, and since sheriff of Lee county. This theatre was called "Houghton's Varieties."

Judge Ralph P. Lowe also held the District Court sessions in the same building, which was a hall capable of containing a thousand people. Houghton was the "lawyer Greasy," of history and of old Daniel McCready's poem. W. F. B. Lynch and Harlow H. Belding were his principal actors, and after them, the ranting Thom. Duff. The same room was used by the old "Charity balls" when Wm. Timberman, Jo. Patterson, Jakey Landes, Ed. Booth, Harry Fulton, John Scroggs, Iron Clad Stannus, and others "tripped the light fantastic toe!"

Duff used to play Richard III, Claude Melnotte, in the Lady of Lyons, and Lynch played Iago to Belding's Othello.

Mrs. Duff played Pauline in the Lady of Lyons, and Lucretia Borgia; she was the sister of the Mormon Elder Adams, a theatre actor.

The old varieties was not grand enough, and Belding & Lynch got up a joint stock company, and built a theatre of their own, the "Atheneum" on 2d street, where Shook played Toodles, and many celebreties fretted their brief hour upon the stage.

Belding married the "lone daughter of the house and heart" of Anti Christ!

Houghton went to Tarrant, Henderson County, Texas, and his last letter in 1857, said: "Any man who comes here and has his health, and is industrious, can make a fortune in ten years, without a cent of money, my case!"

Belding was full of humor, had a keen sense of the ridiculous. Possessed of a good memory, he could commit a speech by hearing it once or twice. Having an appointment to make a temperance speech at Hamilton, Ill with Lynch, whose speech he had heard read, and he committed from hearing it. Lynch insisted on Belding making the first speech, which Lynch listened to dum founded, and when his time came to speak, begged to be excused. Belding had stolen his speech!

When Judge Clagett was a candidate for Judge in 1858, Gerrard, Edwards and Marshall were opposed to him, and Belding claimed to be with them. They appointed an anti Clagett meeting, and before the night came on for their speeches, Belding interviewed them all—they hated Clagett, and some of them hated each other. A crowd was collected that night at the corner of 5th and Main streets, and Belding opened the meeting, telling all they had told him, and talking of all of them, ridiculing their weak points in a most amusing manner, convulsing his auditors with merriment for over an hour, at the expense of the anti-Clagett lawyers, most of whom walked off cursing.

But when they got over their pet, all of them enjoyed it, as no one could stay in a bad humor with Belding.

THE FIRST, FIRST-CLASS HOTEL—THE LACLEDE HOUSE. PRESSELL & ALLYN. THE OLD STAGE COMPANIES. METHODIST AND BAPTIST CHURCHES. THE GUYGER FAMILY.

The "Laclede" was always a popular name for steam boatmen.

Captain Daniel W. Pressell, afterwards Quarter-master in the 21st Mo. Infantry in the late war, and Thomas H. Allyn, for two terms the popular County Treasurer of Lee County, opened this house as a first-class hotel in 1851 and kept it over five years.

Charles H. Guyger first built it, and Madam Guyger kept it. When Pressell & Allyn became proprietors, all the first-class travelers stopped there. It was the headquarters for the Stage Companies, Frink & Walker, and the Western Stage Companies lines, when Samuel Patrick, John Devolvus, A. K. George, Charley Mead and Wm. Potter were general agents at Keokuk, Dave Remick at Burlington, and Harry Cleghorn at Montrose, and Homer Judd for the Missouri stage company.

The Holliday house was just below it, where billiards and cards and ten pins, attracted all the fast men who took mixed drinks.

Just across the street was the May Flower, kept by Neuse & Barlow who started the first "Kino" table.

Game was then plenty, deer swam the river, and were frequently caught by men rowing skiffs in the midst of the stream, and quails were so plenty that flocks of them flew into town and striking against the sides of white houses fell down dead. On the 5th of February 1855, a meeting was held at the old "Bee hive," now "Banner Mission" Methodist Church, of which Rev. R. S. Robinson was chairman, and D. W. Pressell secretary, at which it was resolved that the trustees of Chatham Square Methodist Episcopal Church, proceed to build said Church as soon as $1.000 in addition to what was then subscribed was collected." The money was collected and the Church was built out of the money subscribed exclusively in Keokuk.

While speaking of Churches, the first Baptist Church ever used in the city, stood on the corner of the alley on 3d street, underpinned or propped up, standing on pieces of logs, sawed in two parts about two feet from the ground; hogs would run under it and squeal in the midst of the service.

The Guyger family consisted of the Madam, who was the "boss," her husband a little old man with a large scar on his forehead, and as he was not remarkable for intelligence, had probably been sometime kicked by a mule! Oscar was the only son, a sleepy, slip shod nonentity, and though he had no scar on his head, there are strong grounds to believe that he had at some time in his life been *kicked by a mule too!* The madam was a slattern, odoriferous with dishwater, and had never become very intimate with soap and rain water, but she slashed about like a man and she and Mrs. Rollman, a buxom round faced pastry cook, ran the "masheen," and were the subjects of much gossip, as they were very frisky, if not fragrant—and like Dr. Mary Walker that lively walking mummy, had a chronic hankering after breeches.

HON. JOHN N. IRWIN, MAYOR, a native of Ohio, was born in Butler County, Dec 25th, 1845, graduated with high honors at Dartmouth College, New Hampshire, studied law in the office of Rankin & McCrary, was admitted to the bar in 1869, and formed a partnership with James Hagerman, one of our most promising young lawyers, and continued in the practice but a short time, long enough, however, to exhibit his superior legal capacity which would have made him an eminent practitioner. The wholesale dry goods firm of Irwin Phillips & Co., of which his father is the head, offering him superior inducements, he quit the law with regret, and commenced life as a merchant entering the office of that firm.

He organized the Loan and Building Association of which he has been an active member, and helped to make it a success. In 1871 he was married to Miss Mamie Rankin, the beautiful and accomplished daughter of that astute lawyer and popular citizen, the late Judge John W. Rankin, by whom he has two children.

He was elected a member of the General Assembly in the fall of 1875, as a republican, the only member of that party elected in the county, which is largely democratic.

As a member of that body he was soon conspicuous, advocating such measures as he deemed to be for the interests of the State at large, regardless of party trammels, and at the same time, he interested himself in every measure of value to his own constituents.

On his return from Des Moines, he was elected Mayor of Keokuk in April, 1876, the youngest man who has ever yet held that office, the arduous duties of which he has filled with great administrative ability, and to the satisfaction of people of all parties.

It has been his ambition as mayor, to pursue such a course as would best promote the financial interests of the city, now on the highway to prosperity, after being for years under a cloud of debt.

As a public speaker Mr. Irwin is graceful, and fluent in delivery, and sometimes indulges in classical quotations, and poetical flights of oratory abounding in beauty, originality and pathos. Without political aspirations, the positions he has held have not been from his seeking, but unsolicited. And thus far as a public officer it can be said of him, well done thou good and faithful servant.

"Kilkenney" Perdew, was defending a case, when he was sued on a promisory note of $5.00 before an old bald headed justice: he had no good defense but plead want of consideration but failed to establish it.

In his speech before the court, he said this is a clear case, and if you decide against me here, I will take it up on appeal to the District Court, and from that to the Supreme Court of the United States, from there to the Court in Bank, and if I am beaten there will take it to the high Court of E-e-h-e-e-q-u-e-r! He won the suit.

John Gaines had a trial in the winter of 1837-8 before him, in Rat Row. The Wrights were arrested for hog stealing—he called a jury who sat on a long bench, got a tin cup full of corn whiskey, put brown sugar in it, took a drink first himself and then handed it to the jury who passed it along from one to the other till they all had a drink. In the midst of the trial there was a free fight out side and the court adjourned to let the jury see it, and when it was over, passed around the cup again, and went on with the trial; Gaines was born December 23d, 1803, at Bloomfield New York, and died at Keokuk, April 21st, 1839.

John Judah had a suit before him, in which a party was sued on a note for $10; the defendent put in a set off of ten cents. Judah took the account and note, and figuring it up said, ten from ten and nothing, and this court decides the constable pays the costs.

JAMES F. DAUGHERTY, ALDERMAN, is a native of Ohio, came to Keokuk in 1841 with his father, one of our old and enterprising merchants who died of cholera on the Missouri river July 16, 1852. He was also extensively engaged in running hacks and towing boats over the rapids.

By his premature death his son James F, then but 17 years of age, was left the head of a large family, and continued to prosecute the business of his father.

Since then he has been engaged in the confectionary, and laterally in the wholesale liquor trade; he was deputy clerk of the District Court under Charles Doerr, and made a popular officer. At the breaking out of the war he raised a company for the 10th Missouri Infantry, and was made captain. All Iowa regiments having their quoto, compelled him to enter a Missouri regiment which was at once put into active service in the interior of that state, then filled with rebel guerrillas, was ordered thence before Corinth, Mississippi, was engaged in the siege till that place was evacuated. His regiment being consolidated with the 22d Missouri Infantry, he was mustered out, having made his mark as a gallant and efficient officer.

He is now alderman of "Hoop pole" ward and when a boy, attended the first school ever opened for white children, taught by old "Anti Christ."

Captain Daugherty is extensively acquainted, has traveled and read much, is a close observer with quick perceptive faculties, and has an inexhaustible fund of humorous anecdotes. An old settler, who came when our city was a village in the woods, he has helped to build it, and make its history.

General Browne was reported dead, and said he could whip the man who started the report.

Jim Hardin left the Democrats and joined the possum party, of which Daniel F. Miller Esq. was the leader. Jim McOlgan a drayman, was a possum and early one morning, Hardin was going down town to get his bitters, when he saw McOlgan stealing hay out of Millers hay mow, and went and told him of it, supposing he would be very indignant, but Miller said, I always knew he was a thief, but never mind, say nothing about it, HE VOTES WITH US!

Jim Hardin left the possums and went back to the democrats, and told this story at a democratic meeting.

D. F. Miller, Esq., the Nestor of the Lee County bar was defending the son of the widow "Alie" for murder.

With a long serious face and a pathetic voice, he was reading to the jury from the Bible, the story of the widows son and commenting on it. Tears came to the eyes of many by standers, and jurors, and among the rest lawyers Rankin and Marshall were overcome with emotion, and wept. Millers son was listening and saw them all cry, and went home and told his mother about it who said, did you cry my son? The boy was up to snuff and replied. No! ma, I knew pa too well! The widow's son was acquitted.

Edward Cole a Keokuk J. P. had a whiskey case before him, Clagett & Browne defended, and the prisoner was discharged in the face of a decision of the Supreme Court. The Gate City attacked Cole about it, and Clagett wrote out a learned opinion for him, in which he overruled the Supreme Court, which was published, and signed E. Cole, Justice of the Peace.

AN IRISH BOY'S ADVENTURES, AND GOOD LUCK.

The Green Emerald Isle was devastated by famine caused by the loss of Paddys staff of life, the destruction of bread, caused by the potato rot in old Ireland. The corn meal sent to them from America made them sick, and when they spoke of it they no longer licked the blarney stone, they thought it was poisoned. Many of them resolved to leave there, and our young broth of a boy came to America, to Keokuk, in 1851.

From reports which came to the "ould country," he thought it must be a great city of 20,000 inhabitants, with splendid buildings, graded streets and pea nut stands at the corners, with music from Italian vagrants with trained monkeys, but judge of his surprise, when he found only a few hundred people living in log and frame houses. He was discouraged, but in a few days thought better of it and concluded he could live here; he went to work digging a cellar at 50 cents a day, this over, he got sick and disheartened, but Supervisor Anthony employed him to drive a cart on the streets for four weeks at fifty cents a day and forgot to pay him; next he tried it again at the same price, wheeling dirt and boarded himself; in 1853 he bought a saw buck and saw, and charged on wood piles at 50 cents a cord. James L. Estes offered him a town lot on Main street to saw five cords of wood; but he had no money to build on it, and did not take it. Winter came on, he went to pulling out ice at 75 cents a day; the first day his boots froze so, the next morning he could not get them on, and next day he went out in his sock feet, it was cold but he stood it out.

He saw much for a boy and witnessed the raid of the settlers, 400 in number, coming into town threatening to burn it. His description of them is unique and graphic—they were on horseback, some with saddles, others with a sheepskin as a substitute, and many riding barebacked. They wore all kinds of clothes, many colored as a rain bow, with caps and hats worse of the wear, some wore beards, others had none, their faces being sunburnt or the color of a boiled lobster, many were painted, others had their faces blackened so as to disguise them. Some carried pitchforks, others clubs, and many shot guns that looked at though they had been used in the battle of Brandywine, thus they paraded the streets and blew off steam, but no body was hurt and they left and went back to Sugar Creek, and all was quiet in Cateraugus. In 1859 he started a little grocery on the market on $50.00, he was well acquainted with the Irish and did well; the banks broke, the war came, and he broke too; he smelt blood and went to the war, fought and bled at Pittsburg Landing and at Corinth, came back after two years, singing that good old song

"Whose been here since I've been gone."

Clerked for **Daugherty**, made $250.00, bought out Thom. B. Patterson & Co., for $2,000, gave his notes at 12 and 18 months at 10 per cent and paid them off when due, and increased his stock at the same time, and got married and went on swimmingly till he bought the big brick building at $2,500 at the corner of Johnson and 5th streets, and now does business under the hall where the "Sons of Malta" held high carnival, and in summer time sits under the shade of the old elm tree; but he will not eat corn meal since the famine in Ireland. The lucky Irish boy is James Martin of the Elm Tree Grocery.

LEWIS R. REEVES, was in his time the ablest practicing resident land lawyer of Lee County, and was born in Trumbull County, Ohio, May 21st, 1817, was first a jeweler, then studied law, practiced first at Fort Madison, and then removed to Keokuk where he died of cholera September 18th, 1854. He was largely interested in half breed lands, and purchased the property on which was laid off Reeves, Perry & Wolcotts addition, Col. Perry and Arthur Wolcott as partners.

He practiced law with great success, was a partner of the law firm of Reeves & Miller then having an extensive collecting business; after his death his widow whose maiden name was Eliza Winter, daughter of a Unitarian minister of Knoxville, Ill, married Judge Samuel F. Miller, her husbands late partner, now one of the justices of the U. S. Supreme Court, once of the law firm of Rankin, Miller & Enster; Judge Miller when practicing stood at the head of the bar in the state, and now has a national reputation and should have been Chief Justice. Mr. Reeves amassed valuable property and personally had many friends. He had a long law contest with one "Garry Lewis," and finally beat him, and in consequence was given the sobriquet "Garry." Reeves had much sly humor at times, and it was he who gave the name of the "Land Pirate" to M. M. Morrill of Nauvoo.

Mrs. Miller is a very estimable lady of winning manners, and brilliant parts, of quick perceptions, and decided character, handsome, graceful and accomplished; she is the acknowledged leader of Washington society.

THE HERO OF BLOODY RUN.

An old setler Butcher, came from Baltimore, Maryland, set up shop with knife and cleaver, and located his slaughter house at the lower end of Bloody

THE OLD SETTLERS.

Run, sometimes called Maiden Run and again, Jiggery's Branch, near the rivers bluff, just beyond it is low ground, and not much further on the river, into which it empties. The butcher always went down to the slaughter house in the mornings at day light.

One night there came a tremendous rain storm—next morning Bloody Run had overflowed its banks, and the heretofore sluggish stream was running in torrents. The butcher started to the slaughter house, driving his favorite old grey horse "Gramalkin," and in trying to cross the stream, horse wagon and driver were carried down with the flood.

He said his prayers, expecting instant death, but in passing on, the friendly branches of an over hanging elm tree were seen and seized by him and he was saved. The horse and wagon were carried onward by the mad waters of the resistless tide, and the wagon was found weeks afterwards four miles below at Alexandria, Mo. But the faithful "Gramalkin," now food for cat fish was never seen or heard of more. Like a faithful soldier he died with the harness on.

He could have no funeral procession, no tomb in enduring granite to perpetuate his memory, and his master growing pathetic, instead of an epitaph wrote a poem which rhymed very much like those sweet and euphonous words Frederick and May pole. The butcher then rushed into speculation—bought two cub bears, was offered fifty dollars for them at home, but took them to St. Louis to market. He marched up street holding the chain fastened to the colar of each pet in either hand, feeling good, and stepping higher than a blind horse. A crowd followed him, he was offered $100 for the bears. But no! that was not enough—he had set his heart on a higher figure. The boys now resolved on sport, got sharp sticks, and prodding the bears in the ribs they grew frantic. When he ran at one boy who tormented one bear, some one on the out skirts prodded the other But he held on to the chains while he was alternately jerked by the infuriated beasts first on one side and then on the other while he plead and protested to no purpose. The boys were hard hearted, and resolved to have a free menagerie of their own, and they had it.

The owner of the bears got sick, exhausted and disgusted, there was no rest for the wicked. A stranger now came along and benevolently offered him five dollars for the two bears, and John Hiner of the "Peoples Market," sold out his show and came home with his eye teeth cut, resolved to stick to hogs and horned cattle and let wild beasts alone.

A French milliner brought on the crisis and hurried up the sale, coming out at her door just as one of the cubs was about to charge on her show window.

DAVID G. LOWRY, ALDERMAN—3d Ward has been a resident of Keokuk continuously ever since October 1855, and when quite a boy carried the Keokuk Daily Post for fifteen months, was after this for several years a news boy on the Des Moines Valley Rail Road, and part of this time there was no express company running over the road, consequently he was intrusted with thousands of dollars in money by business men, and acted as a private messenger, carrying valuable packages which he stowed about his person, never loosing a dollar. In 1862 he bought a news depot, that business being then in his fancy. Employing an army of news boys he supplied the public with the latest papers and the latest news during the war of the rebellion, and by his rare executive talent, and tireless personal attention to his business, made it a decided success, constantly enlarging it to meet the growing demands of the public. In 1872 he was elected alderman of the 3d ward and again in 1866, and now holds the responsible post of chairman of the Judiciary Committee. In 1875 he was nominated for Mayor, but after an exciting contest was defeated, as he refused to make certain pledges to discordant elements of his party. Too independent to be a time serving politician, he is essentially a business man. With a thorough knowledge of details, quick perceptive faculties, he is methodical and thorough, with the military talent to organize and direct, with executive ability of high order, and is unassuming in manner, affable and courteous to all, and has a high appreciation of the humorous inherited from his native Green Emerald Isle.

He has amassed much valuable property, and ranks amongst the first business men of the city.

The reading public are more indebted to him than to any other man, for his untiring energy in establishing a literary depot through which they are daily furnished with every thing new and interesting in the fields of literature at rates which are in the reach of all classes of community.

DR. MILTON F. COLLINS, was the first president of the first Medical Society in Keokuk, and one of the oldest medical practicioners in Iowa. He was the Lieutenant Colonel of the 60th Regt. U. S. colored Inft. in the late war, and recruited nearly the entire regiment himself.

Both of his sons were in the army, William B. Collins, now one of our leading lawyers, was major of the 7th Missouri infantry, and a gallant officer. Joseph A M. Collins, was a sergeant in the 2nd Iowa infantry, was in the Signal service at the capture of Fort McAllister near Savannah, Georgia, and was every inch a soldier.

DR. JOHN F. SANFORD, in his time a most eminent surgeon, as Senator from Van Buren County, introduced the bill making a medical department to the Iowa State University, at the first session of the state legislature in 1847. In consequence the College of Physicians and Surgeons of which J. C. Hughes M. D., is now Dean, was located in Keokuk, in 1850, and held its first session here that winter. Dr. S. administered chloroform in a capital surgical case for the first time in the west successfully, manufacturing it himself, and performed the first operation of Lithotomy on a male in the state, Little Jo Hardin of Fort Madison.

HENRY DeLOUIS, a half breed Sac and Fox Indian, the son of Henry Barone DeLouis, a Frenchman, and an Indian woman, now living at Keokuk, is the last and only half breed of that tribe in the city; he has one sister, Octavia DeLouis, a fine musician, residing at Des Moines.

ANTI-CHRIST was the name General Browne gave to the first school master, John McKean.

He kept the first white school in a round log house in the hazle bushes, sixteen by eighteen feet square, and it stood on the same ground now occupied by the Wabash Railway office, at the corner of Johnson and 3d streets, which operates 800 miles of railroad, and of which our genial fellow townsman B. J. Fine, is the superintendent.

Anti Christ's school house had a log cut out for a window—later it was succeeded by a sliding sash.

THE FIRST LAW JOURNAL.

The Iowa Legal Inquisitor, Vol. 1. No. 1. edited by the Bar of Iowa, was published by Morgan & McKenney at Burlington, Iowa, August, 1851, a monthly periodical.

General J. M. Morgan was a spicy writer and edited the Telegraph, and was called "little red," McKenney, was afterwards Captain in the U. S. army, and the sheriff when the Hodges were hung

KEOKUK'S FAST TIMES OF 1855-6-7. THE QUEENS OF SOCIETY.

The rise of property which came up to fabulous prices in Keokuk, commenced in 1855. In 1856 people went wild, and strangers from abroad came in hordes. Speculators in real estate, had offices on every street, and could be seen in consultation on every corner. At the public hotels they filled the tables, and champaign flowed like a river. We had fast horses, fast men, fast women and many adventurers and dead beats.

Fast men drove fast horses, and elegant turnouts. Fast women splurged in splendid dresses and were decorated with costly diamonds or snide jewelry.

The worst dead beat and confidence man, was one P. C. Wright a lawyer and speculator without money but on his cheek, hailing from New Orleans. Paper towns became the order of the day. It was like the times of the golden dreams of the South Sea Bubble.

Wright had a great sale of lots and bought his champaigne from R. F. Bower, and never paid for it. Every little penny dog looked lordly as he sat at the hotel table at dinner, and talked of corner lots. Lemmon & Burbridge, Morrison, Jim Robinson and others, came from Kentucky. Winder, Wootton and the Schleys from Baltimore. Ficklin and Lucas, Dr. A. C. Thorm and Metcalfe from Virginia, Dimond and DeWolfe from Rhode Island, New York and Massachusetts sent G. Washington Mears, besides these were many others we could name equally conspicuous.

We wish we had time to describe some of them personally. Wright was elegant and elaborate in his make up, was handsome, polite and smiled sweetly, and lied like Annanias. Kentucky, Virginia, Rhode Island, and New York, all went under; property went up like a sky rocket and exploded.

Theatres were patronized liberally, ministers went into speculation and were called trading preachers, every one made a speech or gave a toast; the livery stables were well patronized, public entertainments were crowded, and private parties were frequent, and in brilliancy and splendor have never been rivaled

In the high circles of society we will not speak of the beaux, but of the belles alone.

Some of the queens of society, we cannot name them all, were Mrs. Dr. John R. Allen the sister of Judge Buckner of Lexington, and her adopted daughter Miss Lou Pattison, Miss Ellen Floyd, daughter of Major John G. Floyd, Miss Em Greenhow of Vincennes, visiting at Géneral Reids, now Mrs Geo. W. Doane of Omaha, a beautiful blonde who made many conquests; Miss Mary Sullivan, of Madison, Indiana, a brunette, Mrs. A. T. Walling, wife of Congressman Walling of Ohio, editor then of the Times, and her intellectual and brilliant sister Miss Mary Burns, both interesting and beautiful; Mrs. Nannie Jeffords, wife of ex-Judge Jeffords of the High Court of Errors and appeals of Mississippi, afterwards, then a lawyer here; tall, elegant, graceful and queenly, the witchery of her smiles, and unassuming sweetness of manner, won the way to every heart. Then, there was Miss Mary Higby of New York, with her sweet smiles and rosy cheeks, the picture of health, blooming and beautiful, she was quite a belle, and made a conquest of one of Keokuk's now prominent business men, Vice President Wm. A. Brownell, of the Keokuk National Bank.

And there was her cousin, the charming Mrs. Col. C. K. Peck, with cheeks of the roseate hue of Aurora, and lustrous sparkling eyes of deep cerulean blue. Mrs. Huston of Kentucky, a dark eyed queenly beauty and she knew it. There were a few ancient maidens looking for husbands, one married Diamond, and we wrote her a valentine which she never showed, of doggerel poetry about

    Little Diamonds little dresses
    Tiny shoes and shining tresses,
    As you sail along life's shore
    Will, in a dozen years or more,
    Like young blue birds spread their wings,
    And play their harps of a thousand strings.

VALUABLE RELICS.

J. B. Knight Esq., has in his possession the furniture used by the officers of the old military post at Fort Des Moines, now Montrose.

They consist of two heavy cherry tree falling leaf tables, a large old fashioned hair cloth sofa which opens out and can be used for a bed stead, as when opened it has a hair mattrass inside, also a large hair cloth covered rocking chair, in which Generals Scott, Robert E. Lee, Sumner, Browne; then a Captain, Lieutenant Roberts, Jeff Davis, Harney, Kearney, and many other distinguished men have been seated. They are all in a good state of preservation.

On the 1st of February, 1877, Governor Samuel J. Kirkwood, U. S. Senator elect resigned, which made Lieutenant Governor Newbold, Governor of Iowa and Senator Hon. Henry W. Rothert, our Lieutenant Governor.

WILLIAM C. RENTGEN.

Prominent and conspicuous among the old settlers of Lee County, when we first knew him at West Point, and afterwards from 1849 till a short time before his death, was William C. Rentgen. He was born in the Arsenal grounds at St. Louis, Mo. where his father was armorer, and died of consumption at Minneapolis, Minnesota, in May 1869. A member of the firm of Burns & Rentgen, who did an extensive commission business, his house met with financial reverses in the crisis of 1857, and on account of the many bad debts they made in the country, failed. Being of a sensitive nature and proud spirited he felt it deeply, and his nervous system met with a shock from which he never recovered. When the war of 1861 broke out he went as a clerk on the steamers of Captain David White who had charge of many government transports, was present at the siege of Forts Henry and Donnelson, and the Battle of Shiloh, and afterwards was sutler at General McPhersons head quarters, during and after the siege at Vicksburg, and was highly esteemed by that gallant and distinguished officer. After the fall of Vicksburg, he engaged extensively in cotton buying, made money rapidly but meeting again with reverses failed, loosing fifty thousand dollars.

He became dispirited, morbid and melancholy and was attacked with consumption. A change of climate was thought advisable by his physicians, and he tried New Orleans, Cuba, Philadelphia and finally Minnesota, without relief. Born a poet, he was a poetical writer of much merit, and his contributions occasionally to the press were highly appreciated, and he had many warm personal friends. He left many unpublished manuscripts of rare beauty, some of them gems, not surpassed by the first poets of the world. He was a great reader, and a fine German scholar, spoke that language fluently, and translated into English some of the masterpieces of Shiller. He had an extensive acquaintance with business men and authors, and was widely known as a gentleman of literary taste, and in business as the soul of honor. Full of wit, kind hearted and generous to a fault, at public entertainments and private social gatherings, he was a leader, giving tone to such assemblies where all were gentlemen. We wish our space would allow us to say more, and that we could publish some of the grandest of his beautiful poems, which would give us much pleasure, for he was Keokuk's great poet, and the brother of that estimable lady Mrs. John Burns of this city. May the turf grow green above him.

OUR FIRE COMPANIES.—The "Young America," was the first. This company was organized dating from October 9th 1856, the "Rolla" and "Union" were organized afterwards, and then "Hook and Ladder." Col. John Adair McDowell, was the first president at its organization, Francis H. Wootten half nephew of Reverdy Johnson, secretary, and acting Governor of Utah, killed in the rebel army at Fredericksburg, its first secretary. "Dick" Magruder was afterwards president, Captain W. H Appler vice president. George W. Montague, treasurer. Frank Bower an active and popular member, was struck on the head with a key by a rough, and died from inflammation of the brain.

H. C. Landis for nineteen years a member of the "Young America," has held every office except treasurer, in the company, from foreman of the hose when Sam M. McEveny was assistant up to president. Sheriff George L. Higgins, one of our old settlers, has been an active fireman in both the Young America and the Rolla, which he helped to organize before the war of 1861. Ed Booth was one of the first firemen, and helped organize a society, where every member had to carry a stick of wood as the countersign to get admitted called the "Forty Thieves."

The first supervisor in Keokuk, was John Waters, who had enough brass to make many kettles, in his face and could talk the legs off of an iron pot.

When a steam boat landed he boarded it and collected road tax from the passengers, and put it in his pocket.

"Mark" Anthony his successor, did the same.

"Uncle Billy" Graham, present supervisor, is the first who has plowed the gutters, and has lived in Iowa since 1839, is known as the "Blacksmith," went to California for gold in 1849, and afterwards to Pikes Peak, and is one of our oldest settlers.

ROSS B. HUGHES, was born in Maryland, and when he came to Iowa, was for a time a farmer, and owned the farm, on which what was called the Rail War took place, when James L. Estes was sheriff. Farming was not to his taste, it was too dull and prosy a life for him, he was better fitted to mingle in crowds, so he sold out and came to Keokuk. At different times he had a mill, a cooper shop, and a store, sometimes all at once, and later was a steamboat captain.

He had the largest cooper shop west of Cincinnati, which was destroyed by fire on the night of January 3d, 1848. The first election for mayor took place that day in which "Devil Creek" defeated Dornicks, and at night, dressed as a "big injin," Devil Creek followed by his braves, marched up town in single, file! The same night Hughes and Co's. cooper shop was burned, and the old fire company, a bucket brigade with leather buckets, turned out and formed a line from the river to the shop on the hill, just below Johnson street, $3,000 worth of tools, potatoes, beans, onions, corn and a large quantity of staves were burned. In ten days it was rebuilt, and that event celebrated by a dance. While running his cooper shop, it was a favorite maxim of his that hoop poles were a legal tender for debt. His shop was located in the 2d ward, which has ever since been called hoop pole ward. His wife died, and while a widower he was at a party and challenged any one who dared, to marry him. A tall girl, a Miss Barnum, got up and accepted his offer. He sent for a minister, and they were married in fifteen minutes afterwards. He was the father of Mrs. Cram, the wife of Daniel Cram a commission merchant, and contractor on the Des Moines river improvement, he went to California in 1853, and is now living in Salt Lake. She was the eldest daughter, much of a lady, and a tall elegant handsome woman, and had many warm friends.

Kate his second daughter, is the present Mrs. Ex-Attorney General Geo. H. Williams, and in disposition much like her father, and a much handsomer woman than her sister. She has had a chequered career, and first married one Ivans, and growing discontented left him and was divorced. She next married A. K. George, a dashing stage agent who dressed in flashy style, and was a fast man. They crossed the plains for California in 1853, where George afterwards died, and she was again a dashing widow.

The world was now before her, she was invited to visit her husbands brother and family in Connecticut, and went, was afterwards a music teacher in Keokuk, and finally went on a visit to her sister Mrs. Cram, then in Oregon where she married George H. Williams, who as Judge, once granted her a divorce. Williams was in the Senate and the height of her ambition was now reached, and a new field opened at Washington, for her talent for intrigue which she inherited from her talented and enterprising and unscrupulous father. As the wife of a senator and attorney general, she has had her day, and the Chief Justiceship and mission to Spain, were lost to Williams, who is now a played out politician.

He was a green gawky overgrown, long chinned young man when he came to Fort Madison, without money or friends, and hard up for clothes. When we first saw him he was crossing a street on a trot in warm weather, and wore an old worn greasy bell crowned hat, a grey tweed frock coat, and pants of the same material, which were too short by several inches—his clothes looked greasy. He wore a pair of slippers once black, but they were worn, and of a yellowish tinge, and socks once white but very much soiled, and very much resembled an escaped lunatic. D. F. Miller Esq., took him into his office, fed and clothed him, and made him his partner, and he was elected judge, but never felt under obligations to Mr. Miller.

In 1852 he was made democratic elector at large for Iowa, was appointed to carry the vote to Washington, and was appointed by president Pierce, chief justice to Oregon.

Since then his career is well known. His wife is a woman of more talent than himself, and has figured largely in Washington, making it lively for the wives of cabinet ministers and other government officers.

Hettie was the youngest daughter of Captain Hughes, she ran away and married a cabin boy on a steam boat; got tired of him soon, and left him. She was bold, dashing, of with much of her fathers disposition, but she was not pretty—she had an adventurous career, and lived a fast life. Hughes went to Central America, contracted fever at Chagres on the Isthmus, returned sick, and died in St. Louis, before the war of 1861.

www.ingramcontent.com/pod-product-compliance
Lightning Source LLC
Chambersburg PA
CBHW020254170426
43202CB00008B/371